BECOMING JANE DOE

From Train Wreck to Recovery:

The Secret Life of Being a Prisoner to My Own Mind.

BY LAUREN THATCHER

Copyright © [2024] Lauren Thatcher
Legal Copyright Holder: Lauren Daniels

All rights reserved. No part of this book may be reproduced, distributed, or transmitted in any form or by any means, without the prior written permission of the publisher, except for brief quotations used in reviews or critical articles.

ISBN : 979-8-218-55197-1

Edited by Michele Mencer
Biography written by Jacklyn Mcqueen

Publishing Consultant, Designer, Book Manager, Social Media Strategist, and Photographer:
Charley Kvell

Published by Lauren Thatcher
Self-published through KDP & IngramSpark

Content Warning:
This book contains discussions of sensitive topics, including abuse, addiction, and trauma, which may be distressing for some readers. Intended for mature audiences aged 18 and older.

Becoming Jane Doe is a work of non-fiction. While the events and experiences described are true to the author's life, certain names, locations, and identifying details have been altered or fictionalized to protect the privacy of individuals. Any resemblance to actual persons, living or deceased, beyond these intentional changes, is purely coincidental.

Printed in the United States of America

With Gratitude

To my loving parents for never giving up on me, always believing in me, and being amazing parents.

To my Susan, for showing me what true unconditional love is and always being there

To my brother, for all your support, especially when we were doing our workbooks.

To my best friend, Nancy, you have inspired me to be a better person. You have saved me from myself countless times and taught me to own my A-Zs with dignity and grace.

To Jimmy, for giving me love and patience when I needed it the most.

To Beige, my ride or die, for literally everything. I am so sorry that I poured vodka in your purse.

To two individuals in my past, you may have taken part of my childhood, but because of your actions, I became the strong woman I am today.

Lastly, to everyone who was not listed but was included in the text, whether it was big or small, you played a part in leading me to where I am today.

Thank You!

When I woke up Thursday morning, I glanced down and saw that my lower body was covered in handprints. "It must have been a crazy night," I thought to myself. My mouth was dry and tasted like stale beer and cigarettes. I looked around the room. There were holes in the walls, chips in the beige paint, and empty beer cans all over the floor. I was lying on a bare mattress on the floor. I didn't remember how I got there or where I was. Then I rolled over and saw Spencer. Spencer was a guy I had been flirting with behind my boyfriend Cameron's back. I got up, walked into the kitchen, and grabbed a cold beer from the fridge. There was no way I was going to let this hangover ruin Thanksgiving with Cameron's family. I thought of Cameron, and honestly, I did feel bad. I had to face him today, and I did not know how I was going to do it. I drank the rest of my beer, then set it on the table with the large collection of empty cans and cigarette burns and left to go home.

Chapter 1

Misery was a feeling I became accustomed to at a very young age. Having my hands tied behind my back and a mushroom shoved in my mouth is where my crooked teeth, glasses, and teenage acne led me at age 12. Tears fell down my face as all my friends left me after tying the ropes tighter. I wasn't happy in that chair by any means, but I was being noticed. That was a compromise I made with myself at an early age. All I wanted was to feel like I belonged somewhere. That year was difficult. I contemplated taking my life by age 13. I had no idea how to, so I didn't do it, but I wanted to be in another life. I just wanted to be someone else.

It's amazing what contact lenses, braces, and growing into an attractive body can do for a young girl. By the time I got to high school, it was like I hadn't been the laughingstock of our class for the past seven years. My awkward personality turned into humor, and I had actual friends. I had finally gotten all I ever wanted: to fit in somewhere.

When I was a sophomore, I was nominated to be on the homecoming court. My weekends consisted of going to the movies, getting ice cream, and going to the parks. Life was good, but it only took the attention of one guy to completely turn everything upside down. His name was Hunter. I met him through a girl at work, and he went to a different high school. Hunter was very short and skinny. He wasn't bad-looking, but he wasn't good-looking, either. But I really liked him. He asked me out on my first date to go to the Riverwalk, which was located about 20 minutes from where my parents lived. They warned me that he wasn't a good guy because he didn't even get out of his little green Mazda Miata to meet them when he picked me up.

But what did they know?

The first date was everything that I thought it would be. We got hot chocolate and just talked and held hands down the Riverwalk. We spent the next couple of weeks talking on the phone after school for hours. I really liked the attention that I was receiving.

I honestly did feel like I was falling in love with Hunter. So, one day, at his house after school, I told him how I felt. He definitely did not feel the same way and was very vocal about it. He broke up with me and then didn't talk to me for two weeks. I felt lost.

I didn't know what to do. I waited by my phone every day for those two weeks.

Finally, he messaged me, and just like that, I went back to him. That was when I started to get pressured into having sex. I had never done anything but kiss my first boyfriend, and even that was just a very dry peck on the lips, which I was made fun of for later on. After some thinking, I decided that I would spend the night at his house after Homecoming. Which, of course, he didn't attend with me. I lied to my parents. I went to the after-party that I said I would be going to and took a bunch of pictures so I would have proof to show them I was there. After about 50 random pictures, I left and went to Hunter's house. His best friend, Jake, was over there, too.

They were drinking beer, and I had never had one before, so I tried one. I hated it! I thought it was disgusting. But I didn't want to seem lame, so I drank a couple anyway. Then they started smoking pot, so I decided that I wanted to try that, too. They lit up the bong for me, and I inhaled deeply. I immediately started coughing so hard that I couldn't stop. Then, the high hit. I was out for the count. I went to lie down after some time. I hated being high. I went upstairs to lay in Hunter's bed and woke up to him kissing me, and then we talked about me giving him a blow job. I didn't really want to, but I felt like I loved him and wanted him to love me, so I did it. Well, I should say that I attempted to. I had never talked to anyone about how to give one. So, I did what I thought the term meant. I blew on it. Literally.

He laughed and instructed me how to do it, and then he finished in what felt like seconds. We laid there for a while, then fell asleep. I woke up the next morning feeling a lot closer to him. I woke up early to go to work, got a kiss goodbye, and went on my way. We did that every time we hung out, even if I didn't want to. I wanted his attention so badly that I did it anytime he asked me to.

After some time, the topic of sex came up. I did not feel ready to have sex at all, so I declined multiple times. Hunter flat-out told me that if I didn't soon, we wouldn't last. So, being the people pleaser that I was, I caved. One night, we went to his friend's house and had a couple of beers. I had to force them down. I hated beer so much. He was different that night, though. He was so affectionate in front of his friends, kissing and holding me. After some time, we drove to his house and held hands the entire way. I honestly felt like he loved me that night. We went upstairs to his room to lie down and make out like we always did. The kissing got heavier, and he started unbuttoning his pants, but I stopped him. I wasn't ready. He told me that it was okay and slowly started pulling off his pants. I didn't want to say no because I knew he would break up with me, so I let him lay me down on my back, lift up my favorite brown skirt, and pull down my favorite Victoria's Secret polka dot underwear.

I was so uncomfortable, but he just kept going, so I let him. It hurt at first, and I told him it did. He just pushed harder and harder. No matter how much I put my hands on his chest for him to stop, he wouldn't. It didn't last long, and after he was done, he laid there for a minute and held me. I felt so weird. I didn't know what to feel. I couldn't stay the night, so I left. I went home, talked to my parents, and just pretended that nothing happened. I went to bed with a text from Hunter saying he had a great time. I was so sore, but I took it as a sign that he did love me. We had sex a couple more times after that. He never touched me. He never even took off my shirt or acknowledged any other part of my body with his hands or his mouth. It was always quick, and then I would go home. I honestly thought that was how it was supposed to be, so I kept doing it.

I started hanging out with a new crowd at school. I hung out with all the girls that everyone at school thought were bad and slutty. I liked hanging out with them. I had lost all of my old friends once I started drinking, smoking pot, and having sex. They all looked down on me. Just like in middle school, I just wanted to fit in. And with this new crowd, I did. My new best friend, Maddie, started dating Jake. They hit it off right away and started having sex all the time, which made me feel normal. I found out through Maddie that the first night Hunter and I had sex, he kept all the blood on his sheets to show off to his friends. I felt so embarrassed, but I just pretended that it didn't hurt me hearing that.

I went to Florida every year to see my aunt. Hunter became very distant while I was there, so even though I tried to have fun, it was hard. All I did was think about him the whole time. A couple of days into my trip, I got a call from his friend Nikki. She was someone he slept with all the time before me. She told me that she and Hunter had been sleeping together for days, and she thought that I should know. I was in my aunt's spare bedroom and just laid on the floor when she told me. I cried quietly and just isolated myself for the rest of the trip.

When I came home, Hunter apologized so much and was so sweet with his words. Feeling like I needed him, I eventually accepted his apology. We went to a party and smoked and parked my car. We didn't even go back to his house this time. We just had sex in the car. It honestly just felt like he was just having sex with me, no emotion. It felt different. It felt like I was being used.

But did I stop?

No, I didn't.

After a couple of minutes, he finished, and we got in my front seat. I drove him to his house; he kissed me goodbye and told me that he would call me later. I went home, talked to my parents, and then immediately got into the shower to clean off. When I got out of the shower, I saw that I had a missed call from him, and he left a voicemail. I was so happy and excited to hear it, so I quickly played the message. He told me that he had a great time with me, but it wasn't working out, and to have a good life.

Have a good life?

Are you kidding me?

I immediately tried calling him back. No answer. I left him a tearful message begging him to call me back and asking what the hell happened, but there was never a response. I finally understood what it meant to have your heart fall into your stomach. I fell to the ground, laid on the cool, brown-tiled floor, and just cried. I felt so lost and confused as to what I did wrong. I was devastated.

Despite being heartbroken, I still hung out with Jake and Maddie. One night, Maddie and Patrick, a guy I didn't really know who went to our school, went with me to drink in a parking lot. They had a blue bottle of vodka. I had never had anything other than a couple of beers, but I was so miserable that I just wanted to get drunk. I took a long pull from the bottle and instantly wanted to throw up. It was so gross and burned my throat, so I immediately chased it with a cherry soda. I started to feel warm and fuzzy, and I liked how it felt. I took a couple more pulls from the bottle. I felt like I was floating. I was hammered. I could barely talk but loved that I didn't hurt anymore. I didn't know what to do with myself. Patrick asked to see my boobs, and I didn't hesitate. I lifted my shirt and loved the attention I received. I stayed the night at Maddie's and then woke up the next morning to my first hangover. It was terrible.

We were sitting at her mom's kitchen table, talking about how much I missed Hunter, so we decided to call him. No answer. Then I texted him from Maddie's phone. Again, no response. About 10 minutes later, we received a call from Nikki. This time, she told me that

Hunter said not to call him again, ever. He wanted nothing to do with me. Not only did I hate her, I wanted to be her at this point. I just felt hollow in my own skin.

That was when my drinking started to get really bad. I found a new love to replace Hunter with. Vodka. We partied all the time, and I drank only to black out.

I got caught a couple of times by my parents, got repercussions, took them, and then just did it again. I was so jealous of Jake and Maddie. They texted each other and had sex all the time, and he actually stuck around. Patrick told everyone at school that I got drunk and showed my boobs. He told everyone that I had pepperoni nipples and that they were disgusting. I just tried to act like it didn't kill me that everyone thought that. And also that the first guy who saw my bare chest thought it was gross.

We would always go to a club that somehow we could all get into at 17. It was a nasty club in a bad part of town. It was a trailer with a long, wooden deck as the entrance. We would wear our shortest skirts and tightest shirts, then sweet talk our way in.

We would drink before we got there. Most of the girls there were 16 to 18 years old and also showed up drunk. But there were also guys over the age of 21 who would buy us drinks. We used to think they were so cool. I had no idea how much of a loser and perverse those guys were until I got older.

One night, Maddie, Jake, and I drank, then went to the club. We parked her silver BMW in the car dealership parking lot across the street. I was still in such a bad place, mentally and emotionally, so I was looking forward to partying and blacking out.

The club was full, but we found our "old men" to buy us some drinks. Maddie and I got on the bar top and started dancing and making out in front of everyone. We made out all the time. I think I made out with her more than Hunter. We were a shit show. We were soon asked to get off the bar. We took a couple more shots, then went off by the pool table in the back. Jake gave Maddie a rose that they were selling there. I was so envious. So I had some 22-year-old boy buy me some drinks. But he was so gross. I wanted nothing more than just the drinks from him. I noticed that one of Hunter's best friends, Trent, was there. He was tall, full of muscles, and very good-looking. He was a star football player. Lucky for me, it turned out that he was one of Hunter's best friends, and I caught his eye. I had a mission to make Hunter jealous. I played my cards right, and the next thing I knew, we were making out all night. Not long after, his hands were up in that little brown skirt, and I let him continue in the middle of the club. He saw Maddie and Jake leave, and he wanted to follow, so he led me outside.

There was a wooden, broken-down shed
outside behind the building, and we all walked
into it. It was dark and musky, and I wasn't
even thinking about what could happen. Jake
and Maddie went to the back, and we heard
them start to have sex. Trent started kissing
me, this time very aggressively. He pushed me
onto a wooden bench and started unbuttoning
his pants. I told him that I did not want to do it.

I tried to get up, and he stood in the way and put a
condom on. I was almost begging him to let me go
down on him instead. He didn't say anything.
Instead, he forced himself on me. His penis was a lot
bigger than Hunter's, so it hurt. And just like my first
time, I kept telling him it hurt and begging him to
stop, but he didn't. He did not even acknowledge that
I was talking. It was like I was just a body. Next
thing I know, I hear a loud, "What the fuck is going
on in here?" Trent immediately jumped up, put his
dick back in his pants, and stood far away from me. I
couldn't find my underwear and stood up, and my
skirt fell in place. It was a police officer. I felt a

sense of relief. He told us all to come outside. He already knew what we were doing, so he did not ask.

He looked at me, and I was teary-eyed. I was really hoping that he would say something to protect me so I would feel okay. Instead, he said in a stern voice, "What the fuck would your parents think about what you did tonight?" He never even asked me if I wanted it. At this point, I knew that if I said anything, I wouldn't have anybody to back me up. I would lose any connection I had to this whole group. So, I just stood quietly. Jake and Trent got into a black Tahoe to leave, and I overheard Trent complain that there was blood on his jeans and that he was going to "fucking burn them", because it was so disgusting. I immediately thought I was gross and felt disgusted that I bled like that. I didn't even know what to do about what happened. Maddie was hammered and couldn't drive, so we had to wait for her mom to come pick us up. I rode the whole way home in silence. I told Maddie and her friend Autumn what happened, and they almost didn't even want to hear it. I didn't have anyone to talk to, so I just took on the persona that they made me out to be. I became proud of what happened.

He was a hot football player, so I added it to my new list of sexual partners and persuaded myself that I wanted it to happen and that I chose it. Then I started drinking even more. I had at least one drink every day from that point forward.

I worked in a pizza restaurant at this point in high school. Every night, I would take a Corona into the bathroom with a to-go cup, a straw, and a bottle opener. I would pour the beer into a cup and drink it while I worked. I would have a couple a night. Not enough to get caught, but just enough not to feel the pain from Hunter and Trent. I would drink with Maddie every weekend. I barely had any friends left. Just the ones who lived the way that I was heading. They did drugs, had sex, and partied every weekend. I found where I thought I fit in.

I wore the tiniest outfits out to the clubs and parties. Since I was not allowed to get my belly button pierced like all my friends had, I agreed to let a friend pierce my tongue instead so I could hide it. She said she had done it multiple times.

So, of course, she knew what she was doing, right?

I trusted her.

What could go wrong?

We went to the movie theater parking lot by our high school. I sat in her backseat, facing outside of the door. I watched her take the thick, long needle out of a Ziploc bag. She held my tongue with her thumb and forefinger and told me to breathe in deep. Then, she quickly slipped the needle into the center of my tongue. It was the weirdest kind of pain that I have ever felt. I almost passed out. Once we were done, I had a purple sparkly ball on top of my tongue as a result of my pain.

My new look was complete. It was crazy to think that just a year prior, I was "Little Miss Innocent. "I had never smoked cigarettes, smoked pot, drank, or had sex before, but in that small amount of time, I had done all of them.

 I pretended to be okay, but I wasn't. I started feeling even more alone and depressed. One day in class, I was sitting next to Maddie while she and some guys were talking about me and what happened with Trent. They were all laughing, so I just played along even though it felt like knives were stabbing into my heart and stomach. Then Maddie said I had a "bloody pussy" and they all laughed harder. I had finally had enough, so I told her that I would rather have a bloody pussy than a loose one. That immediately backfired. No one took my side. I couldn't take it anymore. I felt so overwhelmed with shame and pain. I excused myself from class and went into the bathroom.

I was full of tears and stared into the mirror, just like I did when I was little.

I felt empty, I felt regret and embarrassment, and I felt so damn alone. I didn't know what to do to relieve these feelings, so I went to the bathroom stall, knelt down by the toilet, and stuck my fingers down my throat until I vomited. I just cried and then felt an immediate sense of relief. I wiped my mouth and rinsed it in the sink. I didn't even bother looking at myself in the mirror before I left. This moment led to my months of self-harm.

Chapter 2

I found out that there was a guy I worked with at the pizza restaurant who was friends with Hunter, so of course, I latched on to him. We started to party together, and I was introduced to a whole new group of friends. They were nicer to me than Maddie. We actually did normal stuff, not just smoking and drinking. It was nice. One night, we went to hang out at the car wash, and I met a guy named Nick. He was a goofy guy and made me laugh. I didn't see him for a while after that, but I thought about him a lot. The guy from work and I went to a party at our friend Adam's house and ran into Nick again. We talked all night and exchanged numbers. He was so nice. We would spend all night texting and talking. The next thing I knew, we were dating. This was different than it was before. It was actually dating. We would hang out after school and all weekend. I finally felt what respect was.

I still had a deep black hole in myself, so I continued to drink alone a lot. I would drink so much that I'd pass out or get sick, and Nick would take care of me. One night, I drank half a bottle of vodka in my closet. I did that often until the day my parents caught me and took off my closet door. I went to bed plastered and just quietly cried. I felt so lost and sad from what I had been through. I felt so empty, like I was just existing. I started spinning, so I put one foot on the ground to balance my spins and just laid there. I could feel my breath getting deeper and deeper, and I fell asleep.

My parents loved Nick, so they let him in. I didn't hear him come in, but I felt a kiss on my forehead, and then he moved my heavy head into his arms. For the first time, I felt loved by someone other than my family. I felt safe.

Feeling safe didn't stop me from drinking. We all partied every Friday and Saturday, and I would drink everyone under the table. I started drinking so much and then making myself throw up so I could drink more. I was very familiar with how to do that after my months of self-harming. I thought I had found the secret to drinking and was so proud to show other girls how to do it. If I wasn't drinking, I was thinking of the next time I could drink, and I was always finding a way. I started to fit in more and feel more comfortable and respected with this new group of friends. One night, Nick and I were watching a movie at his house, and he just looked at me and told me, "I love you." I had never had a guy tell me that before. I kissed him, and I said, "I love you, too." He probably had no idea how much he saved me from myself.

Senior year was my best year in high school. I didn't give two shits about what anybody thought about me. I rolled out of bed five minutes before I had to leave, brushed my teeth, and left for school. I felt comfortable in my own skin. I hung out with everyone at school, and the girls who were snooty with me before liked me now. I honestly think it's because they started having sex and drinking.

Nick was great. We got along great and had fun. I partied every weekend, and I actually had a good time. I didn't go to that dark place where I would go when I drank before. I thought to myself, "Now, this is what it's supposed to feel like." I loved how I felt when I drank. I talked a lot to anyone that I could. I was later nicknamed Gabby. I had the courage to do things I would not normally do, and I had confidence that I didn't have before.

Nick had never had sex before we met. He had someone attempt a blowjob, but she also didn't know what she was doing, so it was never officially done. Luckily for him, Hunter taught me how to do that, so we did that a lot. His mom let us drink at the house. When I would stay the night, we would sleep in separate beds. One night, his mom had a Halloween party, and I got hammered, of course. Nick and I went back to his room and were making out and cuddling. He said he was ready to have sex. I was so happy to share that moment with him. I got on top of him, and our eyes locked. I mentioned that it hurt, and he asked me if I wanted to stop, but this time I did not want to. I wanted to share this moment with him. But then, all the alcohol I had before hit me, and I started spinning and had to stop. We passed out together. This led to countless nights, days, and afternoons of sex and growing as a couple.

At the end of the school year, it was time to graduate. I was mad that none of my friends wanted to get drunk for graduation. I wasn't sure where I was going to go to college. I had no idea what I wanted to study, either. But Nick decided to go to Oklahoma State University, so I followed. The best part of college was that everyone drank like I did. I finally blended in. Another good thing about college was that Thursday became part of the weekend. We would party every Thursday, Friday, and Saturday. We lived at a party house, so we always had people over. We constantly had alcohol in the house. There were a couple of days where I was drinking beer by 10am. I did this solely because I did not want to drink water. We only drank Keystone Light, so it was like water, but it was cheap, and so were we. Nick threw me an awesome 19th birthday party. It was a kegger, and we had Jell-O shots and everything.

The day after, Nick and I were lying in bed with our new little black lab puppy that we named Bentley. We were tending to a terrible hangover, and out of nowhere, he said it wasn't working out anymore. He wasn't happy, and we needed to break up. I was so surprised and devastated. I pleaded for him to please stay and work this out with me, but he told me he couldn't as he shut the door and just left. I was at a loss for words. At first, I thought it was just out of the blue, but then, after some thinking, I realized that there's no such thing. I just wasn't looking closely enough. I took this break-up so damn hard. I spent days watching SpongeBob crying and leaning on my little Bentley. He didn't want him, and little did I know, that dog would become my best buddy and save my life.

I decided to take a couple of weeks off from drinking so I wouldn't make an ass out of myself and cry when I got drunk. Once I started back up again, I immediately picked right back up where I left off. My roommate and friend still hung out with Nick, so just like before with Hunter, I was always trying to impress him or win him back. We all partied at his house one night, and there were lines of white powder on the glass table, just like I had seen previously in high school. The guys were sitting on the couch, and each one grabbed the rolled-up dollar bill and snorted the powder. Nick did it, so I wanted to, too. I asked what it was, and they said OxyContin. I didn't even know what that was, but I snorted it. I hated how it made me feel. It slowed everything down. I liked my prescribed Adderall and alcohol. What I did love about it, however, was snorting it. I loved the burn that it gave the inside of my nose and the drip afterward. After that, I did it one more time with them. I have never touched it again since.

I tried to run into Nick at parties as much as I could. One day, they were doing something called Salvia, and just like before, I had no idea what it was. We were all sitting in a circle on the carpet in an empty bedroom, and someone said it makes you hallucinate. Everyone was doing it, so I did, too. I grabbed the pipe, smoked it, and waited, but nothing happened. Then, out of nowhere, I couldn't see anything. It was all black. Then, there were lines of purple and blue crossing each other, and then I saw a school bus. When I came to, I was on the other side of the circle. No clue what happened during that blackout.

It was only a couple of months after we broke up that I found out one of my good friends, Amber, slept with Nick.

I spent a whole day hanging out with her and crying to her about how brokenhearted I was, and she slept with him multiple times the very next day. I was so hurt and felt so betrayed. Every year, our whole group went on a float trip on the river, so I was really happy to hear that Amber was not invited this year, but Nick was. I started the day off with two double shots of Patrón at 7am. I wasn't the only one doing it, so I thought it was okay. We packed over seven cases of Keystone Light and Natty Light, and he decided to fill a water bottle with Montezuma tequila. Only the classiest tequila for floating the river. I laughed and said that someone's gonna regret bringing it.

I was drunk when I got there. We were all drinking and having a good time. I avoided Nick and just hung out with the girls. Next thing I knew, we ran out of beer. I was the sucker who remembered the Tequila. The last thing I remember was holding it up to my mouth and saying, "Hey, Andy, watch this." I remember glimpses of standing by a cop car, crying in the front seat of a cop car, and waking up by pulling on my handcuffs. I woke up in jail, hearing myself screaming and yelling. Then I saw Andy and Tyler, another one of my friends. I stopped crying and just looked at them. Then I realized I could fit my hands out of the cuffs, so I slid them off. They yelled at me to put them back on, so I did. Then, I blacked out again. I woke up to my mom and her best friend, who ironically was my old grade school P.E. teacher. They came to the drunk tank to pick me up. It was a blur of a ride home, but when we got there, I just went to sleep. I woke up the next morning to Nick calling to ask me if I was okay. We talked for a little bit, and he apologized for what happened with Amber, then told me he would see me around.

To my surprise, the current girlfriends I had stopped inviting me to parties because they couldn't stand how I would get around him.

Luckily, I had friends from work and roommates who took me under their wing and started my good old crazy college years. Lots of sex and drinking. My friends made fun of me because I would put perfume on my ankles before we went out. I was in my own little world. I worked every day and would drink after work and go to bonfires and parties. I had the time of my life. One night, I was all dressed up, and I ran into Nick while I was with another guy. It was the best feeling. He called me that night, but I never returned that call. I was officially over him, and I had moved on.

Chapter 3

I lived with three other girls in my second year of college. One day, my roommates decided that they were going to do mushrooms. I never considered them before, but I was curious, which got the best of me. There were four of us: Lina, Sarah, Becca, and me. It was a Saturday, and it was bright and sunny outside. I was nervous to do it, so I didn't take a lot. I had just eaten them flat out. I waited, then started to feel the best body high I had ever experienced. It was like my skin was vibrating in a soft and gentle way. We all went to Sarah's room, sat on the bed, and started talking about deep, intellectual thoughts. I wasn't really listening, though. I was too busy staring out the window. The tree just looked so beautiful. The way the leaves were swinging back and forth. It had rhythm like there was music. The girls talking was really starting to ruin my trip, so I left and went back to the living room. Lina was sober to keep an eye on us, and I told her I wanted to do more. They say that orange juice intensifies your trip, so I poured a glass of orange juice. I had the mushrooms in one and the glass in the other, then dumped the mushrooms into the orange juice. Lina asked, "Why the hell did you do that?" I honestly had no idea. All I knew was now I had to drink orange juice with chunks of mushrooms in it. I laid on my bed and felt my body just sink into the mattress. I turned my head and noticed the little penguins in Santa hats on my sheets were sliding off my sheets. Then I looked on the ground, and the dog hair on the ground started to blow and swirl. Everything looked like it was breathing. I loved how I was feeling and decided to take a walk. The air and sunshine felt so good on my skin. The wind was intensely blowing against me. I felt every bit of it. I turned to the house and saw my dog on the porch. He looked so majestic and bold, like a lion. His bark shocked me and made the vibrations against my skin more intense. I started walking. My thoughts were light, just observing nature before I made my way back home, and the trip wore off. I felt like I saw the world brighter and saw the beauty in everything.

 I started sleeping with this guy named Logan, who lived a couple of doors down, and my friend Hazel was dating his roommate. I really started to like Logan. I wasn't 21 yet, so we would pre-drink with the guys, and then they would meet up with us afterward. Logan and I would go to Wendy's, which became our thing. We were not officially dating, but it was understood to me.

 One night, they wanted to do mushrooms, and since my last trip went so well, I was all for it. It was getting ready to storm, and I hated storms. Plus, it was at night, which I didn't like either. We put the mushrooms on pizza, and I did a little extra this time since I ended up doing more the time before. I sat on the couch in front of the TV and waited. My skin got really warm, and everything in the house had an orange hue to it. I was starting to feel uncomfortable, like waves of a feeling of impending doom, so I went to the front porch to get some air. I sat on the step and felt the cool breeze as the storm came in and started to calm down. There was a huge tree across the street, and I started watching it sway in the breeze. Just like last time, it had rhythm. I was completely enthralled with this tree. Then, all of a sudden, there was a sad face in the leaves with X's for eyes. I panicked. I looked to the sky, and all the clouds had the same sad face. The vibrations were now in waves. Heavy waves of impending doom. I went in, pulled Hazel aside, and told her I was having a bad trip. She said, "No, just turn it around." I told her it was too late, then walked down to Logan's room in the basement and shut the door. I wanted this to stop. The paint on the walls looked like hot wax dripping down the walls. The walls were white, and I felt like I was in an insane asylum. I felt like I was stuck in the room and couldn't get out. It was terrifying. I actually almost called my mom to come rescue me. I was so scared. I then saw the Guinness conehead poster on the wall. "He" didn't want me in the room. He didn't like me. I spent most of my time there talking to him, and he made me afraid because I could "not make him happy with my presence." I decided to just try to go to sleep, so I laid on the bed, turned out the lights, pulled the covers over my head, and closed my eyes. When I closed them, there were hundreds of green dead skulls that were coming closer to me from under the covers. I turned the lights on and began to cry.

Did I lose my mind?

Is this forever?

As I was sitting on the bed, I looked forward and saw the computer lights. They turned into a demon, inching closer to my bed. I tried not to make eye contact. The conehead really didn't want me there. I was still trying to talk him into letting me stay. I would hear all my friends yelling outside. I thought that they must be getting attacked outside, too. I thought of what I could do to calm down. I turned on one of my favorite shows at the time, George Lopez. The figures on the screen were fuzzy and covered in a bright orange outline, but it was able to take my mind off of things and calm me down. The trip started to end, the panic subsided, and I got out of the bed and walked to the mirror.

My pupils took over my whole eyes, I had mascara streaks all over my face, and my hair was ratted and messy. Logan came in and asked if I was okay. I just said, "You have no idea what happened here." We both walked upstairs, and I stood with the group. Everyone was glad I was okay and told me how amazing their trip was. The screaming I heard was them playing in the rain. I, on the other hand, had an incredibly terrifying trip that was bad enough to keep me from ever using a hallucinogen again.

Logan and I had a lot of fun. He was very easygoing and attractive, but he was still in love with his ex. She had sex with every one of his roommates and friends, but he was too stupid to believe what anyone said. One night, I heard that he was with her at the bar after we drank together. I drank tequila, which was always a bad choice. I spent the whole night crying until he came home, and I took him back to my place to have sex. He spent the night, and then after he left, he never returned any of my texts or calls. It sucked because I really did like this guy and was devastated that he didn't even give me the respect to tell me. He just stopped responding to my texts and calls. It was a pretty big blow to my ego, but nothing that more partying couldn't fix.

I had taken Adderall since I was in the 6th grade. Back then, I was having problems focusing and completing tasks, so my parents had me go through extensive tests and put me on it. By the time I was 20, I was taking 20mg extended release once a day in the morning. I loved it. I loved the way the skin of the capsule felt in my mouth. I stopped using a drink to swallow it for that very reason. After feeling it and tasting it, I knew that soon, I would feel the rush that it gives you. Somewhere along the way, it stopped calming me down and started acting like speed. I loved it because when I took it, I could drink so much more. Sometimes, I would take an extra one before we would go out just to party harder. It also helped me with my hangovers. I would wake up to an Adderall, a cup of coffee, and a cigarette on our front stoop every morning. It was my magic pill.

By my 21st birthday, I was dating a new guy named Dustin. We went to "The Strip," which is where all of the bars were in my college town. The first bar we went to was called Dirty's, and that's exactly what it was. Dirty. The couches were old and smelled, the paint had strips missing, and the beer posters were peeling off the wall. But it was where all the frat guys went, so I wanted to go there, too.

The shots started: Royal Fuck, Washington Apple, Tidal Wave, and then, one I wasn't used to, Rumple Minze from my friend Brett.

I came to find out later that it was one hundred-proof mint liquor. That shot took the night up to the next level. I made it to shot number thirteen, and then I blacked out. Being 21 took me to a whole new level of drinking. Drunk became the normal state I was in more than before. I was always drinking. I even started working at the country western bar on the strip in town. Working at a bar changed me. I was in my element and did very well as a bartender.

I was driving back home to see my parents one day and drove over a pretty long bridge. My breath started to get short. I got tingly and then felt a sense of impending doom. I started shaking. The sensation got stronger, and I started to cry. I just wanted to pull over, but there was nowhere to do that on the bridge. I was hyperventilating at this point. When I finally got to the end of the bridge, I immediately pulled over and got out of the car to catch my breath.

What the hell just happened?

I calmed back down, got into the car, and started to drive to my parents' house. I found out later that I had just experienced my first panic attack. It opened a whole new door of panic attacks for me. The bar I worked at had a bar top with ten well stations and then another one upstairs that had four. It was a pretty big bar. It had one bathroom with about fifteen stalls that always had a line. One night, out of nowhere, I had a panic attack because I had to wait in line for about ten minutes. This became somewhat of an obsession if there wasn't an accessible bathroom. I would obsess about it and end up panicking, sometimes going into a full-on panic attack. I had to stop taking the college shuttle bus home when the bathroom didn't work. I was having such a hard time.

Then I came up with an idea. I took Imodium before EVERY shift at work. This brought my anxiety down, but as you can imagine, it brought more problems to my health. So, I decided to go to the doctor, and they put me on an antidepressant for anxiety. This part of my life was strange. I never had to go to the bathroom and couldn't. It was all built up in my head. After about two weeks, the medicine worked, and life went back to normal. Or as normal as it could be.

Dustin and I were together for about two years at this point, and on the outside, we had a pretty good relationship. He spoiled me rotten but hated my drinking. One night, we were at my house after a day filled with tailgating outside in the sun. The whole day was dedicated to day drinking. As much of a tolerance as I had, I could never carry over day drinking into night drinking without something bad happening.

I remember the sun going down and walking off of campus, and then I came out of a blackout to him crying. Stuff was thrown all around my room, and I was yelling that I wanted to go on the limo. Apparently, there was a limo ride back to a nearby town with some friends, and I wanted to go on it. Dustin didn't think it was a good idea because of how drunk I was. So, he told me no. I didn't take that too well. There weren't too many nights this bad, but I was partying way too much for his liking.

He stopped drinking about a year into our relationship because of a similar incident. He was really drunk from another day of tailgating, and we got into a fight, so he went to my house and trashed it. I thought I had gotten robbed. It was him, and he swore from that moment on that he wouldn't drink again. He kept that promise. Some girls would love their boyfriend more because of that, but it made me like him less. He became boring to me.

Chapter 4

I loved working at the bar. My coworkers and I all got really close and would drink together. One night, a new guy came in. He was about 5'3" and had a mean five o'clock shadow. His name was Cameron. He wore cowboy boots and a button-up Jägermeister shirt. It felt like love at first sight. I didn't stop thinking about him from the minute we started talking. He was a country boy, and he would call me "ma'am," which I thought was so cute. I was always so excited when my bar was next to his. Dustin started to become annoying to me at this point. Everything he did bothered me. I knew it was because I started thinking about someone else. Dustin and I started drinking together with some friends from the bar on our nights off. I started to really drift apart from Dustin. Each day, I would feel sad and know that Dustin and I were over. It was almost like I dealt with the breakup before it happened. Cameron and I started texting, but it was innocent, even though we both knew we had mutual interests.

One night at work, I had been taking shots and noticed Cameron went into the walk-in refrigerator to change a keg. I followed him in there, said, "I've been wanting to do this for so long," grabbed him by his black button-up shirt, and made out with him. I didn't go straight home that night like I usually would. I went over to Cameron's instead. Nothing happened. I felt too guilty. But when I came home, Dustin was so upset. I told him what happened, and he decided to stay with me. I really didn't want to, though. I just didn't know how to end things. As crazy as it sounded, I was worried about hurting him. That night, we had sex, and there was zero connection. I knew he was just trying to claim back what was his. It became evident to me at that point that it was over. I knew I needed to end things, but I had never broken up with anyone before. The next day, I was driving home from the grocery store and saw him fixing his red truck in the driveway. He looked so happy. I felt guilty, knowing I was about to ruin his day. I pulled into the drive and awkwardly walked up to him while he was standing out by his truck. He looked happy to see me. I stood in front of him and just said, "Dustin, it's over. I am sorry." He slammed his car door shut and was quick to respond with, "Are you fucking kidding me?" I started crying. I did feel bad. I said, "I am sorry, I am just not happy." He was emotional but mostly angry. I did feel bad, but mentally, I was ready to move on. I gave him one more hug and then got into my car and left.

I was sad for a few days but quickly moved on to Cameron. Cameron let me drink whenever I wanted to, and even better, he drank with me. I moved into a house right behind The Strip, and that took my drinking to another level. Sometimes, we'd go out for a few drinks and end up blacking out on a Monday or go for drinks between classes. There were numerous times I went to class drunk. One day, we were at the library studying, and I suggested we go to the bar and come back. That was a stupid idea. I got drunk, came back, and didn't study. I was actually asked to leave because I was talking so much. I was a total lush, and I loved it and loved being called one.

One night, we were at Cowboy Copper, which was the bar we worked at. The bar is huge and has two stories. Well, Cameron and his friends, Austin and Dakota, were upstairs, and I was downstairs. I was getting my favorite shot, a Royal Fuck, which was Crown Royal, Razzmatazz, and Cranberry juice mixed together. I shot it back, and as I went to turn around, there was this short guy in a red hoodie with dark jeans. He came up to me and said he wanted to buy me a shot. I never turned down drinks, so I said, "Sure," and walked with him to the bar. We took our shots, then he started getting closer. So much so that he was rubbing himself on my legs and said he wanted to dance. I said, "No, I'm here with my boyfriend." He told me that he could show me what I was missing, so I told him to fuck off and walked up the stairs. I was wearing one of my favorite dresses that night. It was black with little flowers on it, had a cut-out zip-up back, and was very short. I didn't know he was behind me until I felt his hand lift up my dress. I pushed his hand away and held my dress down as I walked up the stairs, and he went back downstairs. I quickly told Cameron. One thing I loved about him was that he was not a hothead, just protective. He told me to wait upstairs, and he and his two other friends went downstairs. I watched as each one of them picked up the guy and his two friends and literally threw them out of the bar.

Due to the ruckus outside, the police arrived and asked to speak with each one of us. I spoke with the female cop and told her the story. Her response was, "Well, maybe you shouldn't have worn a dress like that." Her words sent me into a spiral. They triggered what happened with Trent. I started crying and then continued to cry that whole night. I told

Cameron what happened. I realized I had never dealt with my rape. I just pushed it aside because no one believed me. Everything for the following days seemed hazy. The colors and sounds were dull, and I wanted to be alone and isolated. I would lie in bed, stare at the ceiling, and just replay that night and how much it affected my whole life.

There were so many emotions going through my head, and it took me back to that little girl who no one believed or stood up for. It broke my heart. I felt that hole start to open again. The only way I knew to cope was to do what I did best. Drink it away.

Cameron and I moved to where I grew up, and he got a job at one of the main hospitals in town. I had one class left in order to get my degree. It was Calculus, and I was terrible at math, so I put it off as long as I could. I had stayed close with Maddie through college, and she got engaged and asked me to be her maid of honor. I was so honored and accepted. As her maid of honor, she asked me to go with her to pick up her dress. We flew down and went straight to the dress boutique. It was beautiful, sequined on the top, and an A-line fit. We went back to her cousin Colton's house. Her cousin was engaged to a girl named Renee. We started drinking wine with dinner. I had a normal amount of wine, and everyone went in for the night. Colton and I stayed up by the pool, grabbed another bottle of wine, and talked. Then another bottle, then blackout. I came to after being pushed up against the wall with Colton's tongue down my throat. I kissed back, and then I blacked out again. I woke up hammered the next morning and told Maddie what happened. I laughed about it like it didn't matter. I was so drunk that I didn't understand the consequences of my actions or that I was even in a committed relationship with Cameron. We went shopping at Saks Fifth Avenue, which is a fairly nice place. I had to go to the bathroom twice because I was dry-heaving so much. I called Cameron while at the store and told him what happened. He was so upset. I cried while telling him how sorry I was. Honestly, I was sorry and didn't know how it happened. I could tell Maddie was mad at me, but I was so focused on trying my best not to throw up. This carried on into the airport. Again, I had to get out of line because I thought I was going to throw up. Not only was I nauseous now, but I had severe anxiety. I always got anxious when I was really hungover. It was unbearable, and Maddie had enough. This was the start of how I lost one of my best friends to drinking.

I had gotten news a few days before that my grandma was on her last couple of days. I was able to say my goodbyes months before when Cameron and I went up to Ohio, where she lived. After her fight with cancer, she passed. I was very close to her and didn't take it well.

But what do I do to fix feelings?

Drink.

I went to the bar at about 3 in the afternoon and started with my Irish trash can drink, which was filled almost to the top with different liquors, and then a Red Bull turned over and stuck inside, just like a trash can. Then came the shots, one after the other. A pack of cigarettes lasted maybe 4 hours. The last thing I remember was someone brought apple pie moonshine. I shot it back. Then, blackout. According to Cameron, that is when I started crying. I fell to the ground crying, and no one could calm me down, so they called Cameron to pick me up. I woke up the next morning at 8 for the funeral, and I was still drunk. They had the funeral online for people who could not come and see it in the church, which I couldn't do because it was in Ohio. I sat on the couch and stared at the screen. The service started. Cameron woke up, sat next to me, and just held my hand. He never mentioned the shit show that I was the night before, and no one else did either.

Cameron started working nights, so I had a group of friends that I would go out with. One of them was my friend Cole Campbell. We knew each other from grade school and would go to bars together. One of those nights, we were bar hopping downtown and went to Eddie's, which was a hole-in-the-wall dive bar. Everyone knew not to get any dark drinks at Eddie's because then you couldn't see the roaches. I was drunk by the time we decided to go there, so I didn't care. Technically I was drunk, but for me, I had a ways to go. I ordered a tall double Tito's and soda. The vodka filled ¾ of the glass. I got my drink and went to sit down. It was gone by the time I got to the table. So, I ordered another and took a little bit longer to drink this one. Then came the third. I brought it back to my table and sat down, and then I blacked out. I woke up when I fell down against the wall in our bedroom. I threw up on myself, then went to stand up and fell back down again. Then, I woke up in bed the next morning. Cameron was pissed, and Cole didn't answer my calls, and we haven't talked since. We don't know how I didn't get alcohol poisoning. I was embarrassed until I went back out and drank again.

In December 2013, I graduated with a degree in Marketing from Oklahoma State University. I went back to Stillwater to go to the ceremony. One of my best friends, Kayla, lived there, so my boyfriend and I stayed with her. The night before graduation, my two girlfriends and I stayed in with some wine and worked on decorating my cap while Cameron went out with his friends. By the time Kayla went to bed, I was on my 3rd glass of wine and was pretty tipsy. I decided to meet Cameron at the bar. After some shots, I blacked out.

I was told that Kayla woke up to me hot gluing ribbon to my cap with rhinestones everywhere. I woke up that morning so drunk and hungover at the same time. Graduation was at 9:00am, and it was 7:30am. I threw up in the shower, so they brought me mimosas while I was in the shower. I chugged two. They dropped me off at the building, and they told me that they would watch. Cameron drank Rumple Minze for the first time and was too sick to attend my graduation. Honestly, I was too drunk to care. I barely remember the ceremony. I kept talking to the girl next to me. After I received my diploma, not only did I hug the dean, but I walked down the aisle of headmasters of each department, and I high-fived them all the whole way down. After the ceremony, teachers kept talking to me, and I'm sure I reeked of alcohol. I was completely shit-faced. I couldn't find my friends, and my phone died, so I went out of the building, and there were families and graduates everywhere. I cannot even tell you how many family pictures I forced myself into. I then decided to run to the bar I worked at because I knew our friend Corey would be there. The bar was closed, but I begged him to make me a Fireball shot. He told me that I was way too drunk. After he gave me a ride to my friend's house, we went to eat at my favorite place, Red

Lobster. I barely remember that. I immediately passed out when I made it back to my friend's house.

Chapter 5

After graduation, I looked for a job where I could use my degree. I was currently working at a bar called Whiskey's Pub and Grill, which was by far my favorite bar that I worked at. I got really close to all the patrons, and one invited me to a golf tournament that I could potentially get a job at. He told me to wear a purple golf shirt, so I did. I was put in a cart with two women, Lea and Heather. We had a blast, drank, and just had a good time, and it turns out Lea was the manager of a whole brand of skilled nursing facilities and asked me to work for her. So, just like that, I found my new career. I worked as a Director of Marketing for a skilled nursing facility. My job was to fill the building with patients. I would market myself to doctors and case managers in hospitals and assisted living facilities. I loved it. I found such a love and passion for the geriatric field. I had my favorite resident in the long-term care side named Richard. He would dance with me and show me pictures of his family and was always so excited to see me. I did fairly well, but then my drinking started getting out of hand. Lea and I had become pretty good friends, but my numbers began to decline, and she would be tough on me, so being the immature drunk that I was, I quickly put in my two weeks 'notice.

What did I resort to?

The bar.

I got a job at another dive bar. This one allowed you to drink there as long as you replaced what you drank.

How wonderful.

I would have six to seven shots of Fireball a day. What affected Cameron and I's relationship was that he always had to come and pick me up. It got tiresome. So, Cameron and I were not doing well, but I had no idea because I was drinking so much. He was getting resentful and would always get onto me for drinking so much. I hated that.

Maddie's wedding was finally here, and by this time, I had been demoted as Maid of Honor. I would have done a great job if I hadn't been drinking. There was also the fact that I got mad at Maddie the night before her bachelorette party because I was hammered, and she asked me to stop drinking so much so I could make it on time.

I was so offended that I canceled all the rooms at the Omni Dallas. I was so drunk that next morning. Thank God the hotel had openings. I couldn't even drive to Dallas. I had to have my friend Olivia drive. By the time the wedding came, Maddie was really tired of my drinking. Her wedding was at a very upscale hotel. It was the venue that all of the rich people got married in. Cameron and I had a good time at the wedding. It was a full open bar, so there were plenty of shots. I woke up the next day in bed in my long, chiffon bridesmaid dress, and the bottom was covered in red wine. From this point forward, Maddie and I's relationship was never the same. She was the first friend I lost to my drinking, and I was too drunk to notice or care.

I had gotten off of my antidepressants years prior because I just didn't need them anymore, but by this point, my anxiety was back. Just like before, I would hyper-focus on something and then obsess over it. One day, I ate some avocado, and my tongue became slightly swollen. This opened the door to the fear of my throat closing up due to an allergic reaction. I hadn't had a food allergy since I was little, but just like the last time, it started with the first panic attack. I ate something that a jalapeno touched, so it was really hot, and I freaked out. I didn't tell anyone what was happening, but I told my boss I was sick and needed to leave, then hurried home and took Benadryl because it helps with allergies. During the next couple of weeks, I would drink at work to help ease the anxiety. I felt like it helped, so I kept doing it. But then, the mornings after, I was more anxious than I was the night before. The anxiety wasn't just when I would eat. This time, I was always anxious. Eating became very difficult for me, and anything with flavor would trigger a panic attack. I wasn't at a point where I learned to calm myself down yet, so I started taking Benadryl everywhere with me. Any time I ate something that made me feel that way, I would take more Benadryl. Eventually, I was just eating plain bread and water. That's when Cameron had a heart-to-heart with me and suggested that I should be medicated again. I went to the doctor and was put on another antidepressant, and after about two weeks, it went away. Just like before, it was like it never happened.

Chapter 6

One day, I met Spencer Connelly. Spencer was such a drunk. He was overweight and tall, but he was funny and always did crazy stuff. He always came into my bar, and we had fun together. He was always inappropriate and drank like a tank. He always made dirty jokes and said inappropriate things, which I loved. He understood that drinking was fun and that it was okay to drink every day. Cameron didn't. I started texting Spencer all the time, and I became very interested in him. The texts were getting more and more sexual, which created a strong sexual tension between us. One night, I was off work, so Cameron and I went drinking at the bar I worked at. I strayed off and was talking to other people like I usually did. Then, I started hanging out with Spencer. To other people, it seemed normal because we kept everything very quiet. Then he went outside, and I followed. Next thing I knew, I was pushed up against the wall, and we were making out. There was such passion and excitement. I stopped and went back inside. Cameron looked at me and asked me if I was cheating on him, but I assured him that I wasn't. I had been telling Cameron that I needed more passion and excitement for months now, so I was so pleased that I finally got that. Cameron and I got a ride home, and the next thing I knew, he grabbed me and made out with me. We had passionate sex on the floor, and it was great, but it was too late. It didn't feel right anymore. The next couple of days, I was texting Spencer, and one day, I went to our sister bar with him after work and told Cameron that I would be home later. We took shot after shot until I blacked out. When I came out of my blackout, the bottoms of my feet were pressed up against the windshield, the door was open, and Spencer's face was between my legs. I vaguely remember hearing clapping from people walking by. I found out later that we were in the middle of a parking lot. Then I woke up at Spencer's house.

Oh shit, Cameron!

I got a ride to my car and drove home to find Cameron waiting for me. He called in to work because I never came home. He was sitting on his chair in the living room, and I told him what happened. He said he understood how I was feeling and what our relationship was missing, and things could be worked out. It just might take him some time. I really did love him. I just couldn't stop at this point. It was like a drug. I changed Spencer's name in my phone and kept texting him. A few days later, I told Cameron that I was going to stay at a friend's house, then went out to the bar with Spencer. We were drinking, and just like usual, we blacked out and woke up at his house. This time, I woke up naked, and my upper thighs were covered in his handprints.

I was shocked. I actually cheated. I honestly did feel bad.

When I got home, Cameron greeted me, and I said, "Hi," like nothing was wrong. He was actually happy to see me. I felt so dirty. I went to take a shower because we were going to Thanksgiving at his family's house. That's right, I cheated on him the night before spending the day with his family. I took my clothes off and hopped in the glass shower. Cameron walked by and saw the handprints, and all he said was, "Nice." I didn't even know what to say, so I didn't say anything. The ride together was fun. I loved this man.

What was I doing?

He stopped to sightsee, which is something we always did together because I loved it. When I told him how happy I was that we were sightseeing, he said, "I have to take care of my girls," referring to me and his dog, Maggie. Bentley wasn't allowed to come to his family's house anymore because the last time, he rolled in the mud with the cows and covered their house in mud. Cameron was really trying to make this work, and I cheated. Anything nice he did, the more I thought about how incredibly shitty of a person I was. We were almost home, and I told him I kissed Spencer. I didn't have the heart to tell him what really happened. He said it was over, and I had the nerve to cry and expect him to comfort me.

Cameron agreed to let me stay for the next six months because I had zero savings. I was appreciative, but not enough to stop dating Spencer. I spent most of my time at Spencer's anyways. I drank before work, during work, and after work every day. Always had a beer in hand. His house was nasty, like a college frat house. It smelled like cigarettes. He had a long white folding table that was always covered in cigarette burns and empty beer cans, and the whole place was being "renovated" but wasn't. There was zero work being done, just the mess. But I loved being with him because he never told me to stop drinking, and we had so much fun. He was always right along with me and usually even drank more. We had a group of friends who would drink all the time. I thought these guys were really cool and never looked at them as alcoholics because that would mean I was one, too. Tanner was the asshole out of the group, and nobody really liked him; they just tolerated him. He prided himself on getting our friend Noah, who was a terrible drunk, to drink after being sober for two years. Then there was Dylan Moore. He was a great guy, just a drunk like all of us.

Then there was Mallory. She had a "real job" but still drank with us and eventually dated Dylan after sleeping with Spencer. The group was insanely incestuous. We would start the day drinking and just drink until the bar closed. We went to The Marketplace, which is a bar I worked at sometimes in addition to my usual gig. There were so many times I would black out by three in the afternoon. One day, I was bartending at The Marketplace and decided to show my boobs to everyone after I had some shots. No one tipped, but I was too drunk to care.

I was running rampant around town without a care in the world. One night at The Marketplace, I came out of a blackout to Mallory going down on me in the bathroom. I didn't remember much, but loved every minute that I did remember. It sparked a strong curiosity towards women. I had sex in that bathroom probably seven times, but most of the time, it was with Spencer. I was actually banned from using that bathroom because I had sex in it so much. The bar ended up letting me go because I drank too much and caused too much drama. My response to that was, "I think that's the best thing for me." For a minute there, I was finally seeing how bad I really was, but it didn't last.

Chapter 7

I quickly found a new job in home health sales, which was pretty much what I did before, but with home health services rather than skilled nursing. I was actually pretty good at it, and it gave my life direction. It also gave me more money to drink. I was a functioning alcoholic and got my numbers in and did my trade shows. One day, I had a ride around with my boss, and she drove. I told her to drop me off at a bar for a "business meeting." I actually thought she believed me. I was meeting my friend Seth there and was supposed to meet with Vanessa, my boss, later that night to get our nails done. When I walked into the drafty, musky bar, the lights were dim, but I saw Seth sitting at a round bar table with our friend Don. He had a bucket of Budweiser waiting for me. I told myself I would just have a couple of drinks, and I ordered a shot of Fireball. It came in a warm rocks glass. stonIt was a hefty double pour, but I shot it down quickly. One led to six in a matter of minutes. We decided to go across town to another bar.

There was always that recurring feeling of dread I would get from walking out of a dive bar and into the warm sunlight. It always made me question what I was doing with myself, but not enough to stop drinking. We got to the bar, and that is the last thing I remember. I woke up the next morning with five missed calls from my boss.

Why does this keep happening?

The minute I have a drink, I have to have another, and then I drink until I can't anymore. I felt confused and full of regret. I texted her immediately and told her I fell asleep. They ended up asking me to come in for a meeting. I was still trashed from the night before, but I cleaned myself up and drove to work. My regional boss was in the meeting, and they questioned my behavior. I reeked of cinnamon booze, but I somehow talked my way out of getting into trouble.

One day, I just got tired of Spencer. There was a guy named Ryan Mitchell who had been flirting with me at the bar for quite some time. He was mysterious, not as open and boisterous as Spencer was. I wanted to try something different, so one day, I called Spencer and told him that I didn't want to see each other anymore. After work that day, I went to the bar. Spencer showed up with his friends, and I stayed on the other side of the bar and had some drinks. I came up to Ryan and asked him, "So why haven't we gone out yet?"

He said he never had the chance, so we planned a date night. Then the drinks started. One shot after another. Next thing I knew, we were in the back seat of his car making out. He asked if I wanted to go back to his place. I said, "Definitely," and off we went. Drunk, of course. That night was odd. Oddest and most boring sex I have ever had. It actually sobered me up. The chemistry we had at the bar and the times leading up to this became non-existent. I finally fell asleep, then woke up the next morning to his mom knocking on the door. He lived with his mom, too. That morning was awkward for me. He took me to his car, and I told myself I could easily go without doing that again. But blacked-out-Lauren thought otherwise. I would black out and call him 5-10 times a night. I would get drunk and show up where he was. I became obsessed. I came to realize that it wasn't because of him, but it was the idea of him. I didn't like Ryan. I liked the idea of having someone like him to be a partner with. I definitely had problems being single, but those didn't get resolved until years later.

For weeks, I would get drunk and call Ryan. I would be so ashamed when I would wake up in the morning and look at my phone. Spencer's friends were upset with me since I went home with another guy in front of him the day we broke up, but I didn't see a problem with it. I had a new target who was clearly not interested. My friend Abby decided to take me to Oklahoma City and spend some quality time together. The first night there, I dyed my light blonde hair black. If this wasn't foreshadowing, I don't know what is. It's like I became an entirely different person with black hair. Although It didn't stay dark long, it was a dark time. We went out to eat and then went to a bar downtown called Makers and met up with two of her friends. I was drinking pretty heavily but was holding myself together well. I needed attention from someone, though, so I kissed her friend. I held his hand in my hand until we got back to his house. It's like I would turn into this psychotic girl when I blacked out. I got into his bed, naked, and jumped on top of him. He didn't want to play any part in that, but I just wasn't getting it. He excused himself to go to the bathroom, then came back in with Abby and turned the lights on. Abby yelled, "Lauren get the fuck out of his bed!" So I did, promptly. I was too drunk to be embarrassed until I heard it the next morning over brunch. This was after I threw up in the parking lot. I eventually went back to Spencer since he was more than willing to forget about what happened, and we picked up where we left off.

One of my friends in the geriatric healthcare industry was holding an open house at her assisted living facility. I went to show my support, or at least that's what I said. I really went because there was free champagne. I had some cookies and three glasses of champagne, which I loved, so they went down quickly. I immediately wanted more, but they ran out, so I found a group of people who were going out to eat afterward and decided to join them. It was a nice restaurant, and we sat at a table outside. I sat at the head of the table, and my friends Jena and Don were there, as well as some people I didn't know very well. I didn't drink much because, for once, I was worried about driving drunk. I got into my car and started driving home. I lived around twenty minutes from the restaurant. I was crossing a bridge, and that's the last thing I remember.

There were more occurrences like this. Maybe not as drastic, but drinking was affecting my everyday life. One day, I decided I'd had enough of the drinking, Spencer, the blackout calls to Ryan, the shakes, the dreaded mornings after, and just making an ass out of myself. So, I quit. I focused on work, hung out with different friends, and felt really good. I didn't think about drinking nearly as much as I thought I would. I saved money by not drinking. I had gotten an apartment by myself and finally started decorating it. For the first time ever, I was single and living alone, and I liked it. Then, one day, I was trying to hang up the curtains, and I couldn't get them up. I decided to call Spencer to help. He was up at our bar, and he said, "Come meet us here, and then we'll all come help you." They say you can go a decent amount of time without drinking and then come back to the same bar and have the same people sitting in the same spots, and they'll have drinks waiting for you. That was very true. I was off again. Spencer took me back, and I was back to filling that void inside with a guy. I could never be alone for longer than three months.

Having a normal relationship with Spencer felt off. We went on maybe two dates and spent Christmas with his mom and dad. I blacked out after having sex on their bedroom floor that night. I usually feel like I am where I'm supposed to be in my life when I date someone, but with him, I never felt that. But we had so much fun drinking, and I never had to hear that I was drinking too much. I was actually always encouraged to drink more. One day, he took me to eat with his parents, which was nice. After we got done, we immediately went to the bar. We started on our typical day into night drinking.

We were pretty drunk a couple of hours in, and there was a girl sitting next to me named Jillian. Spencer always said that she was the "world's worst lesbian." At this point, I had been questioning my sexuality for a little while. I had made out with more girls than guys. I enjoyed sex with guys, but I was really curious about going further with a woman. Up until this point, I was trying to find a way to do that but didn't know where to start. Then, I sat next to Jillian that night, and we started drinking with her. She was such a drunk, too. Spencer told me to make out with her. Usually, I would do that for a guy's attention, but this time, I really really wanted to. Then, I thought we should have a threesome. That would be fun, and I would get the best of both worlds. The three of us tabbed out and left. Spencer drove, and I was in the front seat. I was turned around, making out with Jillian and clearly enjoying myself. Spencer could not take it. He got so jealous. He slammed on his brakes, and I flew into the dashboard. He called the threesome off and dropped her off at her apartment. Spencer and I had "she's mine" sex that night, and I was not feeling it. I woke up after Spencer left my apartment, and the first thing I did was message Jillian on Facebook, saying, "I still want it." It was around one in the afternoon, and she told me to meet her at the same bar, so I did. I was so nervous, but I was determined to get what I wanted. I showed up at the bar, and she was sitting at the bar top. We started drinking, and I was intrigued by her. She was very plain Jane, had a short haircut, was very little, and was wearing a tracksuit. But the sexual tension between us was insane. I vaguely remember leaving the bar with her, and I woke up naked the next morning. I had a text telling me how good of a time she had, but that was it. I had been waiting for this to happen for years, and I didn't even remember it. This was the beginning of my next obsession. I couldn't stop texting her. I wanted more of her. We played the back-and-forth game for a few weeks, and then she told me she was talking to another girl and needed some time to figure things out with her. Well, I absolutely did not care about that. I wanted her. So I kept pursuing, and the next thing I knew, she moved into my apartment.

Then there was Spencer. I completely left him in the dark. I just stopped talking to him and acted like we never dated. That didn't keep him from calling me and trying to get me back. I simply wasn't interested anymore. It was just like a switch went off, and I wanted nothing to do with him anymore. I was leaving a trail of destruction behind me and couldn't care less.

What drew me to Jillian was that I thought she was successful and a professional. The type of woman I wanted to be with. Well, soon, I found out she had been in a car wreck when she was drunk, so she did not have a car. She also lost her job as a real estate agent. She wasn't working, but I didn't care at this point. I was addicted. Everyone loved us together. We went from bar to bar and drank and drove all over town. Making out at every bar that we went to. We were in our own world. My drinking at this point was out of control. Jillian still didn't work, so I would wake up for work and do my job, and then I would come home, and we'd be off. We would start at one bar and then move on as the night went on. We did this every day of the week. Except on Sundays, we would go for brunch and start with mimosas. We always made jokes that the Eggs Benedict looked like breasts. I made good money, but all of it was going to bars, and she didn't make anything. So, one day, I asked her to get a job. I was completely wrapped up in her. I had never been the one to financially take care of someone else. And I liked it, for now.

I was still letting Cameron's dog, Maggie, out for him because he worked twelve-hour shifts. I had never really comprehended our breakup. It honestly just didn't register. But we talked almost every day, and I thought deep down that we were meant to be back together. I kept these feelings from Jillian, but she knew we talked every day. I cared for her, but in hindsight, she was more of an addiction than anything. Even though I was happy with her, I still felt like she was just filling in until Cameron wanted me back. She wasn't Cameron. No one was.

Chapter 8

My drinking continued to get worse. I would start drinking around three in the afternoon, then take Jillian to work, then go back to the bar, and then go home and pass out. She would get a ride home, and then, sometimes, I would go back out with her. I had the shakes every day until I had the next drink, so if I didn't drink until three, I had the shakes until three. I would tell people at the bars this, and they would make it sound normal, so I thought it was. I began throwing up every morning and then started throwing up blood. I lost a lot of weight and was thrilled to be so tiny. I eventually decided to get my stomach checked out, so they scheduled an endoscopy and colonoscopy. I hoped and prayed it was Crohn's disease. I just didn't want them to tell me to stop drinking. That was just out of the question. It came back that I had damaged my stomach lining from drinking. But, of course, I didn't do anything about it.

Work was going well, and I was bringing in my numbers. Little did I know that a company was watching me, and someone referred me to their company. The representative's name was Jade, and I had only heard the best things about her. She was the top producer in the home health industry, and I was flattered that she thought so highly of me. This company was bigger and would be a massive pay raise. I passed the first interview, so they scheduled a second interview on the phone with Travis, a guy from corporate. I decided to have some wine to calm my nerves. As usual, the first glass went down quickly, then the second. On my third glass, the interview started. It was going great. I had such moxie and confidence. My jokes were witty and funny, and I was charming. I got offered the job. I got a huge raise, and what better way to celebrate than with drinks? We went into town, and I was so proud of myself and could not stop talking about it. I was on a high that lasted for days.

In the beginning, the job didn't go so well. I was given the leftover accounts and was drinking even more than before. I always started my days at ten and ended them at three because I was either hungover or getting drunk. I was not meeting my numbers, and my regional boss didn't think too highly of me. One day, I was 30 minutes late to bring lunch to a main account. But, like most sales jobs, you have three months to build your accounts. So I was riding it out as much as I could.

There was sales training for this position in Atlanta, Georgia. I was so excited to go. It was in a nice hotel, and the first thing I did was find the bar. I sat on the barstool and ordered a tall Sam Adams and only sipped on two the whole night. What an accomplishment, I thought. I did the same thing the next night and the night after. My wallet was happy, and no shakes or hangovers. I made some friends, Jackson being my favorite, but I was usually at the bar alone. One night, I was watching Miss America, and a girl I went to high school with was one of the contestants. I felt so inferior to her. It made me depressed. I hadn't accomplished anything, and here I was, drinking alone. The next evening, we were going off-site to go to dinner. I had already had my two beers and was going to stay in, but Jackson talked me into going. There was this bigger woman who offered me some vodka, and believe it or not, I hesitated, but then I caved. We went upstairs to her room, and she poured me a drink. It was straight vodka, and I chugged it like I usually do. I don't remember leaving the hotel. I have glimpses of being outside at the table, but that's it. I woke up in my clothes from the night before, and I was on top of my made bed, unable to remember a thing. I got dressed and walked into the training room. Talk about a walk of shame. I felt all eyes on me. My seat was in the front. I walked through the aisle, not making any eye contact with anyone, and sat next to Jackson. He informed me what had happened the night before. He said I seemed pretty drunk, but it didn't hit until we were at the table, and then I passed out at the table and fell to the ground. I had my hand in my hair and pulled out a chunk of hair. He took a picture of it to show me the next day. I was mortified, but not enough to keep me from having my beer to settle my shakes when we left later that day. I had about twenty dollars left in my account. We went to a bar in the airport as a group before we went our own ways. I spent all my money on two beers. I went all day without eating because I didn't have any money left over. I found $1.50 in my purse and bought a meat and cheese stick packet, and that was my dinner. My flight got in around 11pm, and Jillian came to pick me up with flowers. We went straight to the bar. We knew my check would hit at midnight, so we lined up our first round of fireball shots and then started the vicious cycle again.

Things started getting darker for me. I would drink and automatically go to that dark place again. One day, we went day-drinking, and I got drunk but didn't black out. I felt completely alone. I hated who I was and what

I was doing with myself. I was sad and hopeless. I got a pair of scissors and closed the bathroom door. I sat down with one leg close to my chest and started to cry.

I opened the scissors and pressed the edge against my skin. I just wanted it to stop. I wanted these thoughts to go, and I wanted relief. I started to move the blade back and forth. Leave it to me to have the dullest pair of scissors. I barely broke the skin. Jillian opened the door and started yelling at me. "How dare you do that? How can you do this to me? You need help!" She gave me the worst guilt trip and made the whole thing about her. I kept my feelings about the whole situation to myself. She took the scissors and walked away. I just sat there and stared at the wall, asking myself, "How did I get here?" I felt even worse than before. But again, this is nothing another drink wouldn't fix.

By the time Jillian got off of work every day, I would be blacked out or passed out. I wasn't drinking to have fun anymore. I was drinking to disappear and didn't want to live anymore. I would do shot after shot. I didn't even care what I drank anymore as long as it had the same result. I kept wine at home to constantly have something to drink. I actually told a local liquor store to keep my favorite wine in magnums because I promise to buy at least a couple a week. He kept up his side of the deal, and so did I. One night, we came home from the bar, and Jillian went to sleep, so I was alone but wanted to drink more. All I had was Night Train, a "wine" that tastes terrible but is 17.5% alcohol. Someone gave it to Cameron as a joke, and he gave it to me as a housewarming gift. So, I drank it. It was disgusting, but it got the job done.

I couldn't tell how bad I was getting, but looking back, I was completely off the wall. At this point, I would do anything to be able to drink more. I would sometimes take three to four of my Adderall 20mg pills just so I could keep drinking. I was such a lightweight to pills so that was a lot to me. Sometimes, I would even snort them in my car in the bar parking lot. At first, I would try to hide it and snort it off my dashboard or center console, but not long after that, I would just snort it off of my hands and eat the remainder. I just couldn't get the rush fast enough. That is, if I didn't sell them for bar money. I was making a lot of money, but I was spending all of it at the bars. I was starting to get behind on all of my bills, and my electricity was always getting shut off, so I started selling all of my clothes, even the ones I liked. Jillian's money was going straight to the bar, too. At one point, I was planning on selling all of my nice Ashley bedroom furniture because that would give me around $500, and that would hold me over for a week.

Luckily, I got distracted and never put it up. Sometimes, I thought I had a problem, but then I thought since I could go all day without drinking, it wasn't actually a problem. It made me think about a guy I saw a couple of years prior who was sitting on the back door stoop of the bar where I worked. He looked rough and passed out as he hugged a liter bottle of liquor in a brown paper sack. It was around 9 in the morning. To me, that was what an alcoholic looked like, and I wasn't like that, so I couldn't be an alcoholic.

I started noticing something happening when I would drink. I would take my Adderall and immediately would feel a warm rush come over me, more so than it did in years prior. I would feel like I was buzzing, and my skin was tingly. My thoughts were racing, and I could not stop talking or sit still. I would have to drink just to calm down and be somewhat normal. Then, I would have around five drinks, and then the depression would hit. I would go to the lowest of lows. It would feel like I was sinking into the barstool. At this point, I was drinking to not feel a thing, which always led to a blackout. This up-and-down cycle happened every time I drank without fail.

One day, I started drinking around three. I had to let Cameron's dog out, but I realized I was too drunk to drive. There was a guy there that I didn't know who offered to take me to Cameron's house, and I thought it was a good idea. I vaguely remember the drive. When we got to his house, I used the garage keypad to open the garage, and we both walked in. We let Maggie out and then went back to the bar. I drank some more, then went to that dark place again. After my 13th shot of Fireball, I remember crying to the bartender that something was wrong with me and I just didn't know what, and then I blacked out. I briefly came out of my blackout while crying on my knees on the living room floor. I exclaimed, "There has to be more to life than this! I need help!" Then went back into a blackout.

That next morning, I woke up in the middle of a panic attack. I had let a strange guy into Cameron's house. He could have seen the passcode and could come rob him of everything. I was completely falling apart, screaming, crying, falling to my knees, and literally pulling my hair out. Then, Jillian started crying and begged me to get help. I secretly wanted help but never said it out loud or did anything about it. I knew that I was living in utter chaos. I was throwing up blood, drinking all night every night, had severe shakes every minute that I was sober, sold almost all of my clothes, some of my friends just stopped hanging out with me because I was too much, and I just completely hated myself and my life. I wanted more for myself, so I agreed.

Chapter 9

By the time I got to the psychiatric hospital, I already wanted to be admitted. I actually panicked thinking they wouldn't admit me. But I got admitted. They said that I was unstable and unsafe to be on my own. At this point, I was very hopeless and suicidal. I walked through the outdoor walkways. I was so uneasy, but it was so beautiful. It was filled with green grass, trees, and brightly colored flowers. Totally serene. Then, we got to the door. I had the stereotypical visualization of what a psychiatric hospital would be. Very bleak, with limited freedom and crazy people. It wasn't that way at all. There were people of all ages, and they were so nice and made me feel welcome: the staff and patients. I immediately spoke with a therapist, and she gave me my first words of advice. "Don't talk to any of the guys here because they are trouble, and then you will be fine." The rooms were semi-private, and I had a seasoned roommate. I'll admit, as off as she was, she did help me get adjusted. She would explain why they did things, and she was just very warm and welcoming to me when I was so uneasy. The first night was hell. I had a cot covered with a sheet, a blanket, and a pillow that felt like a thick piece of cardboard. I don't think I slept at all. I laid awake wondering what happened to my life and where I was going to go from here. I didn't know what to expect.

What if this didn't work?

The nights were harder than the days. Hard to get comfortable, hard to quiet my mind, missing home, and the biggest adjustment, not being able to drink issues like this away. I would wake up to my roommate crying in the bathroom almost every night. I was told to focus on myself while I was there, not other people's problems, so as hard as it was, I stayed in bed, listening to her cry.

I kept to myself for the most part, but I definitely met some people I won't forget.

Denise was a tall woman with a large afro and pale skin. She always had to have a tech with her. She would start laughing or crying out of nowhere. One day, Jillian came to visit me, and she kissed me goodbye. Denise saw that and got very close to my face, which scared the shit out of me, and asked if I was a homosexual. I said, "Yes," and she told me she's a trisexual; she has sex with women, men, and hermaphrodites. Then, she walked off. Another day, Denise asked me to sit with her at lunch because I had been sitting alone. I really didn't want to, but I couldn't say no, so I sat with her. She told me that she marched with Martin Luther King and then slept with him, and she also fought in the Vietnam War. She was 28. It was a lunch I will never forget.

About a day or two into treatment, they diagnosed me with Bipolar II disorder and, big surprise, a drinking problem. I had no idea what a well-mannered Bipolar could look like. I had heard stories of high manias, extreme lows, cheating on spouses, etc. I was not happy with this diagnosis because of what it was, but I was happy to have identified my problem. I felt like it explained some of my behavior from the past few years. I was told that Bipolar II was a mood disorder with more depressive moods, and with hypomania, which is a light version of mania, it could feel like a very good day or a great mood. In these moods, you can have extra energy, be more excitable than usual, and be more productive. They were very hard to detect for me and made me question every good day I had.

Bipolar was something that I was unfamiliar with. I didn't understand what it did to my mind and how the medications I was taking worked to treat it. I wanted to know more about what I had, so I asked. I learned that Bipolar reduces the amount of gray matter in the brain, which is the part of the brain that controls muscle, seeing, hearing, speech, and emotions. Gray matter also controls our decision-making, self-control, and impulses. This reduction happens when we have manic or depressive episodes. When we have Bipolar disorder, we have higher levels of dopamine, which handles emotions in our brain. When we take Bipolar medications such as mood stabilizers, they work to stabilize those overstimulated activities in our brain. Antipsychotics work by blocking dopamine so we have lower levels, and they mellow out our moods. They decided to put me on Lithium and Zyprexa. They told me that Lithium was a hit-or-miss medication, but if it worked, it would become a major part of my recovery. It worked. I had to be monitored via blood work every few days until everything leveled out. I hated needles, so I really hated doing the bloodwork every morning, but once they got the medication to its therapeutic level, I was grateful to be on it.

I ended up finding friends to sit with at lunch. There was Arlene, who was high on Valium all the time, and Richard, an overweight rocker who looked like Tom Hardy. Richard's wife passed away the year before from bulimia. She ended up bleeding out of her mouth, and he found her next to him in bed. That made me grateful to have gotten help when I did because that could have been me. I was throwing up blood every morning. I had a sense of belonging with them, which made my stay more enjoyable. Then, there was Kylie. She came in for postpartum psychosis, and she had been there for a while. She was really nice.

Denise used to go around and tell people that when her dad, who she claimed was a plastic surgeon, saw Kylie for the first time, she looked like a pig, and he made her look the way she did now. She took that like a champ, and she never let the situation escalate. I was so impressed by Kylie. She made tweezers out of a Bic pen and let me use her markers. I became friends with her and actually stayed in touch with her for several years.

One day, my roommate was crying on her bed, and I asked her what was wrong. I couldn't stand not helping at all. She informed me that she was bipolar and had mixed episodes but was scared to try the medicine they wanted her to take, so she gave it to another guy there. I told her I was sorry to hear that, even though I had no idea what she was talking about.

I had taken Adderall for over 11 years, and the day that I got admitted was the last day that I took it. I loved Adderall. It sped up my days and made everything seem to be better and go more smoothly. I found out that the high that I felt when I took it the year before was causing manic episodes. Stimulants can cause mania. So, the day I quit drinking, I quit Adderall.

I stayed at the hospital for eight days. Each day got better and better, and oddly enough, I got pretty comfortable being in a psychiatric hospital. On the last day, during my discharge, the doctor talked to me about the severity of drinking on these medications. She told me you can only have one or two. And, to my surprise still today, I told her, "I can't have just one."

She then told me, "If you don't want to come back here, do not drink." That shook me still, so I agreed and went home.

Chapter 10

Walking out of the psychiatric hospital was a weird feeling. I walked through the double doors and felt the sunlight hit my face. Very surreal. Jillian made coming home very warm and welcoming. She made a welcome home scavenger hunt, and there were a dozen red roses at the end. Things were great at first. The colors were brighter, noises didn't hurt my head, and my spirits were up. Jillian was great at supporting my new sober lifestyle, and we settled in a bit more in this new life. Everything felt like the first time again.

I was placed on an "action plan" at work. Meaning I had one more month to make my quota of eight home health referrals, or else I would get booted. Months prior, I didn't even come close to that. I went back to work with a clear head but was nervous about the action plan. My boss, Alyssa, asked me, "Are you going to work for this or start looking for another job?" I decided to work for it. I had confidence in my work, and I wanted it badly enough. I worked really hard, created strategies, and paid attention to the accounts that no one thought could produce. I did exactly what my boss told me not to do. In my gut, I knew that if you take care of someone and go out of your way, it always comes back around. That one account gave me 13 referrals that month, then three more from others. I had a total of 16 referrals. I don't think my boss, Collin, was happy, but I was ecstatic. This is where my real career started.

About two months after I got sober, I started replaying all the things I did to people when I drank. All the things I did to Maddie and Cameron were the big ones. It was like an obsession that I could never turn off. I was crying all the time and just wanted to turn it off and erase my past. As much as I wanted to drink, I remembered what the doctor said about drinking on these medications. I was living in flashbacks and questions as to what the hell I had been doing for the past year. It was like I did not know myself or where I belonged. Like one day, I just woke up and was here, but didn't know how I got here. It felt like Cameron and I had just broken up. All the heartache, regret, and pain that comes with ending a four-year relationship hit me at once. It had been a year, yet it felt like it had just happened. This made me question my relationship with Jillian. I didn't want to be with her anymore, but I didn't know how to end it. But I did, at the time, enjoy the company. The romance of the relationship died around this time. We started just being roommates.

I started calling the people I wronged and apologized. There were a couple who were completely crippling to me. I was so ashamed. Luckily, they accepted my apology, and when I apologized to Cameron, to my surprise, he just said, "If it took you doing all that to get you better and here, then it's okay." The feeling of guilt was starting to lift.

I would go to the bars with Jillian sometimes and sit with all her friends from work. I had gotten to know them really well. I really liked Shawn. He was really nice and had a dry sense of humor. His mom would always come out with us, and Jillian made a point to tell me how pretty she was. One day, we were at a long table by the back door of the bar where we went. I was sitting, talking to Shawn, and watched Jillian take Shawn's mom's hat and put it on. Then I watched as she told her how pretty she was and made jokes about dating her instead of me. She would touch her arm and then put the hat back on her head. As much as I was over Jillian at that point, I hated her for doing that. It made me feel like an idiot. She had the nerve to get onto me about talking with Shawn, but she could flirt with other women. I didn't want to rock the boat with Jillian and start a fight, so I just didn't say anything.

The relationship with Jillian was starting to deteriorate. There was a lot of fighting, and then came the drinking. She just turned nasty. She told me that her ex, Lydia, would message her and send sexually suggestive messages, and she would play along. She would receive pictures of Lydia naked and comment on how good she looked. She talked about how good the sex was with her. Jillian and I never had sex sober. When I would try, she would tell me that watching me lose my mind was something she could never get past. That was one of the most painful things she could have said. It had been my most vulnerable moment and my lowest point up until that time. I had worked so hard up to this point to be better. It just wasn't enough for her. Even though I didn't love her anymore, I still wanted to be wanted and wanted to feel that she thought I was attractive. She would go out after work quite frequently. She started off with just one or two a night, then turned into coming home blacked out every night. Every once in a while, she would be nice and sweet, but most of the time, she was terrible. There were even nights she would have people over to drink when I had to work the next morning. I became very unhappy, but I only had a few bipolar episodes during our time together. Thank God, because the ones I did have, she made so much worse. Any time I would have one, she would turn things around and make me feel guilty for having feelings and yell at me.

I was assigned a doctor when I was discharged from the hospital. Her name was Dr. Jocelyn Higgins. She was a blonde, younger doctor. She noticed I was gaining a lot of weight on the Zyprexa prescription, so she put me on Seroquel. The medicine seemed to be working perfectly, which was always good news. One of the pills started to make me feel very drowsy and robot-like, so we lowered the dose a little. Eventually, we moved on to try another antipsychotic called Latuda, which worked perfectly. I really liked this doctor. She was so knowledgeable and knew my bipolar like the back of her hand. She knew what would be the best to try and what to stay away from. I enjoyed our time together.

About six months into sobriety, I got invited to a celebration of a friend, Evelyn, who passed away a year prior. I didn't know anyone other than Tony, the host of the party. So when I got there, I was uncomfortable. I found that once I got sober, I became socially awkward. I went around the room and made small talk, with each conversation lasting about two to three minutes, and then I had to move on to someone else or walk off because it got so uncomfortable. I saw Tony, and he was excited to see me and introduced me to a couple of people, but then he had to go because he had things to handle. I stood there alone, and my eyes moved to the bar. It dawned on me that no one here knew I was sober. I could drink, and no one would know. The doctor did say I could have just one. I approached the bar, and the bartender told me he would be with me in a minute. I waited, and then someone tapped my shoulder. An older man with gray hair and glasses. I didn't know who he was. He said, "Don't I know you from somewhere?" I had to think, but nothing rang a bell. Then, we remembered it was from his house a year ago. He had a group of us over after Evelyn's funeral, and I drank so much that I blacked out. I apologized for my behavior from that day and told him I was six months sober. He informed me his name was Gary, and he was over thirty years sober. We exchanged numbers, and I ended up going home sober that night.

With bipolar, the best treatment is therapy and medication. I started seeing a young therapist named Kara. She told me to start tracking my moods in order to figure out my bipolar cycle. But I didn't have any mood swings to track. She actually ended up saying that she didn't think that I was bipolar. Some people are misdiagnosed when they get sober because there's an emotional reaction after coming off of extensive substance abuse. These reactions can mimic bipolar or depression symptoms. At first, I thought maybe she was right. I told Dr. Higgins, and she assured me that I was, indeed, bipolar. I decided not to see Kara anymore.

One thing that she did suggest, though, was alcohol support groups. She gave me a list of ones to go to. For a moment, I considered it, then decided I didn't need it. I had a couple of therapists, and none of them really stuck. We did Cognitive Behavioral Therapy (CBT) with one therapist. CBT is a way of changing behaviors by changing thought patterns. It is very common, and it worked for me for a minute, then I moved on to other things.

By this point, I had gotten close to Jade and her family. I had the biggest friend crush on her. I wanted to be her friend, and I got just that and more. She mentored me in my sales, and her family quickly became my other family. She had three kids that I absolutely fell in love with.

We would take workday trips to the movies and museums. I had found my new best friend.

Chapter 11

Jillian was now drinking every night, and I was paying for everything. Unhappy was an understatement. She started getting really nasty when she would drink. I was really into work, and I hated being at home, so I would always stay late and talk to Alyssa and Callie. Work became my second home, and my paychecks showed that. I would get in bed around 10 or 11, and Jillian would close the bars down. She would come home and yell at me about anything, break things, and throw things. I would lay in bed afraid of her coming home and wish I could just stay asleep when she came home. I was miserable. One of those nights, I had to host a breakfast at one of my accounts early the next morning, so I was asleep when she got home. She was hammered and slurring her words and could barely walk up the stairs. I helped her up the stairs, put her to bed, and went to the other room. When I came back, she was sprawled out across the bed. I poked at her to get up, and she told me to fuck off. I did it again, harder, and it was followed with another "fuck off." I tried one more time, and shook her this time, and said, "Jillian move!" She quickly jumped out of bed, put her hand tightly around my neck, and pushed me up against the wall. I grabbed her hands to get them off me, then she pressed her whole body against mine to where I was completely pinned against the wall. I cried and begged her to stop and let me go. She finally let go, threw her hands to her sides, and walked off. I was crying at this point, then she just went crazy, and I could tell she was blacked out. I didn't sleep that night. When I got home the next night, I told her what happened, and her response was, "I was just drunk." Absolutely no remorse.

If I hadn't been taking my medicine, I would forget I had bipolar. I was not having any mood swings, and the reasons I was changing medicines were because of some side effects. My friend Christina had a friend who was diagnosed with bipolar four years prior. She set me up with her to get some insight. She told me about her mood swings and how the first two years are the toughest. Those years, you are struggling to find your perfect medication cocktail to get you to be stable, which can take time and a lot of bipolar episodes. She also mentioned that everyone reacts differently to each medication. I felt lucky. I wasn't having a hard time at all. I was stable, for now.

I had formed a routine aside from Jillian and her drinking. I would stay late at work almost every day for an hour or two and talk with Alyssa and Callie. Then, I would come home and take Bentley and Jillian's dog, Marley, to the dog park, which was right next to our apartments. The complex wasn't very big, so we all kind of knew each other. I became very close to this guy named Chase. Chase had a Belgian Malamute named Gambit.

We would go every day for hours. The dogs would play, and we would teach Presley tricks, and Bentley would be ready to go after 20 minutes. Chase and I hung out all the time, and we got really close. Nothing weird, either, just friends. He really helped me get my mind off the toxic relationship that I was in. Before meeting him, I would spend time crying or going to bars with her. This friendship was healthy for me.

On my one-year sobriety mark, I decided to go to New York City with my friend Shelby from high school. It was my first trip alone without family to a different state other than Texas. I was so excited and had an amazing time. It felt so good to be doing something so exciting sober and that I saved up and paid for myself. The whole time, I wanted to share with Jillian what I was doing and how much fun I was having. I remember calling her on a walk in Manhattan, and she flat-out told me not to call her for every update of the trip because she was too busy.

Doing what?

All she did was sit at home or go to the bar.

I started to hate her. When I got home, I was unpacking, and it dawned on me. I had had zero confidence in myself before, so I didn't see that I deserved better. But now, I did have confidence, and I decided then and there that I'd had enough. No more emotional torture. I realized at that moment that I had a voice, and I was stronger than I made myself out to be, then I waited for my chance. I came home one day, and Marley had chewed a hole in the wall. She had done it two times before, and Jillian did absolutely nothing about it. We started yelling at each other, and she said, "Fine, we're breaking up," like she always threatened to do. I said, "Fine," and then just let her move her stuff into the other bedroom. I'll never forget how it felt when she moved her last bit into the spare bedroom. I stood in my doorway and cried for a moment, and then felt like I could breathe again.

The fun thing about leases, though? You can't break them for a breakup. So, I was stuck with her. She started dating this guy and felt the need to tell me all about the sex they had. I think she thought I would care, but honestly, I didn't. She told me she had sex with an ex-girlfriend. Again, I didn't care. I was so happy without her and relieved that she was no longer my problem.

Once Jillian moved on to all her victims, I focused on Cameron. I wasn't allowed to talk to him towards the end of my relationship with Jillian, so we caught up, and I thought this was my chance to get him back. We talked almost every day for a couple of weeks. He even invited me to his new house outside of town and had me there to let his dog out for a day while he was gone.

Then, one day, we were talking, and it slipped that he was dating someone. I was driving home, and it was like I was hit by a train. I asked how serious they were, and he told me they were exclusive. I read him completely wrong. I thought he felt the same way that I did. I played it off like it didn't bother me and then just carried on staying in contact, but definitely not as much, and eventually, it ceased. I was single again, and it felt so weird. But I was still living with Jillian, and she was dating men back-to-back. She always had someone and felt the need to tell me about it.

I had stayed in contact with Gary, and we would go eat, and he would listen and give his two cents on what I was going through. Around this time, Gary asked me to go to this alcohol support group. I agreed the day before, but once it was time, I didn't want to go. I sat on the edge of my couch and started typing my excuses for not wanting to go. "I am tired. It has been a long day," and my promise to go to another one. I was almost done with the text when I received a text from him that said, "I'm sitting in the front come on."

Shit, I had to go.

I got in my car, and I ended up going. I nervously walked into the narrow room filled with orange chairs and sat next to Gary. I did not know what to expect. They talked about God, and I itched in my seat. I drifted apart from God a while back in my life. But I was proud to say I had a year sober. The meeting was hard to follow for me. After an hour, we all got up and talked amongst ourselves. Some women came up and talked with me, and I did like that. It made me feel not so alone and unique in my terrible past. But then Gary wanted me to meet the man who chaired the meeting. He introduced himself as Joey with a smile that completely stole my heart.

We started sharing stories, and then we made a joke about being crazy drunks, and I think we were both hooked from that point forward. Like any alcoholic, we were dating within days. At this point, I really wanted Jillian gone. I told her, "I met someone, and I'm not coming home, so I need you to watch the dogs." She walked by, grabbed my crotch, and put her hands all over me. I laughed. We hadn't had sex in a year and a half, and I wasn't interested now. She did this a couple of times during her last month at the apartment. Then, by God's grace, her paycheck was short one month, so she couldn't pay, so we both agreed that it was time for her to go. She showed up still drunk from the night before to move her stuff. It was definitely one of the most relieving and best days of my life watching her leave.

Chapter 12

Dating Joey was a nice change. I was treated better than I ever expected to be. I found that not only was I in love with him, but I was completely inspired by him, too, and that combination was a powerful feeling. He was in sales and did not have much to his name. He would go to alcohol support groups several times a week. I didn't want to go because I honestly did not like it the time I went. Over time, I started noticing how easily things rolled off his back, things that made me go crazy. He was happy all the damn time. I didn't get it. After a while, it dawned on me that it was from going to those meetings. I decided to go once a week to start off and see what I thought. I wanted to go apart from Joey and his routine so I could find myself in the program. There were a few that I sporadically went to, but none really stuck.

I had not been to church in years. I grew up Catholic and drifted apart from their beliefs.

Joey had been telling me about this church that he went to often. It was a church filled with alcoholics and addicts in recovery. It was an atmosphere that sounded comfortable to me. No judgment. I was pretty closed off to my religious beliefs and never really talked about them or opened up to people about them. I was told to "crack the door open for Him and you'll find Him." I started kneeling to pray every morning. I really didn't know who I was praying to, but I was going through the motions and going off blind faith. One day, Joey asked if I wanted to go, and I agreed. The fellowship was great. Everyone he introduced me to was wonderful. We walked into the church, and it was so different than I was used to. There were screens, a podium, and live music. I stayed open-minded. They played rounds of open music, and I just listened. Then something happened that had never happened before. I started having intrusive thoughts about my Grandma, who passed away years prior. These visions or thoughts were just her face, like the last time I saw her, happy. I cannot explain the feeling I got very well to others, but it gave me chills and just the overwhelming feeling that she was happy for me and that I was, again, right where I was supposed to be. I broke down telling Joey about it, and he started to cry, too. It was so refreshing to hear someone understand what happened. I had my first encounter with the God of my understanding, and nothing has ever been the same since.

I decided to go to another meeting across town. There were girls standing outside smoking, and they welcomed me immediately when I walked by, so I felt comfortable. The seats were set up in a large square, and females sat on one side, and men sat on the other side, which I was told after sitting on the "wrong side." You would start off by saying your name and sobriety date, which I loved because I was so proud of mine. The meetings themselves were fantastic. They arranged specific people to share, and everyone who spoke had great things to say. I was glued to what they were saying. To this day, I thank this group for making me want to come back, believing I can stay sober, and finding a deeper relationship with the God of my understanding. I went for weeks to every meeting I could get to, made some friends, and soaked up everything people had to say. I finally got the courage to ask someone to be my sponsor. I noticed that all the girls had the same sponsor, which was another woman in the meetings. She was older and had over 25 years of sobriety. I called her after a meeting and was tested to call tomorrow and ask, which I did, and then I had a sponsor. One thing that bothered me was, at the end of our first session together, she said, "I love you." I have a thing about saying it when you don't mean it. She just met me. It didn't make sense, but I continued to work with her despite that.

Things in the meeting changed after I worked with her. I was not able to converse very often with the males in the group. She would always direct me to go back to the women and converse with them. One day, I was told not to wear a dress except for on Saturdays. I still wanted to go because I wanted so badly to grab this program by the horns. One afternoon, during our scheduled session, I explained to her my bipolar. She then told me that this group was a non-medication group. My heart stopped with those words. I was hopeful she didn't mean what it sounded like. I continued to stay silent and listen. She told me that it is okay to stay on them for a bit, but they are expected to wean off medication and let God do his work and heal us. She also told me that there were people in the group who were depressed, schizophrenic, and had anxiety who had gotten off their meds and were doing fine. I still was stunned and silent. We got off the phone, and I immediately broke down. I didn't understand how or why this could be happening. The one meeting I loved going to didn't accept me for what I have and who I am. I knew better than to get off my medication, so that wasn't an option. I started to build a huge resentment towards the messenger of that group. I continued to go and work with my sponsor, but the resentment grew, and I decided to respectfully cut my ties with her and the group.

Joey got a job at a car dealership. He always talked about how much of an asshole his boss Allen was. One day, I went up to see him and take him lunch during my lunch break, and he said he wanted to introduce me to his boss. He walked me to the front, and I looked up. I knew this guy. He was sitting up front and center at The Market the day I showed my boobs. And I knew his secret. He came every day on his lunch break and ordered three Crown shots with a Monster. It was very uncomfortable, but we didn't say anything about it and went on with the introduction. Joey thought it was hilarious, but I didn't. The person I was today didn't like who I was when I drank, and it was still following me.

At this point, I had been going to sobriety support groups consistently for about three months. I went along with it because I saw how helpful it was to Joey's life, but I still wasn't fully convinced that I was an alcoholic. I told myself and everyone else that I wasn't drinking because I was on medication. I went to a new group with a larger and younger crowd. It was divided into three groups. I sat at one of the tables as quickly as I could. When it came my turn to talk, I said, "Pass." I was nervous and didn't know what to say. Then, there was a girl who looked about my age with dreadlocks. She started to share about how drunk she used to get. Then she started talking about blacking out every time she drank.

Wait a minute. I blacked out every time I drank.

I thought that happened to everyone who drank.

She started explaining the feeling of blacking out and the dreaded next morning and that, despite making a complete fool out of ourselves, we did it again the next night. There was that pitted dark hole in us when we drank that only alcoholics got. She was telling my story, and she identified herself as an alcoholic. That's when it dawned on me. I am an alcoholic. I called Joey after the meeting and said, "Guess what?" He asked, "What's that?" I said, "I am a freaking alcoholic!" I could hear a smile in his voice over the phone, and he replied, "It's about damn time." The crazy thing is, I didn't know this girl from Adam, and she didn't know me, but she changed my life and recovery, and she had no idea.

Chapter 13

Things were going great. I had an amazing relationship, I was going to meetings, work was great, and I was feeling like I was starting to find myself. Joey didn't have much, but I loved him and spent every day with him. My dog Bentley loved him as well, and we had our own routine. He would make me dinner. We would make the appetizer, which was beef taquitos, and then hamburger patties cooked on the George Foreman and then put Heinz 57 on top for dinner. I was so in love and felt on top of the world. This lasted until around December 2016. I cannot remember back to where this all started and the details, but I started off angry. I was angry at Jillian, angry at my bosses for the pressure I was under, and, at the same time, having suicidal thoughts and just so depressed. Racing thoughts of each emotion. I could not turn it off. I did not understand what was going on, so I continued on and did my best to cope while leaning on my coworkers and Joey through this time.

I'll never get this moment out of my brain. I was driving on the highway and was completely engulfed in the song "The Sounds of Silence" by Simon and Garfunkel. I had to keep myself from driving off the road. I just wanted to die. I couldn't do this. I'd had enough. I needed help. I hated this feeling! I felt like I had failed myself, and everyone was supporting me. I felt weak and like I could not do this on my own. I gave up. I called Joey and my job and let them know that I wanted to be checked back into the psychiatric hospital. They were all supportive, which I am still grateful for. Lea ended up being my boss again at the time. She gave me her PTO days so I could get paid as I was in the psychiatric hospital. I was a wreck when I was admitted, crying, and just wanted to kill myself. My mind was racing so fast about harming myself or thinking about everything that was going wrong in my life that I couldn't get a normal thought in. I walked through the double doors. This felt familiar. I waited in the waiting room to be observed. Joey came with me, and it gave me some stability in such an unstable time. After waiting, I was taken up to the unit. But as we were walking, the tech who was leading me took a few turns I was unfamiliar with. We were going somewhere else. I looked at the plaque next to the door of the unit, and it said Watson Unit. We walked in, and it was so nice. There were two TVs in two separate rooms and an open drink station. The previous floor I was on required someone who worked there to dispense it for you. I got put in the room right next to one of the TVs. I didn't have a roommate this time. I got into my room and laid down. My head wouldn't stop. It just kept going until I fell asleep.

I woke up to dinner that night. Mealtime was always a dreaded time. You had to find a place to sit and eat, and this room was set up differently. There were fewer tables, so you had to sit with people. I can't remember who I sat next to, but there was not much conversation. I just couldn't talk over how loud my head was. I just wanted to disappear. Later that night, they gave us our meds, and I went to sleep early. You would think it would be uncomfortable to spend the night in the hospital, but I was so worn out from being so depressed that I fell right asleep. I felt safe.

The first few days were hell. I was scared of myself, scared of everyone else, and just wanted to hide out. I didn't think this mood would ever pass, which slipped me deeper into depression. I met with a doctor that I had not seen before. The doctor decided to keep me on my Lithium and put me on an anticonvulsant called Depakote. Anticonvulsants can treat seizures and help manage bipolar. They work by calming down hyperactivity in the brain. I adjusted nicely to the medication. Each day, I felt like I was crawling out of the mental dark hole I was living in. The racing thoughts slowed down. I wanted to live, I wanted to get better, and I finally realized that was possible. I stayed in the hospital for five days. I left with a new diagnosis of Bipolar I, which is a mood disorder in which you have swings of full mania and depression. Mania can be grandiose and full of life and happiness, or angry and irritable, and have uncontrollable racing thoughts and impulsivity. I found out what I had experienced was my first mixed episode, which is where you are experiencing a manic episode as well as a depressive mood. During this, I felt irritable, had racing thoughts, was suicidal, hopeless, and had increased energy all at the same time. It was terrible. I now realized why my roommate from my first hospital stay was in the bathroom crying. It makes you feel like you have literally lost control of your mind.

I went back to work and continued my life, work, relationship with Joey, and religiously taking my medicine. My days at this job were different now that I was sober. I woke up and went to work on time and worked until 5 or 6. I absolutely loved what I did. I was meeting my quota and making bonuses. I was at the peak of my career. But at the same time, this was when my Bipolar roller coaster started. For the first year of having bipolar, I didn't experience any noticeable mood swings, but after that, they all came at once. Depression always seemed easier until the lowest day of the swing when I got completely hopeless and suicidal. Mania was difficult for me and still is. I didn't experience the euphoric and grandiose highs of mania.

My mania was filled with anger, impulsiveness, agitation, and racing thoughts. In mania, I would replay moments of my past and tell them off or slam their face into the wall. They were always very violent thoughts. I became very familiar with those. The hardest part of dealing with them was how they affected others. I hated it. I hated that I had this, and I wished I was normal. It put a lot of strain on my relationship with Joey and my work. I started noticing that I would have a manic mood swing at the end of each month when my quota was due. It was the same pattern every month. What goes up must come down, and then I would have a depressive mood swing. I found myself disliking myself more and more. I am not sure when that started, but it became painful because all I did was compare myself to others and felt trapped in this illness. I just wanted to be like everyone else.

Chapter 14

After some time, I went to see my physiatrist. I was so tired of all these side effects of my medication. I have always been built little, but I had gained quite a bit of meat on me. I hated how I looked. I did not like being in my own skin. I just wanted to be on my Lithium. I knew that one worked and just wanted a break from the others. She agreed, and we started tapering off of the Depakote. We went from 1000 mg to 500 mg as the first step. I had a terrible time with this and eventually just stayed at 500mg. I was grabbing for anything to help me cope and stay sober. I remembered that an old family friend had a daughter with Bipolar who passed away from suicide. Her father wrote a book about her story. It was an amazing story and was relatable. I finished it in one day. After I got done, I really wanted to contact her mother, Mary, and just see if she had any advice for me. I sent her an email, and she responded almost immediately, and we set up a time to have a phone call. During our phone call, I explained to her that I was Bipolar and was having a hard time. She sympathized with me. She informed me that her husband hosted a Bipolar support group where they lived, and she was an alcohol abuse counselor and an alcoholic herself. She went on to tell me that she could do support phone calls with me if I wanted.

Of course I wanted to!

It seemed like God just put her right in front of me. We began working together, and she soon became the light at the end of my tunnel. We went over moods and my triggers, and it was so nice to speak with someone who had ideas and knowledge. I started writing in my journal around this time. I began writing for therapeutic reasons and also to be used at some point to help others relate to these swings.

2.6.2017

"I'm having a mixed episode following two days of mania. One of those days, I wasn't the one who discovered it first. Joey was. So I am frustrated. I am so overwhelmed and feel like my life is never going to be enjoyable because of this. Deep down, I know that it will pass and it's all in my head, but the dark thoughts are winning today. I feel as if I am a burden to others, and if I share how I am feeling, then it'll be too much for them to bear. It is very difficult to work or even just feel like myself. I need help with acceptance. I want to accept this, I really do. I just don't know where to start or how. It's a scary feeling to me, feeling so lost within myself and at the same time, being out, having to function and keep on a smile.

Underneath this disease, I love myself and my life and it scares me to think so many people lose their lives to this. I don't want that to be me. I want to beat this and fight this. Again, I just don't know how. It is just a numb feeling. It's not that I don't feel anything, it is just no surface emotion. It's just deep and dark and overbearing. I feel as if I am looking in on myself and watching. It's disturbing to me the fucked up and depressing thoughts that are running through my head as I am smiling, pretending everything is okay. It's not okay. I know it will pass, and I will feel like myself. I feel like I am permanently stamped "damaged goods." I'll never be normal or be able to get away from this, ever. That is powerful. This diagnosis is permanent and doesn't cease over time."

It was very hard to have mood swings while working in sales. It would feel like my head was full of angry and suicidal thoughts, and I still had to cater to others 'needs and perform at work. I would pick myself apart so much that any hiccup I would hit on the sales day would be catastrophic to my mental state. But, as always, I kept a smile on and continued bringing in my numbers.

2.7.2017

"I am just ready to feel like myself. These moods scare me so much, and the hard part is voicing them to others. I don't want to burden anyone with my dark thoughts and needs, especially Joey. I am in constant fear that the more vocal I am about needing him to lean on during these, the faster he will be done with me because it is too much to handle. I am at home now in the middle of the day because I could not take the euphoric feeling and voices and visions of suicide. It is hard feeling so scared of yourself. I am telling myself things will be okay out loud over and over in hopes of it sinking in and lowering my fears. I don't want to lose this battle. I am stronger than this somewhere inside me."

"I am exhausted. I can tell this mood is almost over- for now, at least. My thoughts are starting to slow down, and I am no longer suicidal, and there's hope. My depressive *mood swings are like a peaks and valleys chart. I decline down towards the valley to being suicidal and stay there for one to two days, then go on the incline to be at a normal level. The whole swing lasts 4-5 days. I am talking with Mary here soon and I am looking forward to that very much.*

We decided to stay on 500mg of Depakote a little bit longer because weaning off at this speed is hard on me and my moods are a result of that. There are a lot of thoughts of suicide. Those just scare me because I don't ever want them to become a reality. I love my life, Joey, and my family and would never want to put them through that."

2.8.17

"I feel a lot better about my life and where I am going. Talking with Mary really changed how I feel about what I have. I feel like

together we can map this out and help understand my bipolar. I am so very grateful for Joey. He held me all night. As needy as I felt, I ignored the voices telling me that I was too much and that he was going to leave and just laid with him. I feel so supported by him and by Ashley and Callie. I want to remember this next time I go through my down moods where I feel like no one cares. I have people who care and believe that I can make it through this."

"I am just worrying that I seem different. I am having a hard time making sales calls. I am anxiety-ridden, and I just still feel so vulnerable. I am proud of myself for pulling through that, but I am just ready for this to be over."

During medication changes, I noticed that I reacted better to the older medications than the new ones. I was very sensitive to any side effects. Akathisia was one I had on almost every newer medication. Akathisia is a reaction to some antipsychotics. It makes your muscles feel as if they are quivering and like your skin is crawling. It is impossible to sit still. I remember the time when I got put on a brand-new antipsychotic, then had a doctor's appointment, and I had to go out to the hallway and just walk around. I simply couldn't sit still. I was told once that it could subside after two weeks, but I could never make it that long.

2.16.17

"This is odd. I don't think I have ever felt this calm and happy sober. There were plenty of obstacles that came my way today, and it was like they didn't phase me. I mentally separated myself from people being negative in order to keep my peace, and it worked. I am shocked but amazed at how much I feel like my old self. Any doubt that there is a God is completely

gone. He is here, and He loves me and is with me through all this."

"I am already getting so much out of my meetings and sessions with Mary. It's like a weight has been lifted off and I can breathe again. I mainly had all positive feelings today. 1.) grateful 2.) happy 3.) frustrated about something that happened at work, but happy about how I was able to turn it around and move on."

2.24.17

"Had a good day. But starting to notice some racing thoughts, difficulty focusing on a movie and I am talking a lot more than I can control. I haven't really been under a lot of stress so I can't think of a possible trigger. Maybe this is a normal cycle? I am trying to stay positive thinking I can track my cycles and just not let

this upcoming mood take over like it did last time."

2.27.17

"I'm feeling very squirrely and in my head. Today was a very unproductive day. I had a hard time staying on task without getting too overwhelmed and at the same time I was dead tired. I went to a meeting at 12:00 and that helped a bit. But still struggling with controlling these racing negative thoughts I am hoping they pass soon."

2.28.17

"It's like my mind is trying to find something to get mad about or unleash all this pent-up frustration. It feels like I am just a raging bitch. My thoughts are just like a ticking time bomb, my skin is crawling, and thoughts are racing. I am focused on working on one thing

at a time like Joey suggested I do today and that has helped. Trying to focus on little accomplishments and keep turning my thoughts positive. I know energy drinks make my thoughts race more, but I literally cannot make my mind work without them at this point. Trying to keep on moving and not let it win this time."

"I am starting to feel like my balancing act is toppling over. I did one thing at a time and there's still so much more. Bills, cut-off notices, a new clean slate to fill with twenty referrals (for work), and a cloudy and bitchy mindset. It is hard for me because I want to feel normal, and my stress level goes from 1-100 in a matter of seconds. I have been praying all day and just hope that my moods no longer affect anyone negatively... Including myself."

3.4.17

"I've been having a rough time with my moods. I am not sure if they are just normal swings or Bipolar, but I don't like them and just got told by Joey today how hard it's been to be around me. It was upsetting because I didn't feel too off. I just worry that I am too much work and the relationship won't last. But I am trying so hard to be better and do better for myself. I lost track of doing 90 meetings in 90 days and praying every day, so I feel that's the key to staying healthy in that aspect. My head is loud, very loud."

Chapter 15

Joey asked to come over one day, which I thought was weird. But I was excited that he made an effort, so I said okay. He said he would help put gas in my car and then go to my apartment. As I pulled up to the gas pump, he pulled up to the other side and put his card in to fill my tank, and I started pumping. I knew him well enough to know that something was off. I felt panicked, so I quickly pumped my gas, and we drove separately to my apartment. Once we got inside, he sat across the room and started to cry. He said he couldn't do this anymore. He was not doing well in his life. He needed to be there for his older boys and couldn't do that while being with me. He told me how much he loved me, and I just took it in. As much as I wanted to beg him to stay, I wanted to respect his wishes, but deep down, I knew that he just couldn't handle all of this.

Could you blame him?

I couldn't handle myself.

We hugged, and he left. I felt empty. I sat on my couch and glanced out the window.

Now what?

The next few days were hazy. Slow moving, and plenty of tears. I can't remember what it was exactly, but one of us texted the other and started a small thread of texts. I had hope. We didn't talk much, but I hung on to every word. He started talking about having pain in his back, so he decided to go to the emergency room and asked if I could take him. After we pulled up to the emergency room, we got out of the car. I stood by the driver's side door and waited for him to walk by so I could walk by his side. As I did that, he came by and grabbed my hand. As his fingers intertwined with mine, I felt my heart fall to my stomach, this time in a good way. We never talked about getting back together, we just fell into a new routine together. He later told me that he had a hard time with all that came with my bipolar. He said he prayed to God about it, and God gave him that strength, and we went through this together. Thankfully, because things only got worse from here.

3.20.17

"Starting to feel a depressive mood coming on I think. I am exhausted- like a full body weak and tired and overthinking everything. I am going to try to fight this mood off with being and staying positive. Trying to remind myself that it is just a mood, and it will pass."

One of the hardest parts of these swings was that a lot of the time, I could not identify the mood swings myself. I had the hardest time pinpointing when my manic episodes were happening. Joey always told me. I hated them so much. Manic episodes affected those around me, and most of the time, Joey, because that's who I spent most of my time with. I was mean, impulsive, and irritable. My depressive moods, however, I was able to track easier. It took me a while to get all of it together, but once I started feeling really nervous about Joey and I's relationship ending and started thinking no one liked me was when I became aware that I was slipping downward. I would think that I would be a burden if I told anyone how I felt, so I would start to isolate myself. Then I would start thinking of all that I had done wrong and how I was ruining friendships and relationships from being so needy and requiring so much support. I would forget my purpose. Lastly, I would have suicidal days. I would have one or two on average, and they would be complete hopelessness. I played around with the idea of just ending it all. These swings usually lasted four to five days, and the majority of them were spent with the lights off in bed. I just couldn't function or hold a conversation. The thought of being outside of my apartment was too overwhelming. It was debilitating. I remember days when I would miss work because I could not get out of bed. I would lay in the dark and hear my front door open before seeing Joey in the doorway. I didn't even have it in me to acknowledge his presence. I just let him hug me when he came to my bedside. This happened quite frequently. There were days when I did make it to work, and I would sit in my boss's office and talk or cry. One day, it was so bad that I put some chairs together in the conference room. then laid down and just sunk into the chairs in an attempt to quiet my loud mind. I am so grateful to this day that I had a job that was understanding and so helpful. I would not have made it through this without my coworkers, who soon became best friends of mine.

4.19.17

"I feel like I am in a mood. All the feelings of being overwhelmed and drowning I think pushed me to this point. I feel like I could and want to sleep all day. I still feel behind at work. No appetite and overthinking negative thoughts. I am going to try to stay busy this week and just not allow myself to throw a pity party. Mary said that I can manage how low and high they go, and I want to start practicing that now. She suggested that when I am manic, I should start avoiding things that stress me out as much as possible and definitely avoid caffeine. In depressive swings, the most important thing for me to do is not to let my thoughts win. I can get on top of them and control how far down they take me."

I had an appointment with Dr. Higgins, and we talked about some of the mania I had been having. I really wanted to try this other medicine because it helps you lose weight. So, we tried that, and it did just that. I lost a lot of weight. I had been experiencing blackouts in my mania recently. For example, I would be at work, and they would bring up an entire conversation that I had with a coworker over important information, and I would have absolutely no recollection of that conversation. The more frequently it happened, the worse I felt. It scared me. The manic episodes were getting worse, and I was becoming more unstable. I did not address this with my doctor because I lost so much weight, and I thought they would get better. I ended up paying for that decision.

I became very unhappy at the job that I had been working at for the past two years. Ashley and Callie left, and I just didn't want to be there anymore, so my numbers started dropping. I decided to look for another job. I went through an intensive interview process for an independent living community. This was different than anything I had ever done because I would be attempting to fill a building with the first level of care. The first step of decline and needing help. The residents were independent and allowed to leave when they wanted, but just needed some assistance. The training was in Colorado Springs and Portland, and I hadn't been to either place, so I was pretty excited.

6.14.17

"I am frustrated that I had such an amazing day and I am so in my head right now. I went to Joey's and felt like he didn't want me there. I was just in my head about it and offered to go home so I wouldn't keep him up after he went to bed, and he almost seemed offended. Then he asked me why I was in my head when I had such a good day. I don't know! It must be because I was highly anxious and that made me a bit manic. I hate this. I just want to be normal and have a normal relationship. Will I ever be capable of that?"

The first trip was to Colorado Springs. I had only been on a couple of work trips but had never been on one sober, and where I had my own rental car with nights free to explore. I had never seen the mountains, so I was really excited about it. When I go somewhere new, I become a typical tourist. All I need is a camera around my neck. When I got to the hotel, I could see the mountain skyline. I drove to the independent living community that I was working at for the week. I was being mentored by this woman who was a complete rockstar at her job. She went over a lot of things. The days were interesting, but my favorite part was 5pm. She never let me out early, ever. The first night, I went to The Garden of the Gods. They were huge, and the coolest part was that I was seeing them all by myself. Another night, I went to see The Seven Falls. I walked the whole thing myself and climbed up the 224 steps that were next to the waterfall to get to the top. I climbed, thinking that the end of the park would be there. Well, it wasn't on the top.

Instead, there was a nature trail with snake warnings.

No thanks.

So, I had to climb down and walk the whole park again. I was worn out, but what I was starting to realize while we were waiting for the bus was the internal feelings I was having. It was anger, and I was obsessing over feeling irritated. My thoughts were racing. I chose to ignore them and go on with my routine of going to work and then exploring at night because there was just so much to see. Then I went to see my friend Ava an hour outside of town. That's the one that did me in. I didn't get back until close to midnight and didn't get any sleep. Good sleep is crucial to managing bipolar. A doctor once told me that staying up all night just one time can easily trigger a manic episode. And doing that made the next day incredibly difficult. My mind was racing so much. The mentor got mad at me for something, and I just obsessed about it. I was literally obsessed. I was crying in the bathroom and in the car.

 I just couldn't get it out of my head. But I had one more place to see. I just had to because I didn't know the next time I would be there. I went up the mountains. The drive up was sketchy and windy, but worth it when you made it to the top. I looked around, and the mountains were massive. I wasn't even on the largest one, and they were all green. It was so peaceful and quiet. I walked onto the ledge and just took it all in. My mind went quiet for a moment, and I enjoyed the beauty in life. I stayed up there as long as I could, but I wanted to drive back down the mountain before it got dark. As I was driving down, the thoughts came back. The last day there for training, I don't think I understood a word she said. My head was so incredibly loud. I was picking myself apart. I was angry at everything, and I felt panicked about this job.

What if I can't do this?

After training, I went to the airport and flew home. I was incredibly manic by the time I got there. Joey and I never fought, but we did when I got home. He said I was being reckless by not putting my mental health first. But I just couldn't accept that I can't enjoy a trip like everyone else can. I hated being this way.

I had a couple more manic days, but they passed like they always do. Then, I was off to Portland, Oregon, for in-class training. This time, we were staying at the hotel for training. I set it up to have my plane get there as early as possible. I had a friend who lived there, and we made plans to go to the Columbia Gorge. It was far from my hotel, so I took an Uber there. It was so beautiful. We also had time to see the Multnomah Falls. I have always wanted to see them, so it was really neat to see. I got to spend the whole day with her. Then, I had to go back to the hotel. We started class the next morning. The classes were good but very interactive. We had to do a lot of presenting, answering questions, and working in groups, which started off great. I would eat dinner in the hotel. By about the third day, I started to notice a change. My thoughts got loud again. This time, I was attacking myself. I didn't think I could succeed at work; I would ruin my relationship with Joey, and I just absolutely hated myself. Class got even more difficult to participate in. That night, I skipped eating downstairs and took a Lyft to a meeting. It was a small meeting, but it was an emotional trainwreck. They read from the literature and commented on it. When it was my turn, I just cried. I talked about hating bipolar and that I was just trying to survive and had no one here to lean on. They were nice but then felt the need to tell me that I was supposed to comment on the reading. So, of course, I over-thought that! After the meeting, they invited me to dinner. I always talk a lot when I am uncomfortable.

Not only was I uncomfortable in this setting, but I was uncomfortable in my own skin. I don't think anyone got a word in. I didn't realize this until one of the girls jokingly told me about it later that night. I couldn't handle that information. I obsessed over it for days. I would cry and pace back and forth. I just couldn't get it out of my head. The next day at class was even harder. We had to present to the group every day, but each day was more difficult. It was so hard to get words out when all I could think about was wanting to kill myself. I said my part, he made me stand up, my hands were shaking, and I just threw out the words as quickly as I could. I guess I had an angry face, so everyone laughed. Normally, I would laugh, too, but I just took it in and wanted to disappear. I could not stop these thoughts. I wanted to learn from last time, so I stayed in that night. I talked to my sponsor and to Joey. They always had a way of calming me down. I just got food from downstairs and went to sleep. That night might have been relaxing, but the next day sure wasn't. It was one of my suicidal days. I had no one to talk to throughout the day and no one to see. It was incredibly difficult to function. This would have been one of the days that I stayed in bed all day, but I couldn't and wouldn't do that here. I made it through the day and made plans with my friend. We were going to go to town and go to dinner.

Dinner...

I can do that!

  I took an Uber there, and the whole time, I panicked, thinking they were tracking me and that I would get in trouble for leaving the hotel. I had a 30-minute Uber ride and spent the whole time worrying about it and then the first 20 minutes of dinner talking about it. I didn't realize until later that this was when my paranoia started. All I wanted to get from my trip was fresh salmon, and I did. It was worth all the hassle of getting there. I was able to have a good dinner, but then I had to go back. I had one day left. The last day was such a blur, but I made it through it. The end of the trip couldn't come soon enough, but it did, and I couldn't have been happier to be home.

6.22.17

"I feel like my mind is turning against me and spinning everyone against me. I am paranoid. I feel like I am going to lose the job I just got. I feel like I know I am being ridiculous, but I cannot stop it. It just keeps going on its own, and it gets worse and worse. I saw my sponsor today and am going to a meeting. I hate it. I feel crazy. I don't feel manic; I just feel like I am losing my mind, and it freaks me out because I'm just fearful of losing everything I have."

7.28.17

"I am not doing well today. I feel very manic, but to my advantage, I was able to tell Joey

this time, usually he tells me after the fact. I feel as if my skin is vibrating. I feel like I had a Red Bull when I have had no caffeine whatsoever. I want to pick a fight with anyone possible, my thoughts are very hostile, and my thoughts about myself are very dark. I am thinking about cutting my wrists to alleviate the pressure of this, but I know that I never want to do that. Also, drinking has been on my mind non-stop. My mind and body physically have been moving so fast that all I want to do is drink to slow down. I feel like I am able to function for a little bit up until something throws me off. Then I am completely set into a whirlwind that I am unable to control. I am finally at Joey's, and it is amazing what a familiar scent can do to calm my nerves. I still cannot sit still. My thoughts are still racing, and my cravings are still there, but I am feeling more at ease. I made sure to let Joey know I want him around tonight because I do not need to be alone."

7.29.17

"I am still feeling terrible, but at least I feel like I am coming down from mania. It is a scary down because I still have sporadic moments of intense panic and mania it feels like. I think it was caused by things at work, such as a bad phone call with a potential resident and a resident who was pushing my buttons. What scares me right now is I visualize slitting my wrists and the feeling of all this pressure going away. And I must talk my way out of it. I am trying to be as open as I possibly can with Joey like he asked, but I am still scared of his reaction...I am still scared of my reaction. I hate that this mood is happening. I feel like everything in my life was starting to settle in and I had my moods under control. I feel like my work is starting to slip and people could tell. I left work today bawling my eyes out over a mistake, but I feel like I will find out sooner or later if I did make a big mistake. I have no excuse for my boss. I am in a state where I think this is unfair and I

hate what I have. I want my old life back, before this all happened to me.

I feel like I am very depressed but also still a little manic, which scares me. I am hoping and praying this passes soon. And I want to learn how to overcome these moods because this one is knocking me down. I think a lot of this came from working on some work in my support groups and all the resentment and anger I had turned into this. I don't hold those emotions very well. Also, in my session with Mary about why I have low self-esteem and digging up roots from my past. But I know that these steps need to be done in order for me to get better in life."

7.30.17

"I am so exhausted. I feel depressed and very anxious. I am having very dark thoughts, but they are not as manic as before. They still *flash up out of nowhere and I have to talk my way out of it. Work is so hard to do right now because I am expected to do as much as I did before when I can barely keep my shit together. I left my work phone at home again, the second time I have done that. I feel like I can barely put one foot in front of the other and I can't even tell anyone at work what's going on. I feel like I had my moods somewhat under control...until this one. This one is really starting to scare me because it will not go away. I talked to Mary, and she told me I need to calm my anger down and work on my breathing in order to get past this mood. It is very hard for me to do because I have been so freaking pissed off about everything. It has made me feel good that so many people have been telling me how good I have been at handling my bipolar, but now I am a complete train wreck. I can't even handle myself. I feel like I am failing and that I am disappointing everyone around me. I just hope and pray this goes away. One more day of work, then I have two days off."*

"I am embarrassed. I feel so needy because I am afraid to be alone. I know Joey asked to know what is going on, but I am still scared to tell him what's really going on in my head. I am afraid it'll be too much. It is almost too much for me to handle. I absolutely hate having this, I am angry about it."

7.31.17

"I am feeling a lot better right now, but I have been feeling very paranoid today. It's like I am overthinking everything I have been saying and doing the past few days and realizing I cannot take them back. Some of them I cannot remember if I did them or just thought them.

For example, I would apologize for nasty things I said to Joey, and he would tell me that I never said them. I just thought I did. That would go along with stories I told also. I usually repeat myself because I thought that they were just in my head, I didn't actually say it out loud. I am so physically exhausted; I don't know how to describe how I feel. I wonder if this is why the mood is starting to pass because I don't have any energy to be angry anymore. My mind is still going but my body has slowed down. It is odd to describe but my surroundings seem lighter. The past couple days, everything seemed so dark, like a dull color. And today, things are just a little hazy. I spoke with my friends about how I have been feeling recently, and that seemed to help me a little bit being so open about it. I am continuing to be open with Joey. I hate feeling so vulnerable. I am still learning to trust him when I feel like this because, in my mind, I feel like I am just crazy. He's been great through everything, especially this time around. I really can't ask for anybody better. I finally have two days off and I plan on resting, cleaning, and paying bills. Everything I don't attend piles up, and I want to clear my head so I can get back to work."

8.3.17

"I feel like I am dampening Joey's life. I have all these problems, and even though I am working on them, the results aren't coming fast enough, and I keep slipping backwards. I want more than anything to be healthy and accept what I have and that I am an alcoholic. I just am struggling with anger. I am so mad about everything to the point where I am shaking. Who am I? This isn't me. I want to feel better and have my life back."

One thing I did not journal about was the extreme paranoia I experienced at this new job. I signed a waiver saying that I allowed them to record my phone calls on my work phone. For example, they would do a test call and record my sales pitch and techniques. I really thought nothing of it. But after some time, I started to get extremely paranoid about it. I thought they put a camera in my office, and I was obsessed with it. It made me so anxious.

 I would constantly worry about what I said and what I was doing. I was also worried about my work phone. Making calls was so hard because I thought they were listening to all I was saying, critiquing it, and looking for reasons to let me go. It even got to the point where I would think they were recording me when I wasn't making a call, just having the phone on. There was one time that I was freaking out because I thought they were recording me while my phone was off. I would have panic attacks and just break down crying over this. I felt as if I would say the wrong thing, and I would get fired. It seemed so real. Only a couple people knew about this. I was so paranoid of people finding out in fear that I would get "in trouble." It was terrible and truly frightening.

 I struggled with wanting to drink during this swing. I thought about it when I was so manic that I couldn't calm my mind and body. What saved me through these hard moments was remembering what a friend named Wild Bill said. "Live a life you don't want to lose." I had a great life, boyfriend, dog, family, and friends. I didn't want to lose all that I had somehow built despite this terrible, debilitating swing.

Chapter 16

On August 4, 2017, a day before my two-year sobriety birthday, I was still dealing with this mood that was just lingering. What was scary was that when they go that long, it became harder to talk my way out of the dark thoughts and self-criticism. I was simply just too worn out and tired from fighting. Work was hell. I spent the entire day replaying scenarios I wish I could redo and just crying. I had fallen apart. About midway through the day, I realized where I needed to go. I wanted to live but was petrified of myself. It was time to go back to the psychiatric hospital. I finished my day and headed home. There was so much traffic, which made my aggravation so much worse. I was stopped at a very busy intersection and had the overpowering urge to just drive straight into traffic. I was gripping my steering wheel so tightly and just crying. Telling myself "NO" out loud, over and over again, to try to stop the visualizations of how it would happen, and all of this pain would stop. Then the light turned green, and I exhaled. I made it past the light. That moment reassured me that it was time to be hospitalized. Joey met me at my house. As he always did once I admitted that I needed to be hospitalized. He held me and gave me a big hug. These moments became the eye of my storm each time I went. It's like all of it stopped for a moment, and I remembered one of the many reasons I wanted to keep fighting.

I was admitted and went to the same floor I went to the previous time. I was a complete wreck. When we got to the hospital, Joey had to fill out my paperwork for me because I could not piece together the answers and comprehend what he was asking me. Once I got admitted, I did not want to talk to anyone, nor did I really know how to. Anything I said, I felt was wrong, and I was paranoid about EVERYTHING. It was so difficult, and I felt so incredibly alone. This lasted for several days, in fact. But, as usual, you see a doctor when you get there. The first thing the doctor did was increase my dosage of the medicine they put me on for mania. I was so hesitant because we thought that this medicine was making things worse. He said it was something that we needed to try, and I agreed to it. We also went through an extensive questionnaire. He would ask me things about how I was before or starting off in this swing, and I honestly just could not remember. It was so frustrating. I started crying and would snip back at him that I couldn't remember, and I was upset that I could not. I was so uncomfortable in that seat, and usually, I love answering questions, especially if they were about me.

Immediately after taking the increased dose, I started thinking that they were tapping into the phones. I was so careful with what I said. It's hard to explain the feeling I got, except that I felt as if I was trying to tip-toe around a group of very important people sitting around a conference table in suits, and if I got caught, I would be punished. It was so frightening. Later that day, I was looking out the massive window in the main room, and there was a huge tree with tons of leaves. I saw a monkey. I knew I shouldn't be seeing it, and it wasn't real, but physically, I saw it. I told Joey. I was laughing, he wasn't. I immediately told the doctors, and we agreed that the medicine was not working properly. After my bloodwork was done, we found that taking the 500mg of the Depakote was not a therapeutic level, so all I was getting was weight gain. They decided to take me off it and put me on Geodon. I was told it could help with weight loss, so I was all in. This pill spiked my blood pressure, so I had to take Propranolol to lower it. Also, I found that once it kicked in, I would get shaky and sweaty. Not too bad, but enough to notice. The doctor told me one day that when I came in, I was ranked on a scale where 0 is normal and no swings. The first day I came in, I was severely depressed at a 25 and also very manic at a 25. He told me that I was one of the more severe cases here.

One of the days, there was a new patient. As he sat in the chair by the nurse's station to get vitals done, I noticed his face was all bloody and scratched up, and his arm was in a cast. I found out later that he tried to commit suicide by driving into traffic. That could have been me.

Anytime I go to the psychiatric hospital, the first few days are spent in bed and isolated. Once that passed, I made some friends. There was Beth; she had severe Bipolar II. She was always crying and struggling, but I got to be pretty close to her. Kert was an older guy who was very eccentric. He and I got close, too. Then there was this girl named Hannah who had been there for thirty days. She was new in recovery, and her recovery story is amazing. I've stayed in touch with her. She lost her kids and got them back and got an amazing RN job. It was in the summer, so one of the things they let us do was go to the pool. I loved going. It brought realness to my situation. Putting my toes in the water and having the sunlight hit my face brought happiness. The guys were playing basketball and were terrible. It felt good to laugh. It was nice to have so much fun after all that I went through. Life was looking up.

Around day five or six, I was itching to go home, but I did know that I wasn't ready. He ranked me at a nine for mania that day. So, I was going down and adjusting well to the medication. The next day, I felt amazing and felt like myself, or I really should say a better version of myself. Colors were bright, I felt beautiful (even in a psychiatric hospital), I wanted to rekindle all my old friendships, go back to school for nursing, and start some hobbies again. It finally felt like I was coming back to my old self. I was ecstatic. After calling Joey and my mom and telling them all my ideas and how good I felt, I went to sleep.

I woke up the next day still feeling good, but not as good, and I did not want to do any of those things I wanted yesterday. It felt like that switch got turned off.

Shit, I was manic yesterday.

It was the first time I felt that kind of mania. It was great! I see why people have a hard time with it. It was filled with so much impulsiveness and self-confidence, or arrogance, really. When I got to the doctor and slowly said that I thought that I was manic yesterday, he simply said, "You were." I didn't understand why he didn't tell me. When I asked, he told me he wanted me to feel things out for myself. To this day, I love that he did that because I was able to learn to catch myself.

The hospital had a Koi Pond. We walked through the greenery and walkways to get to it. It was beautiful. There was a waterfall, tall rocks, and bright green plants. There were about 20 Koi fish in there. I sat on the edge and just watched them swim. It was so relaxing. There was a large white fish that would perch up on the rocks and let you pet it. It soon became my favorite place to go when I was at the psychiatric hospital. Very healing.

The next day, I really did feel good to go. We got my moods down to a functioning and low number. I cannot even explain the overwhelming feeling of happiness that I felt. This is all over. Joey came to pick me up, and I just wanted to cry when I saw him. My life was back. I was so happy.

Chapter 17

Every time I get out of the psychiatric hospital, I feel a certain way. The colors are brighter, my vision is so clear, and everything is moving a bit slower. I am peaceful and hopeful for the future. I felt this for about an hour or so. Once I got to my apartment, everything seemed unfamiliar, and things were hard to process. I would watch my dog move around and find his movements so off. I unpacked all my stuff and then went back to Joey's. His place seemed even more unfamiliar, and I spent most of my time there. The smell was really the only thing that registered as normal. He always had the same smell at his house. When he came home, it was hard to process Joey. I knew the face, but I had to keep telling myself who he was. Touching him felt odd but helped reassure me that things were really happening. These occurrences felt weird, and I thought maybe something was wrong. But we just assumed that it was me getting acclimated to being out of the hospital after spending eight days there.

The next day, I woke up feeling even more slow-moving. My thought process lagged so much, and there was so much confusion. Everything was hard. Getting dressed, taking a shower, and feeding myself. I would cry each time I got dressed because it was hard to pull tight clothes over me, and I would have to lean on the bed to hold myself up. I could not do my makeup or hair because it just felt too overwhelming. Driving was even harder, but I had to go to my doctor's appointment. When I got there, I told her how I was feeling. She told me that I could just be getting adjusted to being out and getting through a mood that was so severe. So, I just continued on with my day. It did not get any easier. When I got home, I was so unsettled. I started watching cartoons because they made me feel more grounded. I needed Joey now more than ever, but his boys were in town, so he would come by a couple of times a day. I felt crazy and like a burden to him. I was upset about it, but honestly, I was too worried about putting one foot in front of the other.

The next day, I was having a more difficult time getting around. There were several breakdowns throughout the day. I was constantly walking around outside because I felt so fidgety. The colors were still brighter, but now there was some confusion in everything I saw. I had to retell myself what was going on. Now I was starting to panic. I was taking a shower that morning, which I always did when I felt uncomfortable in my own skin. Something about the hot water hitting my bare skin made me feel better. I was listening to music and "Free Bird" came on. Everything in me had me persuaded that that song was telling me to kill myself. That killing myself would make me free from all of this and finally be okay.

That I would be a "free bird." It took every ounce of me to persuade myself that that was my bipolar talking and not a rational thought. I got out of the shower and struggled to get dressed. I could only wear large T-shirts and elastic pants. Everything else was just too difficult. I did not understand what was going on. All I knew was that something was wrong. There were plenty of tearful conversations with my amazing support team of friends. The hardest conversation was with my brother. He told me how worried he was and that my mom was worried sick and wanted to come home and be with me. I denied her before because I didn't want to burden her and her work. But when he said that I remembered something I heard. "This illness doesn't just affect us, it affects everyone that cares about us." I called her and asked her to please come up. I decided then that I was getting worse by the minute, and I needed to go back to the psychiatric hospital. I had gotten pretty close to Jade, and she picked me up and took me back to the psychiatric hospital. Just like every other time, the admitting process filled me with thoughts of failure and being down on myself for not being able to handle this.

I filled out my paperwork and sat in the waiting room. I laid on the chair and just sobbed. I had done this numerous times, but this time felt so different. I was afraid. It seemed like forever, but I was finally admitted. The unit I usually go to was full, so I had to go to a different unit. This one was a bit more severe than the unit I was on before. I sat in the chair by the nurse's station and got my vitals taken. When I looked around, there were just chairs and a TV with a lock on it so no one else could change it without the remote. The colors seemed brighter, and the room looked so empty. There were people sitting around, all of them staring at me. In the state I was in, I did not like the unfamiliar setting and had terrible anxiety. It was hard for me to come up with words and hold a conversation at this point. As we brought my stuff to my arranged room, I was told by one of the techs that they would get me to the other side as soon as a room opened. I had no idea what she was talking about, but I soon found out.

I laid my stuff down and tried to come out of the room and sit in front of the common area television, but I still couldn't sit still. I walked back and forth down the hallway several times. There were some patients who continuously walked back and forth down the hallway at my prior visits. I never knew why they did that, but now I know. I sat down at the end of one of the rows and did my best to not be seen or stand out. Everything felt so strange, and I missed Joey and my friends.

As I was sitting there, a younger boy was walking around rapping and yelling obscenities at other patients. He had to have a tech be with him at all times. I made damn sure to stay out of his contact. But of course, he sat down next to me, and it felt like his eyes were burning through me. He asked why I was there, so I told him. Then he informed me that he, too, was bipolar. I hated every moment of that conversation. An older man came and sat by me and started telling me about an Alcoholics Anonymous book he got. He was worried that because his name was on it, it wouldn't be anonymous. I assured him it would be okay. He then started telling me about a book he was writing. There were several topics for this book, so many that I lost track of them. All I obtained from that conversation was that whatever comes out in his book would have a part about me in it. He also went on to tell me about a medicine that made his penis hurt and that it was cured by a nasal spray. He told me that he, too, was bipolar. I had been in this unit for about two hours and was already filled with fear that this was my future. I then went back into my room, laid in bed, and cried. I felt like my life was over.

This unit worked differently. You did not see a doctor the same day, which made me upset because my anxiety was through the roof, and I feared being unmedicated. There was visitation the first night, but my mom's flight was coming in too late to make it, and Joey could not come either. Lea and Alyssa came to visit me. I am so lucky that I had good friends who came to see me at the last minute. Seeing them in person helped break my confusion and brought some reality to this nightmare I was living in. They also agreed to let my mom come for a special visitation the next day.

When it got close to bedtime, I was to a point in my anxiety that I was full-body shaking. I would walk back to my room and cry, and then try to be social, and this would repeat over and over. When it was time for our nightly medication, my normal medication was all I had to take. No anxiety medicine. All that they gave me was 1mg of Melatonin. I went to bed and tried to fall asleep within the small window that the medicine had. While I was up at the nurse's station, there was a man in front of me who always wore a blanket wrapped around him and over his head. This guy also had a tech with him at all times. From what I could overhear, he needed to take court-ordered Haldol at night. Haldol is one of those medications I pray I never take. Not sure exactly why, but it scares the hell out of me. He was refusing to take it. As he was fighting that off, all of us were told to go back to our room. As I was walking back to my room, I heard them say that he could either take the pill or get an injection.

I knew what that meant. Isolation room and forced injection. I just cried on my walk to my room. I wanted to be home. Not only was I anxious and in a confused fog, but I was afraid of who I was around. I laid in bed for about an hour and listened to the ruckus of that situation falter. I also took the time to pray. I didn't know how I was going to make it through the night. I decided to get up and see if there was anything they could give me for anxiety or sleep. I was desperate, but they said, "No." As I was walking back to my bed, one of the nurses stopped me to ask some questions. One of those being, "Do you feel hopeless?"

I just got out of an 8-day hospital stay and am back just days later. I can barely handle myself. So, yes, I am incredibly hopeless.

He started talking about a trick to help you sleep. During his introduction, he said, "TRUST me with this technique." He put a lot of emphasis on the word "trust." I felt as if God was talking to me. It made my hair stand up, which is something I will never admit while in a psychiatric hospital. I got a feeling of calm, which I thought was impossible with how anxious I was. He taught me a breathing technique that involved clenching your toes and counting while holding your breath, then breathing out and breathing in, unclenching your toes, and breathing out and repeating. I took that for all that it was and went to bed. Unmedicated.

I ended up not sleeping at all. It was one of the worst nights of my life. While there were a few lights on, I was able to vaguely see the picture on the wall. It was a lake view with loads of trees in the fall season. So many different colors, which reminded me of happier times with Joey on our trips to Arkansas. He loved looking at the colors of the trees in the fall. I held onto those thoughts as tightly as I could through the rollercoaster that was the first night there. I was having panic attack after panic attack in the dark room, each time trying my best to not wake up my roommate. I cried, hyperventilated, and shook in bed for eight hours. The breathing technique helped me not go into a complete panic. I was able to use it to take my mind off my thoughts. The staff does 15-minute checks at night, so I used that to help figure out how much longer I had until I could wake up. The sun finally started coming out, and I eventually was able to get up. I felt like complete shit that day, mentally and now physically. I went to use the bathroom and looked at myself in the mirror. I looked and felt like I was on drugs. I was pale, and my eyes were big, black, and blank.

This day was a rough one. Most of it was spent crying in my bed. I tried to socialize but was having a hard time forming words. I had been having a hard time remembering things for the past few days, too. Not big things, like the date or time, but just little things that I would usually remember. It was the scariest feeling to feel so lost and detached in a strange place. The doctor finally came in, and I was all over the place. Shaky, crying, and unable to fully process what he was saying. Just like last time, I couldn't remember anything from days or even hours before. He decided to take me off the Geodon but also told me that I was not there because of a reaction to the medicine. He told me that I have an obsession with meds, trying to find the perfect pill that cures it all. He said that I have a mood disorder; I am going to have mood swings, but medications can help the severity and frequency of them. However, medication will not cure bipolar. I didn't like the harsh words at this point. He put me on Lamictal and Risperidone in addition to my Lithium. Towards the end, I really liked this doctor. He seemed confident and knowledgeable in what he was saying and exactly what I needed at that point. I spent the rest of the day crying and sleeping.

The next few days were rough. I didn't want to be there, and I was miserable. My mind was filled with fearful thoughts. Thoughts of killing myself, thoughts of Joey leaving me because of all of this, and lastly, the thought that I would forever be stuck this way. I was so afraid that I would always have a cloudy head, be unable to remember things, and just feel stupid. I don't know what I would have done if it weren't for my friends. They answered every phone call and lifted my spirits each time. I am still incredibly grateful for them. One thing that felt good was seeing the same staff members. It felt like they actually cared, and they would tell me that they were rooting for me. I felt very comfortable here.

They let my mom come on a special visit. I loved seeing my mom. She always made me feel safe. She was not very familiar with my bipolar because she lived in Florida, so I held it together for the most part. We talked about life and made jokes. I am always laughing when I am with my mom. The visit lasted an hour, and then I had to say goodbye and go back to working on myself.

The doctor had a serious talk with me about the line of work I was in. He stated that I have been on eight medications, and this was my fourth psychiatric hospital stay, and there was one thing in common: being in high-pressure sales. He warned me that if I stayed in that line of work, I would end up back in the hospital, no doubt. I had a lot to think about.

I got moved to the other side of the unit after day three. There were all types of people there that I was not used to being around. There were a lot of meth users there. Luckily, going to my support groups made me more understanding of people with other addictions. My roommate was one of them. She was incredibly overweight but a huge meth addict, which I found oddly ironic. We stayed up all night talking about the program. She said she goes to meetings but still uses meth. To each their own. She was a really good roommate, but after a couple of days, she was discharged. Then Renata came into the picture. She was a middle-aged woman with curly brown hair. She was terrible. She was messy, loud, and never flushed the toilet. She had a bad attitude and took it out on me. I needed to get away from her, so I told the staff that I couldn't be in the room by the TV, so they moved me. Thank God. She was someone else's problem now. The next roommate was a younger girl with bipolar, and that worked out great.

The solar eclipse was happening, and I was so bummed that it was happening while I was in the psychiatric hospital because I love things like that. We had allotted times to go outside every other day, and it just so happened that my time slot was happening at the exact same time as the eclipse. I was ecstatic. We walked outside, and I sat on the steps. They say you shouldn't look directly at the sun.

So what did I do?

I looked at the sun.

It was so bright that I could only look at it for a moment. There were small half-moons covering the ground. It was so cool to be able to be a part of this. Seeing the eclipse was a first for me, and it was during the worst time in my life. It was little things like that that made me enjoy life again.

We would all sit in the main area and watch movies. I rarely went in there, but one day, I decided to. I sat in one of the purple recliners, and we were discussing movies. We were leaning towards Aladdin, and a girl named

Rebecca was throwing a fit about it. A huge fit, but she never gave us a reason why, so we put it on. Within 10 minutes, Rebecca resorted to acting like a five-year-old. Her voice sounded like a little girl, and her eyes got big and innocent-looking. I didn't know what happened, but later found out she has Borderline Personality Disorder, and cartoons are a trigger for her. I had never been around something like that, so I didn't know what to expect next. So, as much as I sympathized with her, I decided to leave the room.

One of the days, Joey and my mom came to see me. This was probably my best day, getting to be hugged by two of my favorite people. I remember in detail what they were wearing and where I was when I saw them. It was hope. They had some important things to discuss with me. They said I needed to quit my job, the stress was too much, and I wouldn't stay healthy. Also, I would need to apply for food stamps and disability because I was not in the condition to work. Lastly, I would be moving out of my apartment and into a friend of the family's house so I could afford to live without working. They sounded so positive about it, but I was devastated. I felt like I had failed in life. This was the best I could possibly do, and it felt like I was losing everything I had built over the years. I just cried the rest of the visitation hour, and we decided to wait on all of it. It just seemed so completely overwhelming at the time. I cried about having to start over.

Joey told me, "You get to start over, but you didn't do anything wrong. You're just given the chance to push the reset button again. Not everyone gets that chance." The significance of that statement was that it was what I always said about my sobriety date. That it's a reset button, and the past stays in the past, and you get to start over. The end of this visitation was a rough one.

It was so nice feeling like I was at home with Joey and my mom for a moment. But I still had a lot of work to do in my recovery.

I was sitting on the phone one day. It was up against the wall, facing the nurse's desk and the entry door to the unit. I saw this guy with white hair look at me, shocked. It was Kert. He rushed through the door and gave me a hug. His eyes were completely pinpoint small, and I could tell he was strung out on something. He was moving so quickly and neurotically. We sat and watched TV together with the group, and he would not stop talking. I got annoyed with him. From that point on, he followed me around. He was in bad shape, and he didn't want to get better. I told him that life was going to be good once he got his mind straight. He told me that he would do it for me, which I thought was really weird and super clingy, so I distanced myself and I stopped sitting with him at lunch. I remembered what I heard on my first visit. "Focus on yourself," and I did just that.

The days got easier. I was participating in more activities, being more social, and I was able to think clearly again. They say when you are on the right meds, you feel the difference. It was like a switch went off. The fear of permanent confusion was gone. I was me again. I had the rest of the stay to reflect on how I would start over and build myself up again.

I will never forget being out at the Koi Pond at the hospital. There was such peace and clarity. The colors were brighter. I made it through the toughest and scariest part of my life thus far. It was time for me to start over. For the first time in years, there was silence.

Chapter 18

I flip-flopped on jobs the next year, but I decided to quit the sales industry. I got a job offer at a new company with the same old coworkers. It was in the same geriatric field, just a less stressful job. I was staying sober and still dating Joey. Joey and I started to struggle after the last hospitalization. We constantly had chaos, so once the mood swings stopped, it was just us two. But we were learning more about each other and spending more time together.

The first week of work, I was doing office help for them before my position opened up. I spent a lot of time on my own and in my own head. I think the combination of my underlying anxiety and downtime resulted in disaster. I started obsessing about small things. Joey was a private person and hated that I spoke about his personal life to others. I caught myself telling a family friend that his son was going to move to Florida and panicked. I was obsessively panicking. Crying, hyperventilating, and begging them not to ever bring it up to him when they see him. I was sitting on my floor with Bentley and curled up with him and just cried. My mind was so loud. I couldn't hear anything else other than the thought that he was going to be mad, and I was going to ruin everything. Joey didn't have a temper. I think he got upset maybe three times during our whole relationship, so my fears and thoughts were very irrational. As I laid there on the floor, I had that familiar gut feeling. It was time to get help, or else I was going to do something stupid. I called Joey and he came over and picked me up, and we went back to the psychiatric hospital.

I would get a sense of calm once I knew I was going. It could be days away, hours away, or minutes away from physically getting there, but I knew help was on the way and felt a sense of relief. This stay was brief, and I honestly do not remember much. But my moods were stable, which was such a good feeling after all that I had gone through before. They decided to put me on an antidepressant. I was told previously to be wary about taking antidepressants and being bipolar because it will make you cycle faster, so I hesitated. But it was monitored, and it worked wonderfully. Day by day the racing thoughts diminished, and I could breathe again. I was there for five days and came out refreshed. So, now I was taking four medications. It was a perfect fit and proved to be so in the coming months.

Chapter 19

Now that my medications and mood swings were stable, I was focused on my first sober relationship. Joey was everything I wanted, and I was still completely swept off my feet. Some could say that's a good thing, but for me, it wasn't. I hadn't taken the time to learn about myself or what I was about, so I just completely latched on and became exactly what I thought he wanted. I dyed my hair platinum, got into running, and was obsessed with being skinny. I wanted to be his trophy. I didn't do anything for myself anymore, it was all for him. He had numerous talks with me about finding my own way, but I just couldn't grasp who I was. It was like I reverted back to that first relationship. I craved his love and attention, and without it, I felt like I was nothing.

Things went so well for me mentally that I decided to get back into sales. I couldn't handle not making as much and still spending like I used to. I was always in debt, so I went back to sales for another skilled nursing facility. The first thing I bought when I started making money again was my hair extensions. I started hard-core dieting and running at this point. I was super involved in my support groups, and my life with Joey was good. I still felt that the dark hole that I grew up with wasn't there anymore. I forgot that it ever existed. When I had my old sales job, I did very well. Somewhere along the way, I lost my touch, and honestly, I just sucked. I never met my quota, but somehow, I didn't end up with mood swings. I think it was because I didn't really care as much as I did at the first one. That first job was my passion, and now I was doing it for the paycheck. When you get a sales job like this, you have three months of salary to build up your clientele, and then they start counting your numbers. Well, it got really tough for me to manage my work around month three. I had this recurring problem. When something makes me uncomfortable, I avoid it, and I did that with my internet and cable bill. I let it get up to $630, and all I had to use at my apartment was my iPhone. Any work that I needed done, I would have to go to Starbucks or have to work on it in the office, so pretty much, it never got done. I was always behind on the marketing aspect, but with actually handling the patient referrals, I was doing okay. One day, I just got sick of it. Sick of sales, quotas, and all the bullshit that goes with it, so I quit.

I was so proud of my decision to stop the healthcare industry, even if it meant going back to the restaurants. I felt good. I was still skinny, running, going to meetings, and just felt good about myself. Little by little, it started to fall apart. Joey had moved into a new house, and it felt like when that happened, his feelings changed. I felt that was he didn't need me or want me anymore. I started feeling like things were one-sided. He would always have to go do things without me, and I started to feel that hole opening back up again. I started gaining my weight back and had to get my extensions taken out. I had to dye my hair brassy blonde because of all the damage. So, the only thing I thought he liked about me was my appearance, which I was losing. It makes me sad to think about how, at that point, I didn't realize how cool of a girl I was. My self-esteem was so low. Joey and I started spending less and less time together. Instead of giving him space, that just made me latch on and try harder.

One thing I loved about waiting tables was seeing people who were in my life previously. One night, I saw a familiar face. It was the guy from the psychiatric hospital who talked about writing about me in his book. He seemed completely out of his mind in the hospital but seemed so normal at dinner with the man who I assume was his dad. Another night, I saw Kylie, the girl who had postpartum during my first stay at the hospital. She was doing really well.

One Sunday, I was excited that I had the day off work. I walked into Joey's living room as he was unpacking some stuff, and he said, "Oh, I have to go to my mom's today." My feelings were hurt that he didn't invite me, but I just left. I went home and just laid in bed. I knew in my gut that things were over. I felt so broken. The whole day was a haze. My best friend Alexis and her boyfriend invited me to Red Lobster, which she knew was my favorite place. I was miserable. I couldn't even eat. I called Joey on my way home, and when he answered, the first thing I said was, "Are we okay?" He just said, "I am not happy, babe." I don't even remember the rest of the conversation. It felt like when Hunter broke up with me. That hole completely opened up. I was in shock. I remember telling him goodbye and then lying down. I took enough Benadryl to knock out a horse and went to sleep.

I woke up to find the yard completely covered in snow, which usually would make me happy. Bentley loved snow, and it was one of my happiest moments watching him play in it as a puppy. It was the perfect day for that.
Everyone was outside playing with their dogs. But I felt nothing. I could barely move.

I wasn't even crying, just existing. I got dressed in a cloudy haze and drove to work.

We were so busy that morning, and I just couldn't take it. I had a group of 10 come in, preparing to run the marathon that Joey was going to run. They made the first round of cuts, and I paid someone twenty dollars to clean my tables and let me go. I begged everyone to take my shift that night. My boss, who no one liked, asked me why I was so persistent. I said, "Well, my boyfriend and I broke up last night and am having a hard time." To my surprise, he let me have the night off.

The next couple of days were a blur. I wasn't even functioning. I latched on to a friend in real estate to take me out and keep me busy, and she helped a lot. I was completely broken. One night at work, my phone made the weird buzz that went off when Joey would text me. There were all these texts about how much he loved me and how amazing he thought that I was. We started talking again after that. We pulled the usual "let me drop off some of your stuff" card and then started having sex again. It felt like he enjoyed my company again. That hole was filled, and I felt whole and happy. I didn't know at the time that I was settling for less than I really wanted. I wanted more than he was willing or able to give. There was one day that we had sex and laid together for about an hour, talking and cuddling. Then he got up and started acting like I wasn't even there. I tried to laugh it off and said, "I feel like a puppy dog following you around." He jokingly said, "Well, you kind of are." Although I knew he was joking, it was at that moment that I realized if we continued this, we would end up hating each other, and I would be destroyed.

When we broke up this time, my parents and I discussed moving to Florida because my whole family was living there. I was so in debt because I didn't make enough money to support myself anymore. Also, I was waiting tables, so I could do that there. So, after that day at Joey's, I decided to move in with my mom in Florida and start over. I called him and told him my decision, and to my surprise, he started crying. He told me he would always want the best for me and supported my move, and agreed to drive me down there.

After I decided to move to Florida, I had my last appointment with Dr. Higgins. It was bittersweet because we spent so much time together. Through all the hospital stays and medication changes, she was a constant in my healthcare. She was so knowledgeable and knew my bipolar like the back of her hand.

She told me that there were three things that she liked about me and wanted me to know.

The first was that I never used bipolar as a crutch or let it hold me back from living my life. Second, I always stayed myself and didn't let being bipolar change who I was, and lastly, I always stayed on top of my illness. I said my goodbyes and was hopeful that I would find a doctor like her in Florida.

I wasn't moving until my lease was up, which was three months away. Joey and I decided to stay together until I left. At first, it was difficult to push it to the back of my mind that I was leaving, but eventually, I was able to forget it and just enjoy the moment. The three months before I left were probably the best out of our relationship. I had a going away party and then was on the road to Florida. Joey took two days off to stay with me and help me get acclimated. It rained every day he was here. It started hitting right when I woke up on the day he was leaving. The drive to the airport was terrible, and the worst was saying goodbye. After a tear-filled farewell, he left, and I was set to start my new life.

Chapter 20

The month prior to me leaving Oklahoma, Bentley was starting to throw up a lot and lost a lot of weight, but I didn't think anything of it. He turned 11 on the way to Florida, and just like every year, we celebrated. Well, once Joey left, things took a turn for the worst with Bentley. He was so lethargic, hadn't had any food or water for days, and I could just tell he felt crummy. I took him to the vet, and he got x-rays and bloodwork done. The bloodwork would take 24 hours to come back, but they told me he had a massive tumor in his stomach that would prevent him from being able to eat and to think about whether or not I wanted to put him through surgery to remove it. They called the next morning and informed me that he was dying of kidney failure. I made the decision to put him down. I had to drive him to Tampa, which was an hour from my mom's house. It was such a long drive. I got him a Puppuccino, but he couldn't eat it because he was too sick. He was in such bad shape that we had to move his euthanasia to as soon as possible and take him to a different vet. I rode in the backseat with him. When we got to the vet, they laid him on a leopard-print blanket. I had my mom, my aunt, and my dad with us, and we all said our goodbyes. When they gave him the first round of shots, you could tell he felt relaxed. His tail even started wagging. Then came the second round. He went quickly. Then I fell apart. I am not used to death. It was so strange to me to see something I loved so much just be a body and leave him behind. I remember walking out of the vet clinic was like something out of an old movie. It was so quiet and loud at the same time. I felt the wind blow and just felt hollow. Bentley had been my best buddy for 11 years, and I was starting off my new life without him. I talked to Joey, and he told me to get to a support group as soon as possible. So, I went to one at 7:30pm, and I poured my heart out to the women there. I got ladies 'phone numbers. I met this one woman named Brooke. She called herself "Chicago Brooke" and took my number. I really liked her, so I hoped she would call. Two days later, she did.

Brooke became my first friend in Florida. We worked together in the support groups, and she took me under her wing and introduced me to some other friends in town. Joey and I still talked, and I planned a trip to come down and visit. We did just that, and just like before, I felt that things were one-sided. There was even one night that he fell asleep on the couch, and I cried in his bed. It was ending, and I knew it. We had sex the day before I left, and it was very loving, it always was.

Afterward, while we were cuddling, I rested my head on the curve of his chest, and I knew deep down that this was the last time. I held it together until I got back to Florida.

After I got back from my trip, we started texting less and less. I stopped calling and texting, and the communication stopped. We talked on the phone one last time, and then there was nothing. It was so painful.

Did he miss me?

Did he care how I was doing?

The days dragged by. Then, one day when I came home there was a package on my doorstep. I thought maybe it was from Joey. It was. I had left my straightener at his house, and he was returning it, and then accompanying it in the box, there was a typed letter. My eyes welled up with tears as I read the beautifully written letter. It explained why he was ending things. He said that he needed to let me find myself and find my connection with God. He ended the letter by telling me to stay close to recovery and that he hopes that one day I see what other people see in me. Then, lastly, the line I read over and over for months. "I do love and miss you." I read this before work and felt good. I was on a high from it. Until I came home and realized what this really meant, and then just cried. It was over.

What the fuck was I supposed to do now?

Saying that hole opened back up is such an understatement. I didn't know how to live my life without him. My whole life and persona were about Joey before that. Posting pictures, clothes I wore, how I did my hair, how I ran, what support groups I went to, what funny stories he would like to hear, and lastly, what I could do to make him love me more. For the following months, the days blended. I would wake up every morning and lay in bed for an hour or two, just thinking about how much I missed him. Then I would drive to the Dunkin' down the street and get an iced coffee. I would just drive and listen to music. I would cry, sing, and drink my coffee. I would drive by the hotel we stayed at and just reminisce about being with him again. Going to Dunkin 'is what got me going and what got me out of bed every day. I was going to my support groups and staying close to my friend Brooke. Brooke listened to every phone call, all the crying, stories, and what-ifs. She never turned me away. I got really involved in the recovery support groups. I was still pretty lost and shattered, but the pieces were slowly starting to come together.

I had to do a lot of driving because my mom lives 30 minutes from town, and I would listen to music. I guess you could call me crazy, but I would hear certain songs that reminded me of Joey, and when they would play, I would think that he was thinking of me. It was totally insane, but somehow helped me manage. One day at the restaurant I was working at, I was holding a bucket of peanuts when a song came on, and I just dropped all my stuff because it took me back to the car ride to Florida with Joey and Bentley. It felt like I was there again. Embarrassed, I picked up my stuff and listened to that song for the months following.

I didn't have insurance, but I needed a doctor. The only reasonably priced doctor was one in Tampa, which was an hour away. I went to see her, but she was a quack. She pointed out all the risks of being on Lithium and wanted to wean me off of it. I had to be firm about this because that had been my staple drug for five years. I know the risks, but it's not worth risking my bipolar taking over. I persuaded her to keep me on it. I am glad that I know you have to know your stuff and be cautious, in moderation, of course, because not every doctor knows what works with your mind and body.

I experienced a couple of minor depressive mood swings recoiled from the breakup and Bentley's passing. I remembered what the doctor told me at the hospital. "There isn't a perfect pill." I am going to have some mood swings. It's a mood disorder. These were not major. They were tolerable, and I knew what to do, so I chose not to call the doctor. I knew that these would pass and were just from having such traumatic things happen. And just like I thought, they passed as quickly as they came.

I met a girl named Claire at one of my meetings. She came over right before Joey broke up with me to do my hair. She was an awesome hair stylist. I had been trying to get to know her more after this. She talked about getting up every morning and going to the gym and needed motivation, so I told her I would go with her. I hated mornings, but I needed friends, and she was pretty cool. So, every morning, I would wake up to go pick her up at 6:00. First, I would get my large Dunkin' energy cold brew, and then we would work out. I hated working out, so I just talked. We talked a lot, all the time. We became really good friends and hung out almost every day. She had a way of being blunt and sweet at the same time. I was always worried about what people thought about me. I was very vocal about it because I always had to talk about my feelings, which I had a lot of.

One day, I was worried about people talking about me behind my back. She looks me in the eyes, smiles, and says, "Honey, you aren't that important." I was offended at first but laughed it off. Then I realized she was right. People had better things to talk about than what I was wearing.

Brooke dated a girl named Diana. One day, Diana just stopped talking to her and moved away. Completely ghosted her. Brooke was heartbroken, and we connected on that level. We spent a lot of time together, and we would go to a place called Bayport and watch the sunset. Bayport was on the water, and it was a big ledge with picnic tables and a large deck. We would get a pizza and sit in the back of her SUV and watch the sunset. We got so close, and she would always, and I mean always, listen to me talk about Joey and all my crazy stories. I knew then that Brooke was my safety blanket for my hard breakup.

My mom and I bought a large mirror to put above my dresser. We hung it up, and she left the room. I stood there and looked at myself. For the first time in months, I liked what I saw. I was finding myself and loving myself. I still felt hollow, but I was healing. For the first time since I got sober, I put my recovery first. I went to at least one meeting per day and started working at the intergroup office doing volunteer work a couple of days per week.

I had a good group of friends that I spent all my time with. I started running again. Life was finally starting to come together after Joey left. I started to feel like Lauren again. I was finally making progress.

Chapter 21

I finally found a job. I started working as a receptionist at a fencing company. I really enjoyed life. Joey was still in the back of my mind, though. We used to talk about taking a year off and finding our way back to that, so I started counting down from the day I got the letter. It was March 3rd. So, every month on the 3rd felt like a mental milestone, and I was that much closer to finding out if we had a future together. In a way, I was still doing things for him. I would think how awesome it would be to tell him I did this. I started running religiously on a planned program, running four times a week. I would run every day after work. Running became my number two, after my support groups, of course. I was eating healthy. I lost weight and kept it off. I was in a good place.

By this time, I had a great group of friends. I had Claire and her best friend Faith. Then Pat,

Melissa, Leslie, and, of course, I can't forget Brooke. I hung out with them often. We had plenty of dates at my friends' rental houses. We went to the pool. We took a trip to Melbourne, and I saw the Atlantic for the first time. Claire and Faith complimented my girly side. We did our hair and nails and always went shopping. The majority of them were lesbians. I didn't consider myself bisexual. I wasn't attracted to women. I didn't even remember sex with Jillian. I made a joke that I would become a lesbian just out of peer pressure.

I had been offered the opportunity to speak at several meetings. I was at the peak of my sobriety. One night, I was speaking at a meeting in town. It was a small meeting, but I had all my friends there. All of my close friends loved me enough to show their love and support. They each commented on how much they loved me. There were a few things that still stick with me to this day. Brooke said, "Of all the places for God to drop you, He dropped you here." Pat said, "I am lucky to call you one of my friends," and then there was someone else there with bipolar who said I helped her, too. I felt a sense of belonging. It was at this very moment that I finally felt at home.

I was always pushing myself to run, so I always ran myself into Plantar Fasciitis. Well, one day, I ran too hard, too quickly, and too much while training for a race, and when I woke up the next morning, the top side of my foot was in so much pain. I thought it would subside in time for my race, but it didn't. I could barely walk.

I had to walk on the side of my foot. I went to Urgent Care, and they said it was Tendonitis. They told me to ice it and take Ibuprofen, and it would heal within a couple of weeks. The doctors told me not to take Ibuprofen on Lithium, but I figured it would just cause some mood swings. I weighed my options and decided I could handle some mood swings better than this pain. So, I took two pills every four hours for a couple of days. I was turning in paperwork in the back warehouse at work, which was a pretty long walk. I started feeling dizzy, disoriented, and very hot. I didn't know what was wrong, but then it dawned on me. It was the Lithium. I looked it up, and I was suffering from Lithium toxicity, which apparently can get pretty bad. I stopped taking the Ibuprofen, and after about a day, I felt better. I didn't take it seriously to pay attention to things like that before, but after this incident, I was always aware of drug interactions.

They say you shouldn't get too comfortable and prepare to live life on life's terms, which we were reminded of when Leslie relapsed pretty badly. Brooke and I decided to stage an intervention, but it didn't work at all. So, as shitty as it was, I gave up and just continued to focus on my own sobriety. Leslie completely fell off the wagon, and so did our friend

Melissa. Brooke and I tried another intervention, and it went terribly again. She accidentally mentioned that Pat was giving her pills, which I didn't know until later. Pat was very immature and talked badly about Brooke and Melissa. I didn't agree with it at all, but I was oddly very intimidated by Pat, so I kept my mouth shut and stopped talking to Brooke. A week passed, which was the longest I had gone without talking to Brooke since I met her. She texted me, and we got into another argument. Eventually, we talked, and she told me what was really happening with Pat. I was disgusted and decided to write Pat off. Brooke and I agreed to meet at a meeting.

That night, I found myself trying really hard to get ready and look cute. I picked up my friend Drew, who I always took to meetings, and parked my car. I sat in it for a minute, then saw Brooke pull up. She got out of the car, and it was literally like my heart skipped a beat and my breath caught.

What the hell is happening?

I couldn't stop staring at her during the meeting. She was wearing a navy blue and white polka dot button-up, and her light brown hair fell into her face as she shined her bright light on her big book. She did this in the middle of a candlelight meeting, which drove everyone nuts— but not me. I could not stop staring at her. She just looked so beautiful. I wasn't attracted to women, so I didn't think much of it, but from that moment on, things felt awkward. I found myself doing anything to see her. Anything.

My days off were spent with her, running errands. She took care of her mom and always fixed things around the house as a stress reliever. She loved going to Lowe's and Home Depot, which I hated because when I was younger, my dad would take us there and trap us inside for hours. Still, I went with her every time. I got nervous talking to her, but I couldn't stop wanting to see her.

I told Claire how I felt. She was so supportive and told me that she would love me no matter what. My mom wasn't all for it. I told her, and she said, "NO." I told her that hurt my feelings, and then she told me she was just worried about our friendship because Brooke was one of my best friends. My dad, on the other hand, had a great response. I told him I met someone, and he said, "Okay, I'm assuming it's a guy." I told him it wasn't, and he simply said that he couldn't wait to meet her. I loved my parents. They loved me through all my years of drinking, and still, now that I was falling in love with a woman.

Brooke and I started flirting, but I kept it very subtle because I still doubted she felt the same way. We went to a Christmas party with our friend April, where they were doing a white elephant gift exchange. Brooke was taking pictures from across the room. I kept glancing at her, but she seemed focused taking pictures, so I focused on April. Then, I looked again, and I noticed her looking at me. My eyes met with her bright green eyes, and at that moment, I knew that she felt the same way. I was excited but nervous about what was going to come next. I had always been the one to initiate relationships, but she made me so nervous, and I wasn't ready to tell her how I felt. Luckily, the next day, she told me how she felt, and I admitted that I felt the same way. We agreed to meet at the hot tub at her mom's retirement community. I made sure to wear my little blue bikini, then hopped into the water and anxiously waited for her to arrive.

About fifteen minutes later, she showed up. My heart was racing, and I had no idea how to act. She led the conversation, and we just talked about nothing— both of us unsure how to act. We hung out for hours until my fingers and toes were completely pruned. When we got up to say goodbye, I gave the most awkward hug, like hugging a piece of cardboard, and then left. I was on cloud nine. I never thought I would get over Joey, but I did, finally.

Chapter 22

Brooke and I talked all day, every day. When she came over to my mom's house, I made sure my bedroom was perfect. I had spent days preparing— hanging up pictures and changing my sheets to blue because it was her favorite color. We sat and talked for hours, but she eventually had to get back home to her mom. I walked her out, and as women do, we looked at the stars. Then I was ready. I held her face in my hands, pulled her close, and kissed her. For the first time, I felt completely comfortable with her, and it felt like a new beginning for me.

I spent every night at Brooke's house. I would wait until her mom fell asleep, then grab my large Dunkin' coffee and drive the 45 minutes to her house. We would lay in bed, cuddle, and talk for hours. We never ran out of things to say. Just like most lesbians do, I moved in after about three weeks— not officially, of course. I just never left and kept bringing more clothes over. I was genuinely happy. Her mother was such a kind lady. She didn't know we were together and often joked about me being a "boarder" at her home.

I wanted to get off of some of my medications because I felt like I was taking too many pills. The Respiratol affected my memory, so I wanted to try to taper off of that with my doctors' help, of course. I had heard horror stories of people with bipolar discontinuing their medication and going off of the deep end or even committing suicide. I took my medications seriously in fear of losing my mind. We decided to go from 3mg to 2mg, and I was told if that was too much, then to cut the pill in half and take 2.5mg. Well, I started taking the 2mg, and I reacted terribly. I began to slip into mania— I was so irritable and nasty. We went to a women's day event, and I could not sit through it. All the noise and emotions were overwhelming. I felt so uncomfortable in my own skin and, even worse, in my seat. So, I ended up sitting outside the whole time. That was the moment I decided to just stick to my medication cocktail. I had been stable for years— so why mess with what was working?

 I was having this overwhelming urge to call Mary. She and I hadn't spoken in about two years. Not since I had that major mood swing back in 2017. I called her, and she sounded so happy to hear from me. We talked for a while, and I thanked her for walking me through learning about my bipolar, triggers, and my tell-tales of my disorder. I told her that she saved me numerous times from just giving up on myself. We talked for a couple of hours, then said our goodbyes. She ended up passing a couple of months later from Lung Cancer. I am forever grateful that I listened to my gut that day.

 Looking back on my relationship with Joey, I realized how codependent I was with him. I didn't notice the same pattern with Brooke until months into our relationship. I've since accepted the fact; that I have a tendency to be codependent. About six months in, I stopped going to support groups, stopped running, stopped dieting, and eventually only attended meetings she went to. I did everything Brooke wanted to do. My mood depended on hers, and I only liked the things she liked. I was completely codependent. Slowly, I started to lose myself again.

We didn't have a lot of free time because we were caring for her mother. Her condition was worsening, and she couldn't be left alone. Brooke and I managed as best we could. We would bond over doing yard work. She would paint lines on the driveway while I sat nearby, and we would just talk. We never ran out of things to say. She would mow the yard, and I would walk alongside her, chatting as she worked.

Some days, we wouldn't leave the house for days, except when I went to work, so we found ways to enjoy ourselves at home. Her mother went to bed at 8:00pm, and after Brooke tucked her in, we had our time together. We would make our dinner, watch movies, or listen to music. We often stayed up late, just talking and holding each other. With each passing day, I fell more deeply in love with her.

I never thought I would date another woman after Jillian, but Brooke just came into my life and completely blew me away.

Chapter 23

Out of nowhere, I started feeling suicidal. I was overwhelmed with depression, anger, and became so afraid of myself. So, I did the only thing I knew to do— I went to the psychiatric hospital. Since I didn't know of any hospitals in Florida, I asked my doctor for a recommendation, and we went there. As usual, I felt a sense of relief on the way, knowing I was taking a step to get help. It was an hour drive, and when I got to the hospital, I had to go to the emergency room first and have a Teladoc appointment to be assessed. I told him I wanted to kill myself, and he asked if I had a plan. I told him that I wanted to take a bunch of pills, and he asked me what kind. I didn't want to say the Klonopin I had just gotten prescribed because then they would take me off them, and I liked them, so I told him I planned to take a bunch of my Lithium. That would have been the most horrendous overdose, from what I've heard and read. I was approved for admission and brought upstairs to the hospital. This place was exactly how I pictured a psychiatric hospital to be. Bleak, limited freedom, and crazy people.

There was one gathering room that happened to also be the kitchen. It only consisted of metal tables and chairs. The unit was square-shaped. They put me in my room, which had a window and two cots on the floor, two feet away from each other. I put all my stuff on the small shelf I had and tried to go outside in the common area. I could only stand it for about ten minutes. I decided I wanted to go. What I thought the rule was, or what it was in Oklahoma, was that if you hadn't taken any of the prescribed medicine, you could leave if approved. I said I wanted to meet with the doctor, then told him I wanted to leave, so he told me to talk to one of the nurses. I went out and waited and waited. Finally, they were giving meds out, and I declined, but she said I can't do that. I told her I wanted to leave, so I didn't want to take the medicine they had for me. She laughed and informed me that I was not going anywhere and that he put me in involuntary confinement. I felt my skin bubble with panic when I heard those words. I started to cry. I had lost all control of my life. It was now up to someone else for me to go home. I no longer had a say in when I could leave. I was stuck here.

I went back to my room, and my brown paper bag with my name and room number was empty on my bed. My clothes were gone, and so were my books. I went back out to the main room, hysterical. Not only was I uncomfortable, but I was unsafe. I saw a girl with my book, and I told one of the nurses.

They took it back, and I got all of my clothes returned. It was my roommate. She was Hawaiian, short, and chubby. I had to sleep next to her, and for the first time in a long time, I was afraid to go to sleep on my first night in a hospital stay.

They gave us our meds, but they didn't even have mine— none at all. They handed me 3mg of Melatonin, as if that would knock me out with all the anxiety I felt. I went to bed still wearing what I had on that day. When I arrived there, my roommate was already in bed. I had the bed closest to the window, so I turned towards it. About five minutes after laying down, my roommate said, "Hi." I said "Hi," and then it fell quiet for a minute.

She finally said, "I'm sorry that I stole your stuff. I thought it was my sister's." I told her it was okay. Then she added, "My name is Sam," so I replied, "My name is Lauren." She then asked, "Can we hold hands for a minute?" Yes, the beds were so close that we could actually hold hands. I don't know why I said yes, but I did. I held her hand for about a minute before saying, "I have to roll over."

There was another moment of silence before she then said, "I love you." At that point, I just pretended that I was asleep. I didn't sleep at all that night. I stared at the wall, listening to her snore, and all I could think about was that I couldn't leave, even if I wanted to.

It was breakfast time, and thankfully there was a table that no one was sitting at, thank God. I sat down and waited for my food. They brought everyone's meals out on a cart, each tray with a lid on top and cups with aluminum covers, like a baby's cup. When they called my name, I went up to the cart, picked up my tray, and returned to my seat to eat. To my surprise, it was great! The best hospital food I'd ever eaten.

Once breakfast was done, I noticed four metal payphones mounted on the wall, spaced about a foot apart from each other. I called Brooke and just immediately started crying. I couldn't say much about anyone because there was absolutely no privacy. She told me she would get me out if it was the last thing she did. I trusted her.

Turning towards the TV on the front wall, I saw Sam dancing in front of it—arms in the air, booty-shaking like she didn't have a care in the world. I decided to go lie down, and eventually fell asleep.

I was woken up to take my meds, so I went up to the counter, feeling relieved that I could finally get them sorted out. But they got my doses wrong and didn't have two of the four pills I was supposed to take. When I saw the doctor later that day, I was irate. I told him I was ready to go home, but he said I would have to wait. I explained to him that my medication wasn't correct, so he assured me they would get right on it.

I honestly didn't know what to do with myself, so I went to sleep. I slept all day, only waking up for lunch and dinner. That night at dinner, I sat alone again. Across the room was an older woman with gray and black hair sticking up about a foot in the air and only three teeth. I wasn't judging— I don't judge anyone in places like this. She started yelling about the food. I overheard a table talking shit about her. I just kept to myself. After dinner, I fell back asleep until it was time for meds—which they still didn't get right. I told the charge nurse, and she assured me they would fix it at the next disbursement. Then I went back to bed.

Sam was waiting for me to go to sleep. We talked for a little bit, and I fell asleep. The one pill they got right was the pill that helped me sleep. Thank God.

There wasn't much excitement the next day. I slept most of the day and read, still wearing the same clothes I wore coming when I arrived. This hospital made me feel like I was losing my mind. There was nothing to do and absolutely no one to have a decent conversation with. I talked to my friends on the phone for a bit, but eventually, I just went back to sleep.

That day, they still didn't get my meds right, and I was getting pissed. One of the pills required a therapeutic level to work— too much lead to toxicity, and too little could cause mood swings. I couldn't risk a mood swing. Then it dawned on me that they never checked my blood levels. Every time I went to the hospital back home, that was one of the first things they did.

That night, I learned why. My psychiatric hospital back home was a private hospital, but now I was in a state-run hospital. I felt the difference, and it was stark.

The next day, I got a call from Brooke. She hired a Baker Act lawyer to get me out because no matter how hard she tried by talking to the hospital, I was not getting out. They weren't even treating me or changing meds, just holding me hostage. I wanted out more than anything. I sat on my bed and read a little bit. It was hard to read because I felt so crazy and uncomfortable. I decided to take a shower because that always makes me feel better, and it would help pass the time. I didn't know where the shower was, so I asked, and he said, "I'll take you there." He brought me to a room with nothing but a shelf for clothes and one standing shower. Everyone used this shower. I was disgusted, but I needed a shower. I made sure to wear shoes and took a quick shower. I felt dirtier after the shower than I did before.

I changed my clothes, and that made me feel better, then I went back to sit on my bed. Sam came in and started just talking about her life. It was a good conversation. I enjoyed it, but then it just got weird. She told me she had a dream that she had all of these babies, and she was breastfeeding all of them. Then she just started sobbing and saying, "I fed all those little babies. They were so hungry." I checked out and went to sleep.

The next day was Sunday, and I asked Brooke how the lawsuit was coming. She said that they arranged for me to go to court on Wednesday.

My God!

I had to be here for another three days.

  I felt hopeless. That lawyer also said that he was working with a couple of patients' families at the same hospital dealing with the same thing. Again, I went back to bed. I woke up to find Sam naked, sitting on the bed.

Great..

She was playing with her breasts and making comments about them. I chose to ignore all that and pretend to be asleep.

  On day three, they finally got my meds right. Other than that, it was the same thing. Sleep, eat, and talk to Brooke and my mom. Sleeping made the days go by quicker. I made sure not to take any anxiety medicine that would make it look like I wasn't ready to go home. I also made sure to tell the staff who did checks that I was not sleeping out of depression but out of boredom. So I slept all day. I was told that I would be getting out the next day. Oh my God! I couldn't be happier.

 I woke up in the middle of the night to Sam standing in the corner sobbing. I said, "Are you okay?" She just started ranting about God knows what. Then the crying got louder. It took a good minute for technicians to come in and talk to her. They calmed her down enough to fall asleep, only for her to wake up about an hour later, screaming and crying in bed. The techs came back in and calmed her down again. At this point, I was awake for the night. I was afraid to turn my back to her. She woke up again and ran to the hallway. I heard her screaming from the room. She was crying and yelling for about ten minutes, then I heard her screaming falter, and then they put her in bed. For the first time ever, I witnessed a Haldol injection. She was out cold.

 The next day felt lighter. I was going home. I went to breakfast and sat next to a guy named Tom. He seemed normal. We started talking about his family and his fishing. He invited me over to spend time with his family. I told him I would, and he was so happy. Then I got his number, but it didn't come home with me. My discharge time was 3:00. I sat in bed and read and wrote thank you letters to everyone in my life. With markers, of course, because we weren't allowed to use pens.

It was 2:30, and Sam was still snoring away. I decided to leave her a note. Despite everything during this visit, she was a really sweet girl—just sick like me. I wished her well and finally got the fuck out of there.

Chapter 24

Taking care of Brooke's mom was challenging, but I loved her and truly wanted to help take care of her. When I was given the opportunity to take time off work to care for Brooke's mother full-time, I embraced it. It was wonderful because I got to spend more time with Brooke and deepen my connection with her mother on a whole new level.

Her mother was an incredible woman. She was Jewish and from Brooklyn. Very tough but had a hidden soft side. I will never forget the day she stopped being Brooke's mom and became Linda. As much as I enjoyed being there, that meant we had less outside help because I was taking more hours. So there would be times we didn't leave the house for five days straight. Brooke and I got closer on a different level. Taking care of her mother was an emotionally stressful job. I never thought of it as a job, though. I enjoyed my time with her. I decided after some time that I wanted to spend my life with my best friend, so I saved up some money and bought matching engagement rings. I called her brother and sister-in-law, whom I was able to meet earlier that year, and asked for her hand since Brooke's dad passed five years prior. They were both ecstatic and helped me decide how to propose. He told me to not think about it and just freaking do it. I had spent most of my money on the rings, so I didn't have much left for a proposal. I wanted to do something different than roses and candles. I got her favorite candy and wrote out, "Marry Me?" on the pull-out mattress we slept on while she was putting her mom to bed. I figured she would immediately come into the room. But she was taking forever, and I was getting more and more nervous by the minute. I was so antsy that I made a pizza and waited so long that I burnt it. She decided to work on the tile in the bathroom for three hours. It killed me! Then, she finally walked into the bedroom and started crying before asking, "Are you serious?" I told her how much I loved her and couldn't wait to see what our lives together would turn into. She said yes, and we started planning for the rest of our lives.

I had stayed close to Jade, Alyssa, Callie, and my best friend Alexis. They all agreed to be in my wedding and come to Florida. We decided to rush the wedding so Brooke's mom could make it. We chose to rent a yacht and get married on it. I spent months ordering dresses online and returning them and finally found my dream dress. It came in the mail, and Linda was the first person to see me in the dress, which was a moment I'll always cherish.

After months of stress and planning, the day finally came. October 17, 2020. We rented a condo on Madeira Beach for all our friends and family to stay in for the weekend. We got ready in separate rooms, and we did a first look. I am the crier of the relationship, but she saw me and didn't stop crying the entire night. We loaded onto the ship and said our "I do's." It really was beautiful. I had always thought that I would feel like I was missing out on not drinking at my wedding. That thought never crossed my mind. I had the best night of my life. There was a lot of food, music, and dancing. My favorite part of the night was when everyone was under the deck, and it was just Brooke and I. She told the DJ to play "Wonderful Tonight" by Eric Clapton, and we danced under the night stars. This was the start of our lives, and I couldn't wait to see what was coming next for us.

Well, things after the wedding got sticky. I started to turn into someone nasty. With Linda's decline, I had the hardest time dealing with my stress, and so did Brooke. All I cared about was myself. I barely did anything for Brooke's mom anymore. I made everything about me and stopped caring about Brooke's feelings. I became unable to handle any stress. I would cry, freak out, and immediately want to drink. There were times when I left to go and drink. It really showed my age that I went to Cheddar's to relapse. But somehow, I was always able to talk my way out of it. Brooke was trying to get me to go to my meetings, but I didn't. She suggested I find a sponsor, but I didn't. She suggested I do something I enjoy to find myself again, but I didn't. Looking back, I was bound for disaster.

I was lying in bed listening to the usual nightly routine. I felt so unhappy with myself, and so lost. I just wanted to not feel. I looked over at the nightstand and saw a bottle of Hydrocodone. They say we have impulsive relapses. I thought about it for about 20 minutes. I weighed out my options, but the pills won. I only took one because I didn't want to be obvious, and then I went to sleep. I went the whole next day not thinking about it or talking about it. Nothing really happened that night, but I got away with taking one, so I wanted more. I wanted to get high, so that night, I took two. I felt that, and I loved it. I was very chatty and felt great. What I liked the most was that it was easier to hide than alcohol was. No smell. Brooke even said something about me seeming high, but I figured nobody would think I would do that. So I just brushed it off.

I remembered that I had a bottle of Tramadol at my mom's house. I found any reason to go and get it. I said I was going to get something for her dog, and then I took one on the way home. I didn't know what to expect. Then I took another, and then another. These were great. I hid them in my trunk so no one would know. That next morning, pills were the first thing I thought of when I woke up. I could not wait to go to my trunk and take some. They didn't make me feel high, but they made me feel really happy and light, and I really liked that feeling. One morning, I was laying with Brooke, and she was being so loving and sweet, and all I could think about was pills. I thought that might be a problem, but it wasn't enough to make me quit. The pills won again. I was upset that they weren't hitting me as fast as I wanted, so I really wanted to snort them off of the center console in my car. That's when it hit me. I have a problem. I called Brooke and told her and asked for help. I was out of town and went to the beach. I took a handful of them and then sat by the water. I felt really good, but knowing I had to stop ruined it for me. For as light of a pill as they are, I got hooked really quickly. Quitting them was very difficult for me. I was so moody and felt that skin-crawling feeling. Brooke helped taper me off, but I was very unpleasant during that process. One day, we went kayaking, and it was beautiful, but all I could think about was wanting to take more pills.

I started getting angry about things. Everything was pissing me off. Everything Brooke did was wrong. It came so slowly yet so quickly at the same time. I hadn't had this kind of mania in over three years. I forgot what to look for, and Brooke never dealt with it, so she didn't know what to look for, either. Usually, when I know it's mania, I can keep it from escalating by taking my Vistaril, getting sleep, doing relaxing things, and just taking it easy. Well, I had no warning, so It escalated super quickly. We fed off of each other. When I get manic, I get mean and say nasty things. I called her a bad wife, told her all that she did wrong, and that I wasn't happy. Brooke would snip back at me, and I would lose it. I hit the wall with my fist, and that wasn't enough to get all my pent-up anger out. I went for the vase next. I had just bought her white roses and grabbed the glass vase and smashed it on the ground. Immediately after that, I felt like I had lost my mind. I started crying and apologizing. That lasted maybe an hour. Then emotions escalated again over nothing in particular. I was so angry, my skin was crawling, and I couldn't stand how I was feeling. I began scratching at my forearms over and over and imagining cutting them open to alleviate these pent-up emotions. My thoughts were loud. So very loud. I wanted them to stop.

I went into the drawer and saw pills. Granted, they were Benadryl, but I just wanted them to stop. I grabbed a handful, took eight of them, and then just laid down. It happened so quickly that it didn't even register what I was doing until after. We learned that taking too much Benadryl can put you into a coma. So Brooke was going to take me out of town, but now we had to stay close to the hospital. So we went to a local beach. I called my friend Jade from the beach, and Brooke told her what I did. I have had mood swings, drastic mood swings, but had never been this violent and destructive.

Jade said that I was manic and it was time to go to the psychiatric hospital. We both agreed, but I didn't stop there. I got so upset in the car that I tried to get out of the moving car. I just couldn't take in how I was feeling. It's the strangest feeling. I didn't want to kill myself, I just wanted out! I wanted out of my head and out of my body and out of the car! I started hysterically crying to Brooke, "What's wrong with me? I need help. I can't do this anymore." I couldn't calm down. I found a Klonopin in my purse and took it, then fell asleep when we got home. Brooke packed up a bag for me, and the next day, I was on a plane ride to Oklahoma to go back to the psychiatric hospital.

  The flight was a blur, but as always, once I admitted that I needed to go to the hospital and had plans to go, I felt a lot better. I stayed calm the whole flight. Jade and Alyssa picked me up, and we had so much fun in the car that I told them I didn't think I needed to go anymore. Alyssa looked me dead in the eyes and said, "You need to go. You have never acted like this. You need professional help." I always listened to Alyssa. So I went.

Chapter 25

I was taken to the floor that I had been on previously. I still didn't feel very manic, even though I knew I was. I just became super involved in all the groups and activities. Usually, it takes me some time to get acclimated, but I did right away. It would typically take me a few days to set up my room and make my bed, but I set everything up the first day. I had my books lined up, folders lined up, a paper cup with different markers in it. I folded all my clothes and put them away. I started journaling. I decided to write all of my entries as a letter to Brooke. I was in complete denial about the damage my mania caused to us. I was so nasty to someone who didn't know that this was part of it and didn't know that I didn't mean it, so it caused a lot of pain. My first couple of pages were filled with I love you's and all that I love about her and talking about our future. They offered me Ativan every four hours, and I took them like clockwork. At first, it was because I needed them to keep me from becoming more manic and to help bring me down. But after that, I took them because they felt good. I really liked Ativan. I loved how it tasted and felt on my tongue. I would purposefully leave it on my tongue so I could feel the edges and let it melt a little. But, of course, I'm not a drug addict. I didn't have a problem.

My journal entries start off with a lot of detailed lists. One of my tell-tales of mania. I made a list of my new routine and things to improve my life. Sometimes, I would write the same list over and over again, just in different words. Throughout this whole cycle, I was promising to be a better person and to get the old me back. At this point in my life, my self-esteem was so low, and I felt like my life was in shambles. They put me on Restoril for sleep, and I fell asleep fast and stayed asleep, but I woke up at 4:00 every morning. They don't serve coffee until 6:30am, so I would wake up and ask for an Excedrin for caffeine and journal or read until 6:30am, then get coffee and continue to journal. I would eventually get a coffee at last call at night and put it by my bed so I could have it in the morning. It would be ice-cold black coffee, but it got the job done. This was my routine. Not only was I addicted to pills, but I was also now addicted to caffeine. I craved that rush and the speed feeling that I used to get from Adderall. Most of the time, when I am manic, I am super sensitive to caffeine, but this time, I was craving it almost as much as I did the pain pills.

They gave us a 30-page packet to work on while we were there. I finished it in a day and even decorated the pages. I still thought I was normal. It was like all I knew from my mania prior went out the window.

I wasn't angry or irritated. I wasn't this grandiose manic. I just couldn't stop. I asked for more worksheets and worked on them constantly, only stopping to make more lists and routines. I never watched TV or sat in the common area unless it was a group. I was hyper-focused on self-improvement, so I was constantly working on something. As focused as I was on filling out all the paperwork and booklets, I couldn't read anything longer than half a page. I should have known I was manic by that alone, but I wasn't paying attention. This went on for days, then one day, I just wasn't interested, and that's when I knew I was sliding down from mania. Then came the depression.

What I was feeling was my mood coming down to normal. You are so high, and what goes up must come down. I hated being bipolar. I hated not knowing how I would wake up and felt so out of control. I hate how I was to Brooke, and even worse, I hate that I couldn't remember what I said. There's part of the previous week that I simply couldn't remember. I wanted to be normal. I feared going through what I went through before. Once I realized I was manic, it was hard to stay positive. Just like I would with Joey, I felt defeated because I didn't even know what was going on with my body.

The neat thing about this stay was that Dr. Barnes was my doctor. She was the one that I went to on my first stay. She gave me a word of advice since Brooke is new to being with someone with bipolar, and I have a hard time recognizing it. She suggested that Brooke simply ask me if I am manic. That'll make me stop and think about it and start watching my actions. I was kept a couple of extra days to make sure I didn't go into a depressive mood swing. I made it clear without one, and they let me go.

I was going to spend a week at Jade's, so she came to pick me up. There's always so much joy in getting your first hug when you get out. We had lunch, and then she dropped us off at her house. Her kids have been like family to me for years. Lilly and Wyatt ran and hugged me the minute that I saw them. Their hugs are the best. I saw their dog Ralph, whom I just loved! And then, they had a surprise in the backyard. Chickens. She was a crazy woman with 11 chickens. Her daughter cooked us a nice dinner, and I went to bed early because I was exhausted.

The next day was a big one for me. Joey and I hadn't talked since that letter. Brooke wanted me to meet with him to get closure and heal my wounds from our break-up. We decided to meet at a coffee shop. He called me to tell me directions, and it was oddly exciting seeing his name pop up on my phone. I told him I would be there in five minutes. I was so nervous, and I didn't know what to expect.

I pulled up, got out of my car, and walked to the door. When I opened it, I saw him sitting in the corner in a black suit with his signature bright, charming smile. I smiled back. He stood up and gave me a hug. It felt so comfortable and uncomfortable at the same time. I was shaking. I was so out of sorts, which he commented on. Then we started catching up and talking. For a moment, it was like I had my old friend back. We talked for hours. Then he mentioned that he was dating a girl seven years younger than me. He was twenty-seven years older than me, and I couldn't believe he dated younger than me. I itched in my seat. I wanted to talk and catch up more, but this wasn't going the way I wanted it to. I knew this would be the only time I saw him, and I wanted to start over. He asked me if I wanted to see his dog again.

Well, of course I did.

I got into my car and called Brooke, crying. She thought I was crying because he dated someone else, but that wasn't it at all. I always wanted him to be happy. It was just the overwhelming feeling that he moved on so quickly, and the love I thought we had was nothing like I thought it was. She begged me not to go to his house, but in my mind, I didn't get my closure yet and needed it badly, so I went. I pulled up to his driveway, which felt very familiar. I walked into his house and was immediately bombarded with memories. It was so overwhelming, so luckily, he asked to go outside with the dog. So we did. This is when the constructive conversation happened. We laughed and had a great time. I told him how I felt. He told me that I was the first love he had ever had sober and that I was very special to him and always would be. He told me that he would always be there and want the best for me. I felt so relieved. He did love me like I did. I got the closure I had been looking for for years. Now I can close that door.

Brooke asked me to come home early. As much as I wanted to stay with Jade and see all my friends, I had done so much damage and wanted to repair what I had done. So, I changed my flight. The next morning, Jade said she wanted to talk to me. She told me that she had never been so worried about me. She didn't like Brooke and I's relationship because we did fight a lot, but she didn't understand that we were both under so much stress with her mom. She told me that she didn't think I was an alcoholic and had been chewing her nails off worrying about me. She pointed out that I was still manic. She knew my swings almost better than me. She was worried about me going back to the environment that brought me in. I denied it and told her that I was fine, and after a long hug from her and her kids, I left.

On my flight home, I was thinking about gratitude. My group of friends have been with me since all of this started in 2015. They picked me up from hospitals, knew my swings, listened to me cry, and watched me lose my mind. They never blinked an eye, and they always showed up. They would come by my apartment when I was too depressed to move. They would bring books and snacks to the hospital, come visit, and make me feel supported and loved no matter how hard things got. Not a lot of people have friends like this, but I am grateful that I do. Brooke and I weren't doing so well after this swing. I still wasn't sure what all I said and did, but whatever happened made Brooke think my feelings were different than they were, which wasn't the case. I just lost my mind. It was time for me to be a wife.

The following days were a miserable blur. So much fighting, crying, and hating myself. My last mood swing greatly affected our relationship. I was crying all the time and just couldn't handle ANY emotion. I started feeling like my relationship was falling apart. I hated myself and was quickly spinning. I couldn't quiet my thoughts. I kept thinking of suicide. I had a bottle of Klonopin that Brooke kept in her purse for me. Every day for a couple of days, I would take two out and take them, never abusing them but hiding them. One day, I had enough of myself, my feelings, and my head being so loud. I was mad at Brooke, for God knows what. I was completely off my rocker. I took ten pills out of the bottle, then put the bottle back in her purse and said, "I'm leaving," but didn't tell her where I was going. I immediately swallowed four of those pills and started driving off. I vaguely remember turning onto the street to head to Bayport. I didn't know where else to go. It's always been my go-to place. I parked the car. I didn't want to call Brooke. I was so mad at her, and I honestly can't tell you why if you ask me today. I called fifteen people. No one answered. I texted a friend from back home and said 911, which was our code, but for some reason, she had Joey call me. He facetimed me, and I barely remember our conversation. He said, "You're just having a mood swing, and the mood will pass." That made me realize that's why I was feeling this way. He was right. This was all a mood swing, just like the previous manic swing. It had been so long that I didn't look for the warning signs. He told me to throw the pills on the ground and smash them. I didn't want to kill myself anymore, but the addiction had kicked in. I hid the screen and took two more, then threw the rest in the dirt and stepped on them. I hung up with Joey and remembered a glimpse of taking the pills out of the dirt and eating them. I literally could not stop. While on the phone, Joey told me to have someone come pick me up.

I texted my friend Randy to ask him, and he came and saved my life. I don't remember him coming to pick me up, but he did and then dropped me off at home. Brooke said I was incoherent. She had to keep asking me the date, my name, the state, and the president. My mom was with her, and they watched me for hours.

I woke up and felt drunk. I laid there, and the sheets felt like I was lying on tissue paper. I was laying in Brooke's arms; but couldn't feel anything. I had no idea what happened the night before. All I knew was that I was fucked up. We threw stuff into a suitcase, and it was time to go back to the psychiatric hospital. She dropped me off at the airport, and that's the last thing I remember. I don't remember the airport or getting to the hospital, and barely remember the first day at the hospital. I have texts to my friends talking about drinking. I mean long threads of text messages that I just don't remember sending. It was a complete blackout.

I have no recollection of being picked up, but I was told that Alyssa and Jade picked me up again and took me back to the psychiatric hospital to check in. When I was admitted, they sent me to a less acute floor than I was in before. I was set up on the calmer side of the unit. Except for leaving to take my medication, I stayed in my room until the next day.

This mood swing was tough. I tried journaling like I had during the last stay, but I had tremors so bad that I couldn't write. The first day there, I scribbled on the page but couldn't read what I wrote. I don't really remember that day, but when it was time to go to sleep, they gave me the Restoril, which is a Benzo, and I fell asleep. I was used to the awkward first nights by now, so I fell asleep quickly.

12.2.20

"Well, it's 4:30, and I am wide awake. There is nothing to do. I am so very much depressed. I wish I could just sleep until the doctor sees me. I can't eat, write, or read, and all I do is sleep. Nothing can pique my interest. I can't even write. I just lay down. Everything is exhausting. Isn't it sad that I am not grateful that I made it yet? I am isolating. I wish I was with Brooke. I don't want conversations with anyone else. As much as people are doing for me, I still feel like a burden. Apparently, I almost overdosed. I had every intention of dying that night, but I was afraid, so I reached out. I am gaining a glimpse of hope, which is good. I just hate being bipolar."

I have had bad mood swings, but this depressive mood swing was the worst I had ever had. It felt like I had cement tied to my arms and legs—I couldn't get out of bed. I was on autopilot. I stayed in bed the whole day, barely mustering the energy to eat. When I finally went to the dining area, I made sure to sit at the table with only one chair, got my food, and kept my head down. I didn't want to have to talk to anyone. I didn't have the energy to. I had lost five pounds in the short time from my last hospital stay. I have never had that happen. The amount of hate I had for myself at this point was unreal.

12.3.20

"Woke up at 5:00 am again. I miss Brooke. I am feeling way better this morning. She wants me to do intensive outpatient, and I want it for substance abuse. It's hard for me to write like I did last time. (I had severe tremors from Benzo withdrawal). *I am so angry, depressed, and*

cold. I cannot stay focused on a book, writing, or making lists. I hope to get better soon. I am not feeling like myself and motivated or excited about anything. I am numb. Not hopeless, but not hopeful. This is the hardest mood swing I have ever had."

"In a million years, I never would have thought I would try to kill myself. It makes me so sad. I don't have my will back. I feel nothing. But I don't want to die. I am afraid Brooke cannot handle me, and that's what's wrong...me. I just want to be normal. I am suicidal again. They want me to go to rehab. I am totally for it. I am stressed. I miss Brooke and my friends. All I have done is lay in bed and cry. I'm numb. I feel so taken care of with Brooke that no matter what, things will be okay. I love her so much."

"I am going to a 30-day rehab in Fort Lauderdale. I am so hopeful. I just made my bed, and that means I am feeling better. I have

such an amazing wife for setting this up for me. I hate being bipolar. It makes me feel crazy. I never know how I am going to wake up. These past swings have been terrible. This depressive one was harder than the mania. I blacked out pretty much for two days. That scares the shit out of me and I still love to have Benzos or alcohol. I feel such disappointment for myself, Brooke and my parents.

I tried to kill myself, and by God's grace, I only managed to take ten pills before Brooke noticed. Anymore, and I would have been dead. I don't want to be another statistic—I want to beat this thing. But what if this rehab thing doesn't work? What if I don't do it right? I don't want to waste any money, but more than anything, I want to get better and be the old Lauren again."

I made sure to go get all of my meals. My appetite was back. I made sure to sit by the window because no one else could sit by me there, but it brought me some light looking outside. I couldn't stand being around anyone. I knew at this point, though, that one day I would, just not now. I sat in the same position I had been in when Joey and my mom told me my life was going to change years prior. I felt a sense of disappointment at that point. I was supposed to start over and succeed, but now, I relapsed and threw myself into mood swings that the doctors were calling "extreme cases." I glanced over to the other window. That's where I sat with Denise on my first visit to the hospital. Then, I felt a sense of comfort. Each time I went, I felt better.

But then I was quick to feel upset with myself because somehow, I always ended up back here.

Later that day, I was back in bed. I was sitting vertically, and I guess I started dozing off because I started dreaming. I dreamed of the color brown, which I have heard means that one is on a search to find their roots and true self. In this dream, I was walking down a hallway, and there were two women's figures at the end. As I got closer, one was my mom, and then I saw my grandma's face. It shocked me so much that it woke me up. I started to tear up. I felt her with me.

12.4.20

"Well this is a new one. I am up at 3:30. I am nervous about what if this doesn't work and I am stuck this way. Today I am grateful that I didn't die. It's amazing to me how I can come here feeling so bad and leave a new person. I am hopeful that will happen at the rehab, too. I want to do something great for myself and defeat the odds. Be more than a bipolar addict alcoholic. One more day until I leave for rehab. I am really nervous about this rehab. I don't know what it's like or what to expect. Today, I am grateful that I didn't die. I can't believe I tried to kill myself. That makes me so sad."

At this point, I was feeling better and on the outer end of the swing. I was starting to find some enjoyment again. They took us to the Koi Pond. I felt the feeling I got the last time I was there. It was where I knew I would be okay. The peaceful waterfalls and crisp air woke up my senses. I had been to the Koi Pond multiple times, and each time, I had a realization that things were going to be just fine. And that is what happened. Just like before, I had a ways to go, but the past is behind me. I am alive and crawling back up to where I was.

I stayed for four days. Overall, I was in the swing for eight days, which was my longest depressive mood swing thus far. I am not typically suicidal for more than a day or two, but I had about four to five suicidal days and one of those almost ended my life. Brooke and case management arranged for me to get on a flight to Ft. Lauderdale to go to a thirty-day inpatient rehab. They let me go a day early because I was going to treatment. I was so nervous. I didn't know what to expect. More importantly, I didn't want to fail.

The hospital and rehab arranged for me to go straight to the airport, so I arrived a few hours early. I wanted to treat myself to a nice dinner because I didn't know what to expect in treatment. I sat at the table and then glanced at the drink menu.

Well, I am starting over anyway. One drink wouldn't hurt. I am on my way to treatment, after all.

I put the menu down and just ordered a steak and mashed potatoes. It was like I could taste the Merlot. I was obsessing. I could easily get away with it. But then I thought of Brooke. She put so much effort into putting me through this, and I put her through hell because I took pills. I couldn't handle hurting her even more. I decided not to drink.

Chapter 26

I arrived in Ft. Lauderdale late at night. A guy in a red Corolla picked me up. He was Jamaican and spoke very broken English. I was so nervous. The car ride was long, but I didn't mind. I didn't know what to expect, and I was safe and comfortable in the car. We pulled up to a black gated yard with a strip of gray apartments.

Where was I?

I got to the main office, and it was nothing like I thought. I saw shows like Celebrity Rehab, and that was my idea of what one looked like. Fancy wooden floors, large windows, and nice furniture. It wasn't bad, just nothing like I expected. I immediately wanted to go home. I met the first tech, Levi. He was cute. He was very flamboyant and gay and had bright pink fingernails. He told me he was a meth addict, and we made small talk.

I didn't want to do this.

They arranged my meds and told me to go to Apartment 2. I walked through a kitchen and small living room to a dark bedroom with a twin mattress.

This was it?

I looked over to the other side, and there was another bed with a person in it. I hated this. I had to sleep in a room with someone I didn't know for thirty days. I was so uncomfortable. I laid in bed for hours. Mainly thinking, "How the hell did I end up here?" They took your phones, so I had no idea what time it was. Someone knocked on the door. It was still dark out, and they asked if I wanted to watch the sunrise at the beach. Brooke and I love sunrises and sunsets. They're our thing. Of course I wanted to go. There were about five of us. We walked the three blocks to the beach. I noticed the sand was tan, not white, and thicker than I was used to. The waves were bigger than I was used to. It dawned on me then that we were on the East Coast. I had been so messed up that I didn't know where I was going. We put our towels down in the sand and read a meditation. We talked about our stories, our recovery, our feelings, and our fears. Then, the sun rose. It was beautiful, and I felt God. I felt a sense of comfort in such an uncomfortable time. I realized then that I was right where I was supposed to be.

We got back to the compound once the sun rose. It was Sunday, and it really started to sink in. I am in fucking rehab. They took my phone when I got there. The rule is that they take phones at 9:30pm and give them back at 8:00am. My phone was like a security blanket, and it never left my sight. I walked back into my apartment, and my roommate woke up and introduced herself. Her name was Caroline, and she was from New York. Her drugs of choice were weed, alcohol, and "party pills," like Molly. She wanted to stop herself before she got worse, so she checked herself in. She seemed nice. They asked u s if we wanted to go to church, and I didn't want to go at all, but I didn't want to say "no" either. At 9:00, we left for church. We got into a big black van, and I sat in the middle row by the window and next to Caroline. I didn't say a word the entire way. I was so uncomfortable, but as uncomfortable as I was in the van, I knew I would be even more uncomfortable at church. But then, I remembered the experience I had last time at church, which opened my mind and heart a little bit. When we got to the church, we all got out of the van, and everyone split.

Well, shit! Where do I go?

I found my way to the back somewhere, and eventually, Caroline came up next to me, and I felt some comfort. I felt like throwing up the whole time. I was just so anxious. I tried to get the message, but all I got from church was that they were having a Christmas service. That made me realize that I would be spending

Christmas alone. I was ready to leave. And after an hour and a half, we did.

When we got back, I didn't know what to do with myself. I found a chair to the right of our front door by the air conditioner and became glued to that seat. I clutched my phone in my hands. It was the only "home" I had. When I looked up, I saw a pool in the middle of the yard, and then across the fenced-in yard were the independent living apartments. In between the two was some workout equipment. I counted seven apartments, and they were in the shape of an L. If I followed the sidewalk down to my right, I came to the main office, where we took medicine. It had a TV, a huge, old couch, and what soon became my favorite room, the kitchen, with the coffee pot. I looked back at my phone. I called Brooke, and we talked for a long time. Very tearful conversations happened that day. If I wasn't talking on the phone, I was texting someone. I was grasping at anything to bring me comfort because I was so very afraid of what was coming the next day. I was told we go to "the center" from 8:00-3:00 Monday through Friday and a half-day on Saturday.

What were they going to do there?

I don't know what it was that made me so fearful, but there was an overwhelming dark cloud over me all day. They took me to Walmart to get some food and my medicine filled from the hospital. I tried to eat clean. I bought chicken, protein powder, and fruit. My goal was to lose weight in rehab. You know, go against the norm. I came home, ate some chicken, and sat outside in my chair. The fear started to grow, and I started to cry. I sent the text to Jade, "How the hell did I get here?" It hit me. I hit bottom. I thought I hit it years ago. They took our phones, and I went to sleep. That night wasn't so bad since I knew my roommate, but still weird.

I don't think I slept for thirty minutes. I tossed and turned. The technician came in to wake us up at 6:30am. We didn't have any clocks in the apartment. I laid in bed, frozen. Today was it. They came back at 7:00. We left at 8:00, so I woke up. I wore a baggy pair of gray sweatpants and Brooke's hoodie to sleep that night, so I decided to wear it to the center. I brushed my teeth, put flip-flops on, got my phone, and sat in my chair. No one was answering my texts, so I panicked. I had a lump in my throat.

Is it too late to go home?

I didn't want to do this anymore. I didn't know I would be so afraid of something that would eventually save my life. They took our phones, and I waited for the van. I brought a protein shake for lunch, my attempt to be healthy. I got in the middle seat by the window, the same seat as last time. Everyone came into the van, and the doors shut.

This was it.

The ride to the center was intense. I was terrified, and my eyes were filled with tears the whole way. When we got there, we walked down the hallway to the group room. The tables were set up in a square with a large TV on the wall. There were positive hand-made posters on the walls and a lot of windows, so it was bright. I sat by the wall and just took it all in. They put rap music on. I hated rap.

How this program worked was that we would have group therapy of all kinds from all members of the staff and see a therapist individually once a week. And a plus, they did massages once a week, too. The day was filled with group therapy sessions, but I honestly don't remember any of them. The whole day was a blur. I didn't want to be here.

Everyone here had a problem. They all did hard-core drugs: heroin, meth, PCP, and pills. They were homeless and had sex for drugs, and I wasn't that bad. I didn't think I needed this. I became angry. I hated it here. We got back to the compound, I took a seat in my chair, and Caroline made dinner while I sat on my phone. Brooke and I started fighting about something, probably because I had such a bad attitude. They took our phones, and I went to sleep.

I woke up in the middle of the night drenched in sweat. I was so hot. I took the sheet off and fell back asleep, and after what felt like five minutes, I was shivering. I only had a sheet, but then I remembered Brooke packed our wedding blanket for me. I put it over me and fell back asleep. Just like yesterday, I ignored the first wake-up and laid in bed until 20 minutes before we left. I decided to wear the gray sweatpants and sweatshirt again. I had a protein shake, but I felt so nauseous. I packed another shake and went to the van. I sat in the same seat, middle row by the window, then started to get anxious.

What if I threw up in the bus?

I spent the whole van ride imagining myself throwing up into my lunch bag, and that just made me feel even more sick. We started groups. Again, I didn't think I needed this. I was never rude, but there was a sense of arrogance about me. I wasn't as bad as they were. I mean, I only used Benzos for several days. I couldn't stand feeling this sick, so I went to the nurse's office and got some Zofran, which helped me feel better. Just like the day before, I was physically present, but mentally, I was somewhere else. Once our day was over and when we got back to the compound, I got my phone and sat in my seat. I felt really sick again. I ate some chicken and decided to lie down. Brooke and I were not getting along. I spent the whole night crying. Caroline was so nice; she would make me tea. I hated not having any privacy. I had to cry in bed while she sat in the living room, which only made me more resentful. I fell asleep, and they came in and grabbed my phone. It happened again. I was so hot and so cold back and forth. I didn't get any sleep, and I couldn't get comfortable.

The next few days were miserable. I felt so sick. I was so nauseous and congested, and my hands were shaking. I couldn't write anything to save my life. I lived in Nurse Lisa's office. I tried my best to be pleasant to others, but I definitely wasn't myself. Lisa told me I was having Benzo withdrawals.

I couldn't believe that. I didn't use that much. There was one day that one of the therapists, Dr. Spears, was giving her group therapy and was calling on everyone, and I was so nauseous that I couldn't talk. I was so angry. I felt like shit. I didn't want to be there. I didn't need to be there. I hated sharing a bedroom with Caroline. I hated myself, and I hated everyone here. I wanted to go home. I wasn't having a good time and was nowhere near fun to be around, either. I had never had to do a drug test in front of anyone before, either, and of all people, they picked Lisa. I had been getting to know her a bit, and it was so degrading. I tried to keep talking and not make eye contact. That part alone could keep me from ever coming back. There was one guy who always made me feel better about myself when I felt so low, though. His name was Brady, and he was an aspiring rap artist. He was so positive and inspiring. He would tell not only me but also others how awesome it was that I went to the sunrise on my first morning here. He said that showed my dedication to my sobriety. I found someone to help me lift myself up when I couldn't do it myself.

I met with Dr. Spears one day as my assigned therapist. I spent the entire hour word-vomiting. I was so angry about Brooke, my home life, my life in general, my friends, and that I wasn't an addict. I don't think she got a word in. I think she felt sorry for me because she told me she would try to see me as much as she could.

That night, after my usual crying in bed to Brooke, I got off the phone with her, and I did something I didn't expect. I prayed. I actually cried. I knew that thinking I wasn't an addict would only end in disaster. I prayed for help. Help to know that I have a problem and that I stick with this. I prayed that I would become happy again and a good wife, daughter, and friend again. I asked to become Lauren again. I closed my eyes until the night sweats happened again.

That next day, I still felt really sick, but not as bad. I went to the nurse's office and got my cocktail that we had created. Mucinex, zofran, Vistaril and Excedrin. Over the week, we found that made what I was going through more tolerable. I sat in my usual seat. We had a speaker that day. His name was Johnny, and he was one of the techs. He started to speak, and his story was good. He was from the streets of New York. His drug of choice was cocaine. He got sober, and because he didn't get into the program and quit his way of life on the streets, he ended up back in prison. While there, he realized he needed the program and started a narcotics support group in the prison and now has many years of sobriety.

I felt like a light switched on. I was fully focused, and my body was lighter. It was like someone took the wool blanket from over my eyes. I wanted this. I remembered what it felt like to speak. I used to be in the center of the program. Just like Johnny said, your life comes together when you're in the center. I wanted to do this now. I now knew that I could do this. It clicked. I ate pills out of the dirt. I am an addict, and I need to be here just as much as they do. Dr. Spears pulled me aside later that day to see how I was doing. I felt amazing. So full of optimism and hope for myself. I wanted to find myself again. I told her my goal was to love myself. As positive as I was feeling, loving myself felt so far away, almost unattainable. She was so glad that I was feeling better. I knew then that we would work out great together.

Things were different after that day. I started to feel like myself again, the old me. I was talking to people. I didn't spend every night crying. I woke up early and got ready. I showered every day and wore makeup. When I did this, everyone noticed. I had numerous people tell me that I looked so much better. I looked brighter and happier. And I felt it. Things were bright and shiny, and as much as people still drove me nuts at rehab, for the first time, I was grateful for being here.

The rehab center takes us on excursions every other Saturday, and the first weekend I was there, we went to the Everglades. I had always wanted to go. I had made a couple of "friends." Troy was one of them. His drug of choice was meth. He was successful and owned his own business, but just couldn't quit the drugs. I spent most of my day with him.

We went on an airboat ride. I sat on the edge of the seat by the water. The airboat started, and it was nothing like I thought it would be. We saw alligator after alligator. The captain was really interactive and funny and made us all have a good time. I found myself laughing, like a good belly laugh. As we were coasting down the water, my eyes filled with tears. I felt happiness, true happiness. I didn't need any drugs to hide how I was feeling or to have a good time. I was healing.

Caroline was a really nice girl. She always made dinner and made me tea when I was sad. But I was getting so fed up with sharing such a tight space with someone. I didn't have any privacy. She wanted to do everything together. We would be watching TV, and even though there was a couch and a chair, she would sit on the small couch next to me. I needed space. She was a smoker, so she was always outside, so I couldn't sit in the chair by the door. I looked across the yard and saw a laid-out lawn chair apart from everything. I claimed it. I found my quiet, happy place.

As good as things were, I started to see all that I did to Brooke and to my marriage. They say you relapse long before you actually relapse. I was selfish, ungrateful, and just a bad person. I wasn't a good friend, daughter, or wife. Brooke doubted that I loved her because of how I acted. I did love her. There were many positives to this relapse, like getting the chance to literally dig into myself and find myself and become the great person we all knew that I could be. But this relapse caused a lot of damage to friends, as well. It was one of the consequences that I thought I would be immune to.

One of the main things I became grateful for was that I was happy to wake up in the morning. I snuck in my Kindle so I had a clock and would set an alarm for 5:00am to wake up and read or watch TV. I got my private time. I usually fell asleep, but I was content having the place to myself while she slept. The book I was reading was about a woman who was addicted to meth and starting ultramarathons. I used to run a lot while I was with Joey and loved it, but I lost sight of it. I was inspired.

I was still nauseous, so I had to eat pieces of bread every morning to calm my stomach. I wasn't having night sweats anymore, but I was having day sweats. It was usually freezing at the center, so I typically wore sweatshirts, but one day, I was literally sweating and had to take it off. Now I know why they kept it so cold. I was also still having hand tremors and could barely write. I was in week three after my last pill and was still in withdrawals.

We were so close to the beach that they took us there on Sundays. Of course, I went. Things were so much brighter and beautiful there. It felt like I was seeing everything for the first time. Once my toes hit that sand, I felt happy. I brought my book and laid my towel down. I was next to some of the guys, but I just focused on my book. I hadn't read a book in so long. I would take breaks and go to the edge of the water. I would let the cold water meet my toes. I hadn't been living. I told myself that this was going to happen. I was going to get this and do it right. I was and had been putting all of me into this thing.

That day, Caroline and I were sitting outside at the table in the middle of the yard, talking. CJ, who was a tech that drove us all around, walked by us and said, "Lauren, you got some meat on your bones. Sobriety is putting weight on you." I looked down at my Flaming Hot Cheetos and sour cream.

I didn't gain a lot of weight the last time I got sober, but this time was more difficult.

I dedicated myself to focusing on my mental health, sobriety, and loving myself, even if that means being a little overweight.

That night, we had a speaker at the compound. They had the tech, Caleb, speak. I liked Caleb. I always saw him when I went to make my morning coffee. He made fun of me because I made the shittiest coffee. We had long talks in the mornings, and he became my morning buddy. His story was intense. He lost everything. He even slept with guys for drugs. Yet, he was so kind and humble. He lived a rough life on the streets. I was so engulfed in his story, then I took a glance up to the night sky. The sky was so clear that you could see every star up there. Then, I saw a shooting star. I had only seen two other ones before this one. I made my wish. God gave me a wink to let me know He's with me.

I was on a pink cloud. A life high, if you will. Life was good. I loved myself, my life, and just life in general. I was eager to wake up and go to the center and saw the good in everyone. One night, after Caroline made me spaghetti, I sat in my chair and called Jade. I made a chicken joke because she has chickens, and then, out of nowhere, she pummeled into me. She ripped on me for being in rehab, didn't think I was an addict or even an alcoholic, and told me that she didn't even go to school and makes triple what I make. Lastly, she ripped apart my marriage and Brooke. I was frozen. I listened to this for 45 minutes. Jade had a heart, but boy, you didn't want to be on her bad side. She's a Virgo. Then I stressed to her how much work I've been doing and that I am different now, and her response was, "Yeah, I've heard that before." I was crushed that my best friend didn't believe in me. I admitted I was very unkind, unpleasant, and ungrateful. I was devastated by her lack of empathy. But deep down, I knew that was part of relapsing.

I told Dr. Spears the next morning, and she told me it was time to shut the door on it and that "being alone is better than bad company." As painful as it was, I did just that. I shut the door. I didn't deserve to be talked to that way and was happy. I was at a point where I saw that. As much as I looked up to Jade and loved having her in my life, I put her behind me and decided to focus on my growth.

The treatment center offered equine therapy. Horses have been proven to calm you down and balance your mind. I was afraid of horses, and I was so upset about my friends that I wasn't very excited to go. We rode to the farm, where we were greeted by two cats at the gate. It's hard to be bitter when you have kittens' faces rubbing against your legs.

Maybe this won't be that bad...

We walked to the barn where there were tables and chairs and two women who ran the farm and were previous patients of the treatment center. A massive rooster was walking around, and a giant potbelly pig that came up to you like a dog. It was really neat, so I became fully open-minded. I love animals. The exercise we were assigned was a grounding exercise. Find something you smell, taste, hear, and see. When you do that when you are panicking, it'll help calm you down. We had 20 minutes to do the exercise, and then we could explore. I rushed through mine. I wanted to explore. I walked up to the corral. No one was there other than a huge white horse. I was leaning on the fence, and he put his big head on mine. I freaked out. I stepped back and then slowly put my hand up and petted his mane.

This wasn't so bad!

I stayed there thinking about all that happened. I was bummed but proud of myself for walking through all that I had. I felt gratitude. Johnny came up to the fence, and we talked. I really liked Johnny. I told some of my story and what I went through, and he assured me that I was going to get this, he just knew it. One of the women from the farm came up to us and told me that the horse's name was

Plenty. She asked me if I wanted to walk her around the corral.

No way.

She and Johnny eventually talked me into it. I stepped through the gate and held the reins in my hands. I held him close. I was afraid of him running and trampling me. I found myself talking to him, which calmed me down. I wasn't afraid anymore. Then, I started talking to God. I thanked him for what He's done for me and for giving me a second chance.

The next day at the center, I got mail. I was so excited! My glasses came in from home, and in my glasses case was a note from Brooke.

"I want to spend the rest of my life with you.

I will never leave. I will never quit you.

You are the love of a lifetime"

Love, Brooke

I needed this. As much damage as I caused my loved ones. The ones who were meant to move forward in my new life will stand by me and forgive me. She did love me, even after all that I caused her to go through and feel. My marriage was coming back together.

Throughout all my journals, I made so many lists. "Things I want to become," "Things I need to work on," and "Things I don't like about myself." The wonderful thing was that I was able to cross things off. The biggest one I crossed off was that I wanted to love myself. Even before I got to rehab, I really didn't like myself. I was hopeless and stuck in this shell of a person. I worked hard, put my sobriety first, and became incredibly close to the God of my understanding. I knew I messed up and lost some friends in the mix, but I was a better person than I was before. I knew my flaws and knew that they made me who I was. I remember putting the pen to that piece of paper and sliding it across the words. I did it. I worked with Dr. Spears to make a new goal. I always wanted to have a goal. I loved the feeling of accomplishing something. I wanted to be more independent.

I had to pee in front of someone three times a week. It was always Lisa, the nurse. It got easier as time went on, but I still hated doing it. It made me never want to come back. I talked to a friend from back home one night. She was someone whose sobriety I admired, and she gave me some advice. I needed to change how I speak. Be more confident, not fearful. So, I started saying "I will" stay sober rather than "I want to." She also told me to eliminate anyone and anything who doesn't support my sobriety...like Jade. It goes to show that I was on the right track. She ended the conversation by saying that she knew I was a good person and that she was privileged to have me as a friend. For the first time in a long time, I believed that that was possible. It showed me that the people who are meant to be in your life will stick with you through your shit.

Caroline and some other people in the program moved to hybrid, which is the next step of the inpatient program. When you are on hybrid, you have to go to the center six days a week, but every day from 3:00-8:00pm, you're allowed to leave campus. All she talked about was wanting to smoke pot.

So, I really wasn't surprised that she did it the first night she had free time. She woke up in the morning telling me she had some wine on the beach and smoked a blunt. I told her, "Oh well, just start over." By this point, I was so sick of living with her. She had no concept of personal space or respect. I rolled back over in my bed, and she then asked me for my pee. I laughed and said, "Fuck that," thinking she was joking. Well, she wasn't. I assured her I was not doing that, and she had to just deal with the consequences.

That day was a Sunday, so we had the whole day to ourselves. I was sitting on the couch reading. For once, I wanted to sit inside. Another girl who was on her 4th stay at the rehab came over and sat at the table with Caroline. They were talking about drugs. Heroin, especially. Sophie, the other girl, started talking about how powerful and amazing she felt when she was doing it and how she would do it again. I decided then to leave and go to my chair in the yard. If you use substances when you're in the program, your phone is taken for twenty-four hours. So, Caroline's phone was taken. Johnny was the tech of the compound for the day, and he let her have her phone to call her mom. After her call, she just wouldn't give her phone back. Like a child. It infuriated me because I really respected Johnny. She then grabbed a packed bag and said she was leaving. Johnny talked her out of it, but I watched her drop the bag off inside the doorway of the apartment, which I thought was odd. Within twenty minutes, Sophie and two other people came to the gate in her car, and Caroline grabbed her bag and jumped in. Within two hours, she overdosed on Fentanyl. She survived and was immediately sent to detox.

As soon as she left, I told them I didn't want to room with Caroline. There was a new girl, Karina, who was a frequent flier at rehabs. She always talked about getting high, but I would rather move in with her than Caroline. They told me to just have the place to myself until someone else comes along. As much as I hated to admit it, I was happy to have the place to myself after finding out that she was okay.

I started experiencing what I thought were mini bipolar episodes. I would feel really insecure and sad and that no one liked me. I would pick myself apart and then, thirty minutes later, be on top of the world. I followed these mood swings and tracked them with what I knew about my patterns. I was told that these were part of early recovery and that they were not mood swings. I didn't remember having them the last time I got sober, so this was new to me. I tried to journal from this point forward.

12.22.20

"I woke up at 4:30 today and finished my book. I am so proud of myself. I finished something. I can't remember the last time I finished something. I wonder if I am a little manic. I am really chatty and sensitive to caffeine and didn't sleep. I am sensitive to others talking. I went to the nurse's office and took two Vistarils. Hopefully that'll help. I am afraid of having multiple mood swings and going through hell again."

"You know, one of the most depressing things to think of is that others just forget about you and you just become a memory, even with people you were once close to. I am down, I don't feel like I matter."

"I feel like I am annoying. I talk a lot and interrupt. I just talk a lot when I am happy, and I'm tired, so I am quiet, but for the most part, I am happy and most people, or some, ignore me or get short with me. I am trying to not care, but I do. I just want to be well-liked."

12.23.20

"I am so depressed. I don't feel important. So many people here have affected and changed my life, and to them, I'm just part of the job. Everyone at home seems to be doing fine without me. They don't call. I must call them. Brooke has so much going on and is in her depression, and I can't be there for her and her hard times. And that makes me feel like I haven't made any progress."

"I have no one here but Troy now. Andy left yesterday, and I know that this is just part of it, but it was still hard. I feel like a burden to

everyone. I don't even want to tell anyone what's going on, but it's getting worse. I'm spiraling down again.

I'll know if this is a mood swing if I feel this way tomorrow or get suicidal. I feel uneasy, uncomfortable, alone, and so depressed. I feel weak for feeling this way.

I am full of all these emotions, and it's overwhelming, and it's like every little thing makes it worse and puts me deeper in this hole, and I can't stop it. I feel weak and not strong enough to handle my emotions, which makes me feel worse."

12.24.20

"I am second-guessing everything I say and do. What if I sound stupid, arrogant, or annoying? I interrupt all the time. I need to get better about it.

I feel really annoying, like I can't carry a conversation. I didn't notice it until after the fact. I need to take 7 seconds and not have a story or response to everything. I'm starting to feel really bad about myself, and it'll be lonely for Christmas tomorrow."

"I miss home but I am afraid to in a way. I hope I'm ready."

Christmas was a day that I was not looking forward to. I dreaded it for days before it came. I woke up that morning, got my phone, called my parents and Brooke and talked to them for a bit, then got my meds. I still had the place to myself, so I felt freedom. I went to the main office to get my coffee and saw all the guys making Christmas ham and dinner. I offered to help, but they didn't need any. So, I sat and watched a movie with some of the guys and Karina. She was the only other girl. It felt good to socialize. When the food was ready, I took my plate and went back to my apartment.

I just felt an overwhelming feeling of gratitude and family. These people have been with me since I started and saw the change in me. At this point, I had numerous people that I had gotten to know who wanted this program and to stay sober. Later that day, there were chairs outside Troy's apartment, so I pulled up a chair and talked to a group of the guys. I felt a sense of belonging. Today was a good day.

12.26.20

"I just shared, and someone scoffed when I said it. I said, "One of the best things to happen was my relapse because I found myself again." But it was, it got me out of my rut, and it woke me up to a better life. I just worry that I sound like I know it all and fake. I don't want to share anymore. I am depressed again.

Well, a couple people said what I said, so clearly, I didn't look stupid, but now I'm just in a negative rut."

That next day, we went to the beach to watch the sunrise. As we walked up to the shoreline, I felt another sense of gratitude. We laid our towels down and started talking. We shared our growth and our fears. I talked about how I was afraid of relapsing when I got home and not being ready. They all assured me that I was going to be okay.

I had grown so much since they met me. When the sun rose, there were some clouds and beams of light that shined down to the ocean. It was God. Again, I was right where I was supposed to be. It hit me then. I did it. I became the old Lauren again.

12.28.20

"I am feeling a lot better about everything. I am nervous about going home. What if I get too stressed and slip up again? I really don't

want to. I need to learn to be by myself. I am proud of myself."

"The two people who took Caroline to relapse are back, and everyone is going to confront them. I mean, ya, they are shitty people, but they didn't force her to leave. She wanted to. I'm over it, honestly. She messed up, and she's okay. Let's move on. I have too much to worry about, deal with it."

"I hope Brooke's happy with who I am today. I am still a little crazy, but that's because I am adjusting to being alone. But I have worked really hard."

"Six more days- this feels so odd. I think I'm ready, though. I was just told that I have good willpower because I don't smoke and didn't start back up while being here. I can and will have the willpower to stay sober and to live a healthy life.

I need to trust Brooke's feelings for me and build my self-esteem to help with my issues with feeling guilty about what I have done...all that I have done. We do need to be more of a married couple, but we haven't had any time to be one because I lost my marbles a month into marriage. I know I will definitely be a better partner. I have no doubt we will be a better couple."

"We just had a women's group session and did the 5 love languages test. Mine changed from words of affirmation to quality time. She said the only reason things like that change is because we gain self-love. So, I did it. That makes me feel good. I feel very positive and optimistic. I'm so excited to start my new life with my wife."

I was feeling so much guilt for what I put Brooke through. We got married, and within a month, I relapsed, went into an extreme manic episode, tried to kill myself, and then went into a depressive swing and then 30-day rehab. I was not there to celebrate our first month of marriage and our dating anniversary. That hurt me, and I felt terrible, but after being in treatment, I learned that if I didn't do this, we would have been destroyed, or most importantly, I wouldn't be here.

12.30.20

"I only have five days left. Still bittersweet, though."

"I won't miss listening to rap every day- all day. But I will miss it here. I've gotten really used to being here and the routine."

"I hope I never forget that as long as I crack the door open, God will take care of the rest. Just like he did for me when Johnny spoke. Just like that, the light switch turned on, and I was out of the dark and back in the sunlight. I

love myself and have such high hopes for myself. I still have doubts and fears that I'll get lazy again."

I used the money left over from groceries to buy thank-you notes. I wanted so badly to show my gratitude for all that the staff did for me. I made my first one out to Johnny and reminded him how much he changed my recovery, and he would forever be a huge part of my recovery story. I wrote one to Dr. Spears and to CJ, and then one to the whole staff. I always liked writing these because I like getting them myself.

12.31.20

"New Year's Eve! I am starting this year on the right foot. I intend to finish it on one, too. Tomorrow, I get my thirty-day chip. I've never gotten a month chip, so this is a big deal to me."

"Brian left last night to get high. Not too surprised because when we talked about what we were grateful for, he said drugs."

"I never want to forget my bottoms:

Pills- completely miserable, mean, selfish, terrible wife, hated myself, and all I did was bitch.

I don't ever want to forget how it felt not being able to stop. That complete loss of control and then eating them out of the dirt.

I blacked out the whole next day. I remember trying to manage my luggage and nothing else.

Alcohol- getting sloppy drunk and driving, not being able to stop after one. Complete loss of control after the first drink."

"It'll be humbling and rewarding to get chips every month, and I'm looking forward to it. I am excited to start this sobriety over. I will be diving in completely, working the steps and

applying them to my life, going to meetings, and sharing and enjoying life."

"I don't ever want to forget how I felt the first week. The night sweats, hot and cold, and the tremors. I was so angry and irritable. I hated every person here. I wore the same outfit for a week and only showered twice. I didn't have one positive thought or thing to say. Brooke and I were fighting every day. I burned bridges with my friends, I was ungrateful, I cried every day, and I hated myself. I never want to feel that way again- good news is that I don't have to.

I hope I always remember that feeling with all of my addictions. That I could not stop. All the willpower in the world couldn't stop me from taking them."

I met with Dr. Spears for my last appointment and gave her a thank-you card. It was bittersweet. She had been complimenting me on my recovery often and really made time for me about three times a week. She talked about how much she liked me, and there was one day in rehab when I reached out to her on the weekend, so she had my number. I didn't think much of it. She started to talk about herself and her life, and I always liked it when people did that because it made me feel like people trusted me. Which isn't something a therapist should do, but again, I didn't think much of it. She told me that day that she really enjoyed our time together, and we covered so much. It was rare for me to be able to open up to someone so quickly, but because I was so willing and with her knowledge, I completed my goal. I received my completion certificate and almost cried. I did it. 30 days, and I put my all into this. I said my goodbyes and thanked her for all she did for me. It was setting in, and I had one more day.

1.1.21

"I am sitting in my chair outside. Tonight, I am going home. All that I've worked for has been building up to this moment. I finally get to be a wife again, a daughter, and have healthy friendships. I am going to go to meetings, get a sponsor, and do this thing."

This was my favorite day in treatment. Not because I was leaving but because of the conversations I had. I really liked Johnny. I liked what he had to offer and how much he cared about us. I sat there and talked to him for hours and gave him my thank-you card. We talked about my life and my story and what I was afraid of. He talked more about his story and details. I felt so relatable, and he reassured me that I would be okay. That I had grown so much since he met me. I was no longer the miserable person in the corner of the room, and he enjoyed talking to me. He said I was shiny and bright, and I made him realize how much he loved what he did.

I sat in my chair and watched Caroline come home. I honestly didn't care, but, of course, I acted like I did. After she relapsed for the second time, I asked for her to move out. So, I had to deal with the awkwardness of her wondering why she wasn't in the room with me. I acted like I didn't know. The best part was that it was not my problem anymore.

I packed up my stuff. It was so bittersweet. I remember unpacking my stuff when I got there. I was so afraid and felt so far away from finding myself. Now, I was someone different. I was me again. As I zipped up the bags, I cried and thanked God for helping me through this. I heard a knock on my door, wiped my tears, and opened the door. It was Johnny. He was holding my thank-you card and told me that it was the best Christmas present he could have asked for and wished me the absolute best. It made me feel so good that he could feel my gratitude. I also received a similar text from Dr. Spears. I felt really content with myself.

They were going to the beach, and I wanted nothing more than to go to the Atlantic one more time. I went with Troy, Elijah, the group of guys, and Caroline. She still had no idea I was the reason she had to move out. It was a beautiful day. The water was freezing, but they were all from up north, so they got in anyway. I sat in the sand and journaled and read. I watched as boats passed by, and I felt peace. My mind was quiet. I felt confidence and love for myself, hope for my future, and a new, stronger love for my wife. Everyone came in from the water, and it dawned on me that I would never see these people again. I guess that's how rehab works, though. You go through the toughest times in your life and help each other out, and then you never see each other again. It was an odd feeling.

Today was my 30th day of being sober. I really wanted my thirty-day chip to be presented to me at a meeting. One of the techs made sure to get me to a meeting, even if it was just me. I asked the group of guys sitting at the table by the outpatient apartments if they wanted to come. Elijah and Troy said they would come. I felt so good that people wanted to celebrate with me. It's amazing how at home you feel at meetings, no matter what city or state you are in. The meeting was over gratitude. How fitting. I didn't share but thought about all that I was grateful for: my parents, my wife, the friends who helped me through this and answered the phone every day, and most importantly, that I was given a second chance. At the end of the meeting, I received my chip, and Elijah and Troy cheered really loudly. I felt so good.

When we went back to the compound, I had about two hours left before we had to leave. I decided to sit with the guys at the table by their apartments. Chad was making dinner and invited me to have some. We talked, and I wondered why I never got to know these guys. They were great, and I came to find out that they would have come to the meeting, but no one told them about it. I really enjoyed hanging out with them, but it was time to go. I said my goodbyes to everyone. I tried to say goodbye to Caroline, but she flat-out ignored me, so I guess she found out. We packed up the car, and as I looked back at the gray buildings, I got a lump in my throat. This chapter is over, for now.

Chapter 27

I got to the airport and waited at the gate. Linda was not doing well at all. So, Brooke told me she would have an Uber pick me up because she needed my mom there, too. The flight home was dragging. I was so ready to see Brooke. I landed, got my luggage, and went to the front of the airport to get in the Uber, which seemed like it took forever. I came home to Brooke in my favorite blue shirt of hers, and she was waiting for me in the driveway. I was greeted with a huge hug and kiss, then got to see my mom. I was anxious to see Linda. I walked in, and she didn't look good. But she perked up and said, "Hello," and told me she was so happy that I was home because she missed me. Brooke and my mom were shocked. They told me that she had been almost incoherent for days, and it was like she waited until I got home to transition. That's what happened because not long after that, she declined incredibly quickly. Brooke and her mom's nurse got COVID. Linda was at the point where she couldn't talk or eat solid food but could eat pureed food. Brooke couldn't do anything, so I took care of her myself. At this point, she was 100% reliant on me. I fed her and laid with her for a minute. She couldn't talk, but I saw so much love and trust in her eyes, and she gave me a little smile. I have never felt so responsible for someone else's life. It was an incredibly humbling feeling and quite frightening at the same time. I told her good night and left her light on, then went to take care of Brooke. I said a little prayer for both of them and went to sleep.

The next couple of days were so tough. Linda was still declining, and Brooke and her nurse were able to help, but it got to the end, and we all knew it. She couldn't drink or eat anymore, and then she was not able to move at all. Hospice was now staying 24 hours. We opened the white box and gave her comfort meds every two hours. My mom took off work to help and thank God she did because Brooke and I were so overwhelmed and afraid of giving her the medication. Brooke and I crashed after being awake for over 30 hours. I woke up to her nurse telling me that she passed. I looked over and saw that Brooke was gone. I hoped and prayed she was there at the moment she passed, and thank God she was. She was able to hold her hand and say her goodbyes after my mom told her that my family would always take care of her and that she could let go now. I laid by Brooke as she held her mom's hand and sobbed. I held her and sat with her until the coroners got there.

She was not doing well with COVID, so she finally went and laid back down because she couldn't stand being there. Her brother, who was in town, overslept and missed her passing but was able to say his goodbyes the day before and was there with me when they took her off. Before they were able to pick out an outfit for her, I picked out her favorite purple shirt and pants and helped the hospice change her clothes. When her brother was saying his goodbyes, I stepped outside. I hadn't cried since she passed. I held it all in. As I walked outside, tears just started falling. I looked up and saw two cardinals, a male and a female. I instantly knew that it was Linda and her husband, together again. I said my goodbyes and watched as they put her in the hearse. This was going to be a new chapter for both Brooke and me.

The funeral was beautiful, and Brooke and her brother both said amazing things about their mother. Since she was Jewish, we did two ceremonies, and we decided what her tombstone would say. Brooke was still so sick, so I spent most of the time doing these things by myself. I had dealt with some death but never in person. It changed me and made me realize how fragile life is and how much I need to make time for my family.

We stayed at her mom's house for several months and then decided to move to Tampa. We spent weeks looking all around for our perfect first home. We went to one in Tampa Bay. We walked into the small 1,000-square-foot condo, and it felt comfortable. We walked out to the porch and saw our view. It was on the canal to the bay, and we saw a couple of manatees outside. We knew this was home.

Settling in was difficult because I didn't know anyone, and I didn't rush to meetings like everyone from back home suggested. I decided to work at a restaurant called Carrabba's. I put on my black pants and button-up black shirt and pulled out my old non-slip shoes. I was ready. Back to the old grind. I waited tables for years back in Oklahoma. I knew how to do this like the back of my hand. I was already a little overweight, and they let employees eat all the bread they wanted. You can imagine how that ended up. I was the oldest person who worked there. All everyone did after work was drink, and when they were at work, they were talking about drinking. I had an awesome boss named Ken, who I got really close to. He was kind of a jerk and didn't like people, but he liked me.

He was my age, so we related a lot. I shared with him that I was an alcoholic.

I liked sharing that with people in a way because I was proud to say how long I had been sober and to hold myself accountable. If I were to drink after work, I would know that someone knew that I was relapsing. I thought that would stop the next possible train wreck.

Brooke and I loved our new home. She got her favorite blue velvet couch she had been dying to get. We hung up all of our wedding pictures and made it perfect for us. Brooke was not the same after her mom died. She was very broken and completely shut down. It was really hard on our relationship. I loved her and wanted to be there to support her and love her through it, but I needed more.

So, what do lonely people do?

They get a puppy. I found the perfect red, long-haired dachshund, and I named him Bodey. He helped me get through such a difficult time. I didn't think I'd ever get another dog after losing Bentley, but he filled that hole left in my heart. With Bodey and Brooke's dog, Sophie, our family of four was now complete.

I got a text from Dr. Spears about her trying to find a way to work with me still, which was odd, but I really liked her, so we did that for a while. Then, a couple of weeks passed, and we didn't talk. It just got really weird, and she became super flirty, so I ended it. A couple more weeks passed, and she reached out and asked how I was doing, so I told her that I was doing great and all that had happened. I received a thumbs-up emoji, and that was it.

I never learn from my mistakes. I still wasn't going to my support meetings. Just working, enjoying my time in Tampa, and being close to the beach. So, I inevitably ended up relapsing over a stupid fight that Brooke and I had. I left the house knowing exactly what I was going to do. I drove to Walgreens down the street, got a small pint of wine, poured it into my blue cup with an orange straw, and chugged it. I immediately felt that familiar warm and fuzzy feeling that I hadn't felt in eight years. I felt really good and remembered how much I liked this feeling. I knew better than to have more, and honestly, I had all that I needed to feel better, so I went home. Brooke was still crying after our argument, but with this liquid mood enhancer, I was able to say the right things and comfort her. I knew better than to get close to her because wine has a very strong odor. We made up and had a great day together. This was perfect. I got away with it.

Chapter 28

When I woke up the next day, I immediately went to "get Brooke some chocolate from Walgreens." Again, knowing exactly what I was really going to do. I got the pinot grigio because there's no way I could chug red wine, even though that was my favorite. I checked out and was excited to get to my car. I did the same thing I did yesterday and poured the wine into my cup. I put the straw in my mouth and sucked it until it was completely dry. Every last drop. I made sure to get a Dr. Pepper to pour into the cup and then dump it so it wouldn't smell. I continued to do this for several days and never got caught. This was great!

Then, as every alcoholic is wired, one is never enough, so I decided to have two, then three. Then, I came home and just started a fight with Brooke over absolutely nothing. She called me out on being drunk, and that's the last thing I remember before waking up on the couch. I felt like shit physically and opened our door to apologize. She was so angry. She told me that I called her names and told her that I was going to go back to Oklahoma to fuck Joey. I knew that would hurt her, and it did. She asked if I wanted to get help and held me when I cried out of shame and regret. I declined her offer and said that I could do this myself, and I did. I went back to work and waited tables for a couple of weeks. But even though I had waited tables my whole adult life, it got hard. I was around wine, and the smell got to me, and the clients made me so irritated and got under my skin so much that I wanted to drink. So, eventually, I did. Again. Starting off slow, and this time, I ended up telling Brooke. I told her I needed to quit this job and start a less stressful job. She was irritated but gave me the chance to start new and supported me until I got another job. I was scheduled at 4:30 the next day and just didn't go in thinking that they would get the hint. I was so well-liked by management that they messaged me. This time, I chose to do things differently. I just told them what I was dealing with; I was in recovery and relapsed and couldn't seem to get it together. They were so understanding and let me go very politely and wished me the best. I told Brooke that I would quit drinking, but of course, I didn't. I had already gotten a taste for it, so I was hooked again.

I found creative ways to hide my drinking. I went to Walmart to get our groceries because I wanted to do more to help now that I wasn't working. I ventured into the wine aisle again and found this cheap wine mixer with 5% alcohol. I didn't hesitate and quickly put one in my cart. I made sure to buy gum and rushed out to my car. I always park far from the door. It annoys everyone I am with, but I like to walk as much as I can.

At this point, my weight was up to 180 lbs., and I knew I needed the exercise. I poured the drink into my cup and chugged it. There's no way I could ever sip any drink with alcohol or caffeine, either. I want the effects to hit me as soon as possible. Well, as cheap and light as the drink was, it did the job. I sat in my car, feeling content and warm, and listened to music for hours. Brooke liked receipts, but I just always said that I had forgotten it or that the machine was broken. I did this for weeks. I figured that the drink was $1.96, and at checkout, it was $2.11, which was the exact price of the energy drinks that I used to get. So it worked out perfectly if she was to check the bank statement, which, to my advantage, she never did.

  I started applying for jobs. I decided to get into the hotel business in a large corporation because there's so much room for advancement, and I wanted a career again. I got a call back from Hilton and scheduled an interview for the next week. Well, I drank every day until then, but by now, I was drinking two of the wine coolers each time. My tolerance was starting to build back up like it did when I drank before I got sober the first time. I actually bought an onion to bite into before I got home so I would smell like onion rather than alcohol. Then, there was the one day when two wasn't enough, so I drank four. I went home and blacked out completely. I went to sit outside on the condo porch, talking on the phone to my friend Callie from Oklahoma while smoking cigarettes.

After eight years without smoking, I immediately picked it right back up the minute the alcohol hit me again. I looked at my phone and saw that my mom was on her way. I knocked on the door, and Brooke opened it. She told me that I was not welcome back inside and my mom was going to be picking me up for the night. I guess I did the same thing as when I blacked out before. I said mean things and started a fight over nothing. This was weird for me. I was usually such a nice drunk. I used to cry and get naked and always made an ass out of myself, but I was never hateful or rude. My mom showed up and didn't say a word. She was pissed. This reminded me of when I drank in high school. I got in her car and rode with her for an hour and a half to her house, and we didn't say a word. I quickly passed out once we got there.

When I woke up around 6:30am the next morning, I had an incredible hangover and so much shame and regret. I texted Brooke, who never went to sleep that night, that I was sorry and asked if I could come home. She said I could, so I had my mom drive me back for my interview with Hilton. My mom was kind, and I promised her I would stop drinking. I went home, changed for the interview, and left the house. I didn't go to the interview and never had any intention to. I had the shakes so bad and was so hungover. I went and drank. A lot.

The next couple of days were the same vicious cycle. I would wake up and start drinking, and I did it all in my car. I came up with different reasons to leave the house every day. I would say that I was going to go running and go buy wine and drink in the parking lot.

This time, I was drinking the little bottles of wine. I would drink all four, and then I would get an energy drink, spray Febreze, and just do my own thing at home or come home late and stay in the other room all night. I eventually got caught once again. She took the debit card, but I was a master at finding ways to drink.

I started returning things we bought at Walmart and used that money to buy alcohol. I was out of control. Brooke caught on and set up an intervention for me. I was very open to it but was hammered when my mom and aunt got there. They didn't say much to help but just trusted that I would stop. I packed my bag, took all the bottles of wine that I had hidden in my car, and we left for my mom's house. My mom stopped at the gas station, and while she was inside, I chugged the remaining two mini bottles that I had hidden in my bag. I was feeling very, very good at this point. My mom was in a better mood because she, as well as everyone else, thought that I was about to get better. Brooke didn't let me take Bodey because she thought I needed to focus on myself, and I agreed. I told her to please take my debit card because I couldn't stop. I got to my mom's and immediately passed out.

My mom worked nights, so she was gone all day. She left me money for groceries since I was going to be there for a while, and I cringed, thinking that I could buy alcohol with it, but I didn't say anything. She asked me if she could trust me with her car. I knew the honest answer to that, and I honestly felt terrible about it, but I said yes. She went to sleep, and I left to get groceries, fully intending on not getting wine. But, I walked past the aisle, and the next thing I knew, I had two 4-packs of white zinfandel in my cart. I came home and just started drinking. I drank so much that I started spinning and threw up. I drank some more, then fell asleep. My mom woke me up to say goodbye, but at that point, I wasn't as drunk, so I was able to compose myself and say goodbye. The next day, I took money out of her jar, bought another 4-pack, and did the same thing. But this time, as I was drinking, I wanted to stop. I really did. So, I did. When my mom got off work, I had her drive me home. I still had two mini bottles, and I didn't have it in me to throw them away, even though I had every intention to stop. When I got back home, I hid the bottles in my trunk and actually went to a meeting.

I walked into the room, and there was a massive black-and-white picture of the two founders of my support groups. I felt a sense of comfort. I sat in the chair right by the front door and didn't say anything in the meeting. I just sat there.

My mind was too busy to listen, but my butt was in a seat, and I knew that was where I needed to be. I came home to our dogs and Brooke, and started over. I felt like I could do this. I started going to meetings again, and things started falling back into place. I received a call back from an even larger hotel chain and went to my first interview. I had so much confidence. I have done customer service my whole life. The woman interviewing me and I laughed the entire time. I glanced down at her sheet, and she was writing 9/10, 10/10, and more 10s. I couldn't believe it. The week before my interview, my life was in shambles, and I was controlled by my addiction. I would have one drink and just could not stop myself, and at that point, I honestly didn't want to. I liked the feeling of being drunk so much. One interview led to another, and then it was time for my final two interviews. I put my blazer on along with some of Brooke's attorney clothes. My heels matched my shirt. Brooke had bought me a Tiffany and Co. necklace because she was so proud of me for taking control of my life again. I was so proud of myself and working so hard on myself and my sobriety, and it was showing. I got to the hotel, then sat and waited for my interview. The VP of the division, Stacy, met with me, and it turned out that she was a runner. We talked about that for a while, and she told me she would really like for me to talk to the president of the division, so I did. He also received a bachelor's in marketing at Oklahoma University. What a small world. I got offered the job of the front desk agent at the hotel that day, and he informed me that after six months, I would be able to move up to any part of the hotel. He started at the front desk, and within about seven years, he moved up to the president position. I had so much hope for myself. The gifts from sobriety and the program were really happening. I got the job. I was a master at interviews. I knew how to look the part and say the right things, even if they weren't true. But I was so proud of myself and excited to start this new career.

I would call women from the program when I would go to Walmart so they could talk me through walking past the wine aisle. I did that multiple times, which helped, and eventually, I didn't need to anymore.

Chapter 29

On our way home one day, Brooke and I were arguing about something stupid.

What do two women do?

We bicker over nothing.

They say you can make it through the hardest and most stressful things in sobriety, but drink over a broken shoelace. Well, I decided then and there that I was going to drink. At this point, I had gained all the trust back from Brooke and my family, so she gave me back my debit card. I told her that I was going to get some Excedrin for the headaches I had been having and that I would pick up her medicine from the Target pharmacy. I knew what I needed to do to stay sober. I kept my one-month chip that I received in the center tray of my car. I knew that I had women I could call. I knew that I could go to a meeting, and I had evidence that the program worked by how well my life was going, but it wasn't going to stop me. I wanted to drink, so I did.

I went and got a pint again at Walgreens, then quickly drank it in the parking lot. By this time in my drinking career, the full-on craving for more hit me right when the effects of alcohol hit me. I drove to Target and got another pint of wine. My gut told me not to do it, but I wanted more. I picked up her meds and called her brother and sister. I loved talking to them when I was tipsy. I was always funnier and more loving. I parked my car in an empty car wash and drank the other one. I got rosé this time, which seemed to have a stronger odor. I got into the house and felt so good and so happy that I forgot not to get close to Brooke. I got into bed and leaned over to kiss her. She immediately knew that I had been drinking. I blacked out at that minute. I woke up with a shattered phone, my necklace was broken on the floor, and I was on the couch. I was spinning so much that I went to the bathroom to throw up. I had to meet with HR the next morning at 9am. Brooke wouldn't let me come into the bedroom this time and told me she would wake me up at 7:00. I felt so sick, but eventually fell back asleep. She woke me up, and I jumped into the shower. No soap or mouthwash in the world could take away the disgust I had for myself. I dried my hair and put so much concealer under my eyes because they were puffy, and it still didn't change anything. I looked like shit and felt like shit. I felt like such a loser and questioned if I was still going to have a marriage after this point. She, of course, took our debit cards again. I got in my car at 8:00 and drove downtown to go to work.

Thank God they required masks so I could hide the reeking smell of leftover wine that was seeping out of my mouth. I was worried that they were going to do a drug test. There was definitely still alcohol in my system. I wasn't sure if that would come up or not, but it made me feel even worse. I worked so hard to land this job that could lead to my new career, and I almost lost it. I had the shakes so badly that I could barely sign paperwork. I had to have a drink. I just felt like I was not going to make it without it. I found a Publix on my way home and scraped up some change. It was 9:00, and I bought a pint of wine with pennies, nickels, and dimes. I was shaking so badly that I spilled the change all over the counter. My eyes were cloudy with tears as I showed her my ID. She didn't say anything, but she put my wine in a brown paper bag. I went out to my car, and then it hit me. I was exactly what I used to think an alcoholic was. I was drunk at 9am, drinking out of a brown paper bag. This was my bottom, or so I thought.

I got home, and Brooke said that this was it. One more time, and she's done. Completely done. She couldn't take me being so nasty and drinking and driving and watching me throw my life away. The wine wore off, and I got the shakes again. I went to the meeting at 8:15pm, and I shared this time. I started crying, saying that I had over five years of sobriety before this, and I couldn't stop relapsing and now absolutely could not beat my alcoholism. It was winning and ruining my life. It felt like I had no way out at this point. Someone in the meeting said that if you start over, you never lose the time you put in, and you can always gain back the knowledge you had. I felt a glimpse of hope. I had a sponsor before, but since I broke my phone, I lost her number. I only knew of one meeting she went to, and there was no way I could wait until the next Wednesday to see her. I needed help now. I walked up to the woman chairing a meeting. Her name was Amy, and she seemed to have good sobriety. At this point, I couldn't be picky. I walked up to her, full of tears and shaking so badly. I told her I noticed that she didn't raise her hand when they asked if anyone was willing to be a sponsor, but I needed help. I needed to find God and work this program. My entire life, marriage, job, self-worth, and love depended on it. For the first time in my life, I was scared that I was going to end up dead from this disease. Amy agreed and told me to call her the next day, and I did, and every day after that.

I had a week before orientation at work and went to one to two meetings a day. I talked to women in the program and really put my all into it. I was so desperate and wanted this so badly. Very slowly, I started to pull myself out of my current rock bottom. It was like I was clawing my way out of the hole, blood and dirt under my nails, just to move inches up in the hole. But it was progress, and I trusted that.

Eventually, I would get back to where I was. I went to work and started training. I had a badge and a work suit that I wore every day. I didn't make any friends, but I liked the work.

As much as I liked the work, I really struggled to learn the computer system they used. I had always had a hard time learning new, unfamiliar things. I was a very slow learner, contrary to what my resumé said, but I figured nobody wanted to hire a slow learner. So, I struggled. A lot. I got paired with Katrina, a woman from the Philippines. She was very blunt and mean and moved very quickly. She moved too quickly for me to learn anything. I asked her to slow down, but she didn't. I felt like I wasn't learning anything. I started to feel stupid because I couldn't get it. The guy who started when I did was already on his own, and I was two weeks in and barely knew how to begin to check someone in. They moved me to the back for training for the work we do on the phone in the back, which I liked better. I was able to put someone on hold and ask questions, and I noticed I didn't make as many mistakes. I felt comfortable and asked if I could stay back there, and they let me, so I was able to feel comfortable in my position.

We had to walk half a mile from the parking garage to work because we worked in downtown Tampa. We would talk and laugh, and I got close to people I worked with. I was sober and happy. Just like before, things were falling into place again.

Every year, it was a known thing in my family that my birthday was a national holiday. I planned a dinner with my family for Sunday. I had to work on my actual birthday, but I had that whole weekend off. I worked that Thursday, which was my birthday, and came home to a surprise. Brooke got me Slim Jims, which were my favorite, pork rinds, and a Monster energy drink, and left them by the door. There was a sign on the door saying, "Happy birthday, we love you, love Bodey, Sophie, and Brooke." I smiled. I felt so loved at that moment. I walked in to find Mrs. and Mrs. cups on the counter with a Cartier watch and a picture of us at our wedding. I went into our bedroom, and Brooke wasn't there, so I glanced out onto our patio overlooking the moonlit water.

She had gotten a string of lights and was sitting in one of the chairs and told me there was a surprise in the freezer. She got my favorite frozen yogurt. Raspberry pomegranate loaded with boba. She invited me to sit outside with her, and I did. We had never spent time together out on our patio. She played our song, "Wonderful Tonight," and we danced under the stars. It was a beautiful night.

That Saturday, we went out to eat with my family: my aunt and uncle, my parents and Brooke. We went to a restaurant on the water and had an amazing time. We took our new boat out, and it was so windy, and the boat was so small that we had to come back. I was petrified and hated it. My stress levels were through the roof, but I was just so happy to be able to feel all of these things sober and have such a loving family.

Sunday was a day for Brooke. We laid in bed and watched movies with the dogs and cuddled all day. Just a lazy Sunday. I did have to go back to work that next day. At the end of the night, she had to work on some paperwork in the spare room, and out of nowhere, I became incredibly suicidal. It hit me like a ton of bricks. I had felt slight depression before, and I assumed it was a small mood swing caused by stress at work and it would pass. Well, it didn't. It got so bad so quickly, and I was declining by the minute. I looked around for pills to take. All I had was Lithium. I knew how horrendous that overdose would be if I made it, and my hands shook as I grabbed the bottle. I was crying. I mentioned to Brooke how I felt, but I don't think she realized how bad it was. She told me she would be in later, but I couldn't wait that long. Everything in my mind was telling me that I needed to die. My mind completely turned on me. I was thinking about failing at work, losing Jade and other friends over the years, and that I was thirty-three, working a front desk entry position making $14.50 an hour. I started to sink deeper. I was twenty-three days sober, and I started to hate myself for all the drinking that I had been doing. I went into deep thought about the relief I would get from taking the entire bottle of eighty pills. I grabbed ten in my sweaty, shaky hands, and as I did that, Bodey cried to come up on the bed. I put the pills down and picked him up. He curled up in my lap and looked up at me with those big brown eyes, and I saw his love, and it snapped me out of it. I needed professional help. I started looking for places to go, but I couldn't find any that weren't state psychiatric hospitals. I looked for an hour and couldn't find anything. My mom was looking, and luckily, my cousin's sister worked at a privately owned facility in Clearwater. Just as before, the minute I knew I was going, I felt better.

Although, I didn't know how this place would be, so I was nervous about that. Brooke couldn't handle me being in this state, so she asked if my mom and my aunt could take me. About twenty minutes later, they came to get me. I packed a bag full of books, long-sleeved shirts, jackets, and long yoga pants. I knew better than to have any strings, so I made sure none of them did. This was not my first rodeo. I knew the drill. They keep the building at about 65 degrees at all times. I grabbed shampoo, conditioner, and body wash. Brooke decided she wanted to take me, and it was a thirty-minute drive that seemed like it took forever. It was around ten at night. I texted my boss and told her what had happened. I knew that if I told them it was medical, they legally couldn't fire me for it. I was as honest as I could be, and she told me that they were there for me and to keep her posted. At this point, I had been talking to my sponsor and informed her what was going on. She told me to keep her posted. In the car, I wrote down all the numbers that I would need since I wouldn't have my phone. After what seemed like hours, we pulled up to a dark green, run-down meeting with a dimly lit sign. I didn't want to go but knew that I needed to.

Chapter 30

I walked into the waiting room. I had taken some of my anxiety meds and my normal medication since most places seemed to hold your meds for the first night. I knew if I didn't take it, I wouldn't sleep. There was a square of chairs and then some more tucked away in the corner. I sat on the side of the square that faced the TV and saw it was playing some alien movie. My mom loved those, and I had seen almost every one of them, so I wasn't thrilled about their choice of movie selection. They checked me in when I got there and told me to sit down and wait until they called me when they were ready to get my information. Then, I would speak to a nurse to see if I needed to be admitted.

I curled up into the seat and glanced across from me. There was a guy with his feet wrapped up in thick bandages, and his face was beet red and peeling. He tried to spark conversation, but I was not having it. I just fell asleep. I woke up to someone coughing up loogies in the corner and then another guy walking behind me and yelling. I could tell he was homeless and very drunk. They took him to the back, and then I heard him yell, "Shit, I pissed all over myself!" I tried my hardest to fall back asleep, but I couldn't at that point. Then, the admissions lady came to me and said she was ready. She took my picture and my insurance information. I looked at the clock, and it had already been three and a half hours. They told me that I needed to sit back down and wait for the nurse to be ready. I sat down and looked up at the TV, and it was the same damn movie. I guess I sighed loudly because the guy across from me told me that he had been there for six hours and he had seen that movie three times already. I said, "Oh great." He said, "You seem to be fairly normal. What brought you here?" I didn't feel like getting into it, so I just told him I was bipolar and having a bad mood swing, which was true. He told me that his name was Jesse and that he drank a bottle of tequila and passed out in the sand for seven hours in the Florida sun. He was so burnt that his skin bubbled. He couldn't walk, and the hospital sent him there. We talked a little bit, but I kept getting distracted because of the heavyset guy snorting his nasty snot all night. Then he jumped into the conversation. He was mumbling so much that I could not understand a word he said other than that his name was Greg. All three of us were having small talk, and I kept getting distracted by the homeless guy yelling and pacing back and forth behind me. He was now saying he felt like he was going to throw up. If he threw up, I would, too, so I begged for them to take me back. After 30 minutes, they called me back, right after Jesse.

  They asked me what was going on, and I told them everything. I was so gone that I couldn't even get myself to cry, but I knew what to say to ensure that I would be admitted. I told them that I felt unsafe with myself and that I wanted to die. That was, for sure, an admittance.

They walked me to the back, and we went to a locked door where they swiped their badge and walked me into a small room set up in a square. There were rooms along all the walls, and couches and a table in the center. There was a small moon-shaped desk with a chubby nurse and an older man behind the counter. The man brought me to the back room to do my admittance questionnaire. He was funny and made me feel comfortable. He told me that they put me on a crisis floor because there wasn't room in the acute psychiatric unit. He assured me that I would be out by the next day. We got done with the questions and paperwork around 3:00 in the morning, and he sent me to my room. The two beds were feet apart. Mental hospitals keep the rooms at around 65 degrees, so I requested two blankets. I hated the loose sheet on top of the three-inch plastic mattress, so I chose to sleep on the bare mattress. I was so used to things by this point. So, I comfortably fell asleep. I was exhausted.

I woke up the next day for breakfast. I was almost comatose. I was so tired. I barely remember breakfast. They brought us boxes of food, and I ate it in a chair. I looked around, and there was a tall black man in a hospital gown pacing the floor, and that made me very uncomfortable. There was an old lady in a wheelchair who just would not shut up. Then, there was a tall, skinny girl with long brown hair that seemed normal. I wasn't in the mood to make any friends. Then there was Don. He was tall and about three hundred pounds of pure muscle. He was yelling at the staff and was so angry that they told us to go into our rooms and called a code. Luckily, they were able to calm him down by giving him a Haldol shot. Just like before, I got out of my room, ate half of my food, and then went back to sleep. I was so used to the chaos that it didn't phase me anymore. I woke up hours later to the doctor wanting to see me. She told me that she was sure I just had a mood swing from stress at work. I felt hopeless, wondering when I was ever going to be able to work like a normal person without having incredible mood swings. She didn't want to change my meds, but I did. I learned over the years that you must take control (within reason) of your treatment. I research every pill and every side effect and suggest the ones I think would work best for me based on my research and what side effects I am very sensitive to. A friend of mine took Viibryd, and I asked for that, and she told me she thought that was a great idea to get this little black cloud out from over my head. I took the pill after a couple of hours, and it made me so tired, so I fell back asleep. I was woken up again, but this time, to move to the other floor. I grabbed the sweatshirt of Brooke's that I brought and followed the tech upstairs. We took the elevator, and she told me I would like this floor so much better. She used the badge to open the door to unit 33. It was a huge area with lots of rooms, plenty of chairs, a TV, two phones, and a huge table surrounded by chairs. I was so out of it from the medicine that I just went straight to the room where they placed me. He told me I had a very sweet roommate and to take care.

It seemed like five minutes, but I guess hours had passed because it was time for dinner, which was in the cafeteria. I always dreaded this. The first couple of meals at a psychiatric hospital are terrible. You don't know where to sit, and you're so mentally fucked that you don't want to talk to anyone. The group lined up at the door, and they divided us apart to take the elevators down, where we waited in another line to get to the cafeteria. Once we were in the cafeteria, we waited in yet another line for the food. I glanced over at the tables for two. Great, I was going to be stuck sitting with someone.

Luckily, I was one of the first in line, so I just sat at a table and hoped no one would sit with me. I was up against the wall, and I saw Jesse in his wheelchair. He was so excited to see me. He asked, "Can I sit with you?" I told him, "Yes." I really did feel comfortable with him. It usually takes one person reaching out their hand to get comfortable. Luckily for me, it was Jesse. He did most of the talking. His wife of 27 years died, and he never healed from it. He wouldn't admit he was an alcoholic, but he definitely was. He drank bottles at a time and went into that deep, dark place that we alcoholics go to when we drink. Dinner was fun. They had smoke breaks after each meal. I wanted a cigarette but didn't have any, and then I found out that they had community cigarettes. I took one and went outside. I sat with Jesse by the door and continued our conversation. I told him about Brooke, and like every old man, they get grossly excited and say something stupid, but I just ignored it.

After the smoke break, we took the elevators back up to our floor. I met my roommate. She was a twenty-three-year-old tiny thing with short hair and had cuts all the way up her arms. Her name was Sadie, and she was incredibly timid. We said hi, and that was it. We took our meds, which, to my surprise, they got right.

I woke up the next morning to the dreaded Lithium level blood test. They sat me down by the phone where there was a small wooden table and two green cloth chairs. I sat down, and she made the small talk that they usually do. She strapped my arm with the band and rubbed the alcohol on my veins. I glanced down at the incredibly massive needle she was about to use and asked why the hell it was so big. She denied that it was and just did the usual countdown, and I felt every bit of that needle entering my arm. It was like I could feel the end of the needle poking inside me. I knew better than to look, and I did my deep breathing, but I saw how much blood she was putting in vials. I started to get lightheaded and told her I was going to pass out.

 I have no idea why this is the usual response that I get when I tell them I am going to pass out. She just flat-out told me, "No, you're fine." She acted like I hadn't done this before. My vision started to tunnel, and I felt all the blood leave my face. I told her, "No, really, I am going to pass out." She pulled the needle out quickly and said, "Perfect timing. We're done." Thank God. I had to sit there for quite some time to feel better. By the time I was feeling better, everyone was starting to get up

for breakfast. That's when I met Jennifer and
Mia. Mia was a younger girl who wore clothes
that were way too tight but was a nice girl.

Then, there was Jenn, who was an older black
woman in a wheelchair. She was such a loudmouth
and just rude to others. But, lucky for me, they were
both kind to me and talked to me. I was feeling better
overnight from that medication, so I was engaging in
conversation.

Jesse woke up, and I just latched onto him.
We went to breakfast, sat in our spot, and just
talked. Then, we had our cigarettes and went
back for groups. I had a love-hate relationship
with group time. Some were great, and I
learned a lot, but some dragged on, and you
are forced to go, or else you get moved to a
lower level, so you are stuck for thirty minutes
to an hour in a boring group. After the group, I
begged my mom to bring me cigarettes. I
hadn't smoked cigarettes sober in over eight
years, but it was literally the only thing to do

on break. For some reason, I could go thirty days at rehab without smoking, but the minute they offered them to me here, I instantly wanted one. She brought me two packs of Camel Crush Menthol, my favorite. I absolutely loved the cool burn in the back of my throat when I smoked menthol.

I started to get to know others in the unit. There was Monica, who was such an oddball. She was a very large woman who always wore tight clothes, and her extensions were a rat's nest. She didn't talk much, but when she did, it was something completely off the wall. No one really talked to her because of that. Then, there was Chelsea. She was a little spitfire. She was angry and let everyone know it. Then there was Luke, who was also called Derek. I wasn't sure what that was about, but he was in a black tuxedo, had glasses the size of his face, and was quite intellectual. Then, the girl who was in the crisis unit came up. Her name was Kaylee, and she was very quiet and kept to herself.

After two days, I received all my clothes and personal belongings. I noticed that none of my toiletries came up. Apparently, there is alcohol in some shampoos and conditioners, so they kept those. They provided me with the shitty three-in-one: shampoo, conditioner and body wash. That stuff was terrible. It reminded me of the lice shampoo that they used when I went to the drunk tank.

For some reason, they kept my brush, or I forgot it. Either way, all I had was a small comb to use. At this point, my hair was quite long, and I was not looking forward to washing it at all. But Mia had been there for a while and suggested putting some of their lotion in the shampoo mixture and mixing it together. I did that, and somehow, it made the process bearable. I would put more lotion in my hair to force the comb through my long hair. I changed and felt better. I loved being able to put on clean clothes and shower when I was in a place like this.

Jesse and I were watching a movie. He was my best buddy there. We spent all the time together. Kaylee was sitting in the row of chairs behind us, and he turned around to talk to her. She and I hit it off and ended up talking for hours and hours that day. Turns out, she was severely bulimic, along with having borderline personality disorder and depression. She also self-harmed and wore long, baggy clothing. She was probably ninety pounds soaking wet. She was so nice, and we had so much in common. We related to so much of our mental distress throughout our lives. She became my new meal buddy, and we just kept the conversation going. She didn't smoke but would sit outside with me while I smoked.

My mental status was great at this point. I felt amazing. I talked to the doctor on Friday, and they told me that they didn't do discharges on the weekend, which wasn't unheard of, and I would be discharged on Monday. It was only a few days away, and I felt in good company, so I stayed.

I sat down and watched a movie with Kaylee. She excused herself to go to the bathroom, and her room was across from where we were sitting. The bathrooms were very awkward and similar to stalls. There was a large, open space on the top and the bottom. Zero privacy at all. I watched as I saw her feet point to where the toilet was. I felt sad for her. She hid it well, but I knew what she was doing. She talked to me about being borderline and told me that she would go through different moods/personalities, sometimes three to four times a day, and that there was no cure for it and it was only treatable through some mood stabilizers and therapy. She didn't have any friends at home, so we agreed to hang out. She was twenty-one but so mature for her age. I looked forward to hanging out with her. We exchanged numbers, and she left later that day. Our party of three turned into two. It was just Jesse and me.

I moved my focus to Derek. He always had a side smirk on his face, and he was so loveable and charming. Almost drawing people into him. He was a genius, no joke. He would debate, but not in an immature way. He stated facts and was not attached emotionally to anything he said. I was drawn to him, but not at all in a sexual way. I wanted him to like me and become as close as you could to friends in a mental hospital. I heard from someone else that he had multiple personality disorder and schizophrenia. Derek was his number one personality. He was the main character of his twelve personalities. He was always writing stories and drawing gruesome pictures.

He offered to read them to me. They were written so well for how gory they were. The explicit detail and imagery of his personalities was incredible. Quite a few of his personalities were cannibals, and that's actually what brought him. Not only was he mentally ill, but he was also a crack addict. He went off the wall and threatened to eat someone. I was always suicidal, and that is always what I heard other people say. He was the first person I had ever met in my years of hospital stays who came in as homicidal.

Even though part of me was completely freaked out by reading his stories, I was fascinated by how his mind worked. I would catch him talking to his personalities in his head. When he was Derek, I noticed that his eyes were beady black, which I found incredibly eerie. Then I met Luke. He wasn't as charming and had a temper, but that's who he really was.

On Saturday, a girl named Jamie came in. She was so nice and came in for a mental breakdown after the love of her life ended things. At this point, angry Chelsea and I became close. I don't know what it is about me that draws people in who normally don't like people. Maybe because I am all personality. Whether I'm doing well or not, I don't shut up. Jesse and I sat at meals together, but Chelsea invited me to her hidey-hole where she smoked. By this time, I had mastered snatching three to four cigarettes at a time. She wore a jacket with a chest pocket that always had cigarettes in it. She, Jesse, and I would sit on the covered stoop, far away from everyone, and smoke and talk. It turns out that what I thought was anger from Chelsea was actually just her protecting herself. She was an alcoholic who lived on the streets because the only place she had to go was her mom's, and she was a drunk, also. She told me she had been beaten, sexually assaulted, and raped. And underneath the tough exterior, she was a beautiful person. She loved God and nature. I really enjoyed Chelsea's company.

On Sunday, I woke up at 4:30am. I went to get coffee, sat at the table, and just waited for someone to wake up, and Jamie did. We stayed up chatting until everyone else woke up. There was not one negative thing I could say about her. She was a gem. At this point, I was feeling like I was going to conquer work and my life. I felt like I was on the right meds and was finally stable. I felt so good about myself and my life.

There was a window that we would all go by to look out like we were prisoners. We would play Rummy there, which I was terrible at, but that's all Chelsea did to keep her mind off of being in the hospital for her depression. I oddly really enjoyed being in this hospital. I hadn't made any friends since we moved to Tampa, and suddenly, I was surrounded by people who felt like friends.

After dinner that night, I went into my room to journal a bit. Sadie was sitting on the bed. I looked at her arms, and there were horizontal slices, inches apart, up both arms. I asked her what she was in for, and she said she was bipolar. She would get so manic that she wouldn't know how to handle it and would cut to alleviate the pent-up manic energy that comes with bipolar.

I had felt the need to do that before, so I completely understood why she would feel the need to do that. We also talked about how she dealt with her mood swings. We both dealt with them the same. It was refreshing to be able to talk to someone else with severe bipolar. I had finally found someone who understood the years of misery and pain that I had been through and all the obstacles that I had to push through to just live a semi-normal life. She understood that no matter how hard we try to be normal, we won't ever be.

It was a lot better staying in our room once we started talking. The whole group got close-knit, and we all talked and spent time together, except Monica. She came up to our circle one day and asked if she could sit with us. I said of course and made sure to include her in our conversation. Then, out of nowhere, she blew her nose into her hands, and a massive snot rocket came out, and she wiped it on her pants. Everyone else made her feel so gross, and I just made a joke out of it and tried to make her feel normal. I told myself a long time ago that no matter what happens in a psychiatric hospital, I will never judge because I need to remember where I am and that we are all here to get help. She and I kind of bonded after that. She was actually quite a talker and very funny. Poor girl had a hard life and was homeless.

She was so positive about life, and I admired that about her. She talked about living what seemed like a normal life, and I am not sure what happened along the way, but she was not the same girl she described.

Monday rolled around, and I was ready to get out of there and continue living my life with a healthy and clear mind. Sadie and I were both supposed to leave that Monday, but they had six other discharges, so we got pushed back to Tuesday. I mean, I was pissed, but I knew that there was nothing I could do about it.

They tried to fabricate it as much as they could, but it all came down to being short-staffed. Sadie fell apart. She was so ready to get home and had to go to therapy and work. She was hysterical. I took her into the room and told her that she had to watch what she said or did because we were under a microscope there. I told her we were in this together, and it was just another day, and we did a countdown until it was the next day.

Tuesday was actually a sad day. I really liked being around so many people that I liked, and they liked me, too. I got really close to Jesse and Chelsea and wanted to make sure I would be able to stay in touch with them. Jesse and I shared our last lunch together and our last smoke break. We had our routine, and I was almost crying, thinking about having to say goodbye. It felt like hours and hours waiting to be discharged. But I finally was, and Brooke was coming to pick me up. She was always fashionably late, so I assumed she would be, and she was.

She was late enough that I was able to get another smoke break in. Mid-cigarette, they said Brooke was there, and they walked me out. She absolutely hated cigarette smoke, so I knew then I would get caught. Which I did. She was very happy to see me, though. We made the thirty-minute drive home and started over.

Chapter 31

I got excused from work for a week from my psychiatrist. I told work, and they told me to get all of my paperwork together and that they were ready for me to come back. Now that the time had finally come, I was very nervous about work. They put me in the front on my own, and I was not ready for that. I tried to stay positive and live the day. Home life was good. I was in such a good mental place. Brooke and I were doing well, and I stayed in contact with Chelsea and Jesse. My special birthday gift came in, and it was my favorite wedding picture put on a canvas to put over our bed, which I had always wanted. I took time to go to meetings and to meet with my sponsor, Amy, for coffee. Amy was nice, but I wasn't connecting with her, so I decided to just give it more time. I agreed to give Chelsea some clothes because I didn't need all of mine and she didn't have any. I gathered the clothes and drove to the psychiatric hospital to drop them off. On my way home, I was listening to some Elton John, getting my mind ready for our concert, and out of nowhere, it was like I hit a wall, and I immediately went into a deep depression. In minutes, I went from what I thought was a normal level to suicidal depression. I went into autopilot. I drove to Walgreens, grabbed some wine, and resorted to what I knew best. That day was day thirty of not drinking. No one knew about it this time, so I hid it from everyone.

I started drinking White Claw because it was light and didn't have a strong smell. I would start drinking at 9:00am. I would tell Brooke I was going to meetings, meeting with Amy, or running, and I never did any of those things. I eventually just stopped coming home and just stayed out all day. I would get drunk and park my car in our visitor parking lot. There were tons of trees, and the more drunk I got, the more those leaves blended together. I called everyone in my phone book over the next couple of days. I made friends with the gas station guy and would buy one or two drinks at a time because I was "going to the pool." I drank all the time, from 9:00am to around 7:00-8:00 at night, but mastered not getting too drunk. There were a couple of times that Brooke thought I was drinking and smelled my breath, but somehow, I got away with it. The drinking on bipolar meds and being bipolar started to catch up to me. I slipped into a depression but hid it from everyone because I didn't want anyone to know that I was drinking.

I knew Brooke's Valium was at the pharmacy. I told her that I would help her by picking them up for her. She didn't like to leave the house much due to her depression and feared getting COVID for the third time. I picked them up and immediately took out six and put them in my pocket. They were ten milligrams, and I am such a lightweight with pills, so I knew this would be enough to knock me out and hopefully keep me asleep for a very long time. I don't think I wanted to die at that point, but just to not feel the pain and depression anymore. I got another drink on the way home. It was always the last drink that my gut told me not to drink that did me in. And it did just that. Brooke caught me drinking, and the rest was blurry. I told her that I wanted a divorce, so I was pretty much choosing to drink over her. She freaked out. I guess all the resentment from my drinking and all the mean things I said caught up to her. She called my mom to get me. I immediately reached into my pocket and took all six pills. I passed out for a while but then woke up to my mom there. I was so messed up. They kept yelling at me, and when they were talking to each other about what to do with me, I found five dollars in Brooke's purse and left to buy more drinks. I don't remember leaving the house. I came to hitting the stop sign by our house and hitting the one car in the visitor lot. I guess I hit our gate, too, which would cost around five hundred dollars if I broke it. I got out of my car, and someone yelled, "Are you fucking drunk?" I turned around and saw a cop standing with him. He said again, "Are you drunk?" My response was, "No, I took Valium."

What an idiot!

He took me upstairs to talk to Brooke and thank God I picked up my new Viibryd medication. The label said it could cause dizziness and should be used with caution while using motor vehicles. Her lawyer brain never ceases to amaze me. She told him it was the first day I tried that, and I seemed out of it when I left. I think he knew better, but he told her I would have to pay for the stop sign, and I got a ticket for no insurance. With how much I had been drinking, I forgot that Brooke took me off of her insurance until I got sober for thirty days, and by then, I wasn't able to get thirty days sober. He told me that if I went to a psychiatric hospital, he would let me go. We both agreed, and I put my head in his car and told him thank you for being so nice. Brooke had to force me into the house because she knew I would talk my way into a DUI.

Once I got into the house, shit hit the fan. I didn't know who to call, so I called Chelsea and cried to her about what happened. She told me to get my ass back up to the hospital. My mom took me this time since Brooke wanted nothing to do with me. I don't remember the drive, but luckily, I never unpacked my bag because I was drinking so much. I took that bag, my mom got me some cigarettes, and I was on my way back. I don't remember being in the waiting room at all. I came out of my blackout some five hours later upstairs on the detox floor, which was directly across the hall from the unit Chelsea and Jesse were on. I wanted to be there so badly, so I immediately asked to go there. They told me they would ask the doctor tomorrow, and I would most likely get to. They only put me on this unit because the other one was full. I was very quick to fall asleep. I didn't even realize until the next morning that I had the room to myself.

I woke up in a haze the next day. It was a Saturday, so I saw the weekend doctor and told him all that happened. Apparently, the Viibryd took me into a hypomanic state, which I thought was just a good mood that whole time. So even though it was a little high that I got on from it, I crashed hard and very quickly. He immediately said that he wanted to change all my meds, including my Lithium, which I had been on since 2015. I was scared to but just wanted to feel my kind of normal again, so I agreed. My psychiatrist and I talked about the new medication called Vraylar. He was quick to agree that it was a good choice. He told me he was going to take me off the Risperdal, too. I was happy to get off of that one. All it did was make me eat a ton and make my memory terrible, but it did help me sleep like a baby. I was out cold within minutes of taking it. I didn't have to put any effort into falling asleep. He asked me if I wanted to be put on Wellbutrin or Zoloft. I had already been on Zoloft, and it made me have zero sex drive and an increased appetite, so I chose Wellbutrin. I heard that it could be a magic pill and help you lose weight, quit smoking, and give you energy when mixed with the right medication. I was hoping I would be so lucky. I never met that doctor again, but little did I know then that he would change my life with his decision to change my medication.

I spent two days in the detox unit. I kept to myself and lived in so much anxiety, regret, and shame for all that I had done. I had flashbacks and would wake up in a cold sweat thinking about how I could have easily killed someone. The days dragged on, but finally, I was able to move to the next floor. I could not wait to see Jesse and Chelsea, and they welcomed me with open arms. I felt safe now.

Apparently, Jesse had started acting really weird. He told Kendra, a girl who came in while I was gone, that he loved her, and he tried to kiss her. Chelsea took his long hug with me and him rubbing my back as sexual, so she and Kendra complained. I wasn't bothered by him, and I should have stuck up for Kendra, but I wanted to be with my buddy, so I denied him doing anything to me. The next day, he was asked to leave the unit, and they moved him to the detox unit that I had just been in. I missed him, and after that, I only saw him through the small window when he was in line to go to lunch.

It was just Chelsea, Kendra, and me, and all we did was play Rummy. I was so sick of that game but wanted to do something. This time wasn't as fun and entertaining, but I had them, so I was content.

But out of nowhere, Chelsea was discharged, and then Kendra, so I was on my own. I was feeling better mentally, but by this point, I was just getting stir-crazy. The days dragged on and on. On the eighth day, I was able to leave. Before I left, they had me sign a waiver saying that they informed me of the warnings on drinking on Vraylar. It could cause a stroke, seizure, coma, or even death. I signed my name and honestly thought nothing of it. I went home to my destroyed marriage and did my best to repair it. I couldn't handle all that I did to her and that she wasn't forgiving me.

So, what did I do?

 I went straight to the gas station and started the deadly process again. I knew I was playing with fire with these meds, so I started drinking very cautiously. The days started off with just a couple, then, of course, led to more. I think at this point, Brooke just didn't care anymore because she wasn't even bringing up the times when I had too much or would pass out or slur. She was just mentally checked out, and I wasn't out of control, so I was able to do what I wanted. She did, however, take away my debit card. But I knew she didn't check the bank statement, so I would order a DoorDash to bring me alcohol. I would meet at the gate like a drug deal. I did this for a couple of days, and then I got the balls to put the drink in a glass and drink it in the spare bedroom because, at this point, Brooke and I were not sleeping together. I was too drunk to care about that.

My mom came to visit because I ran out of gas, and Brooke wouldn't fill my tank. She gave me a one-hundred-dollar gift card for gas and told me to please not spend it on anything else. Well, I wish she didn't trust me so much, because...

What did I do?

I went to the gas station, and now I could buy cigarettes. I went in to start my day the next day and bought two White Claws and a pack of cigarettes. It was 8 bucks!!

What the hell?

The guy at the register looked at me and said, "You get these all the time." I had always been so drunk when I got them that I never knew how much they cost.

At this point, I started abusing a friend's prescribed Adderall. At first, it was because I liked how much it made me focus. It actually worked like it was supposed to and didn't send me into mania like everyone in the medical field always said it would.

But, shortly afterwards, I was taking three to six a day so I wouldn't get sloppy drunk. I had stayed in touch with Chelsea, and she was living in a halfway house and had been dying to go to the casino. I didn't tell her that I had been drinking that day when I came to pick her up. She sat down at the machine once we got to the Hard Rock, and I immediately went to find the bar, but I told her I was getting a Diet Coke. Which I did, but I also got two shots of Fireball. I came back and sat there for a while, then wanted another shot, so I offered to get her a Diet Coke, then I had two more. I went back one more time and had another shot, and then the gift card ran out. Then, I pushed Chelsea to leave. I was completely shitfaced. I got in my car, and we were singing and dancing, and I turned left and missed getting pummeled by a semi by about one hundred feet. To this day, it still makes me sweat at night, thinking about how close it was. I dropped her off and got home, and it was a dead giveaway that I had been drinking. My mom was crushed that I did that and was finally done with me. Brooke thought that I would stop because of how bad I felt and sorry that I was, but she should have known better. If hitting a car, a stop sign, and our gate, and almost getting a DUI wasn't enough to make me stop, then this sure as hell wasn't. I just kept drinking and taking Adderall.

I found out that Lea lived directly across from me. It was a small world, so she came over with her dog on one of my sober days, because I did try to stop on my own a couple of times. We agreed to have dinner one night. I continued on with my drinking and taking Adderall. I was losing so much weight because I just wouldn't eat anything. All I did was drink and smoke cigarettes. I was pretty big before that and started having clothes fall off of me. I had been drinking for some time one day and decided to hang out with Lea. I told Brooke that I was leaving around 3:00 and told her I would be home after dinner. The next thing I remember is us in the hot tub. Then, I woke up the next day on her couch with my phone dead.

I never told Brooke where I was and just never came home. When I did get home, the door was locked, but luckily, I had a key. I walked in and could tell she had been crying all night. I did care, but I didn't want to admit I was drinking. We both knew that I had been, but I think she was just done as well. My marriage was crumbling, and I was too wrapped up in my addiction to care.

One day, I had about five to six White Claws and took some Xanax that I bought from a friend. Looking back, I realized how much I affected Brooke's sobriety and mental health, but I just took it as a way to get more messed up.

Being bipolar already makes us impulsive and act insane when we stop taking our medication. I didn't stop taking my medication, which honestly probably would have been better. Drinking on this medication brought me so very low. I couldn't take how I felt, and Brooke finally called me out, and I snapped. I grabbed a knife, locked the bathroom door, and just started slicing up my arm and upper thigh. I went deeper each time and just kept going higher up my arm. Brooke caught on to what I was doing and told me to open the door. I didn't, so she kicked down the door and took the knife, but I wasn't done. I laid down in bed for a minute, then got up to go to the bathroom, grabbed two knives, hid one, and then used the other to start again.

There was blood everywhere. She came back crying and begging me to stop, but at this point, I felt like I had lost my mind. I could not stop. I went back, grabbed the knife I had hidden, and kept going. Then, Brooke picked me up, helped me get back to bed, laid me down, rubbed my hair, and calmed me down. I was hysterical, but I eventually fell asleep in her arms. When I woke up, I still felt like I was losing my mind. I could not stop and didn't want to. Brooke took my keys, but I wanted to drive to the hospital. I knew I needed help.

 I was going crazy. She agreed that it was time for me to go back and drove me there herself.

Chapter 32

I walked through the familiar doors yet again. As messed up as I felt, I felt such shame in coming back for a third time in two months. I was tired from all the chaos from the night before. I gave them my bags that I still hadn't unpacked since the last time I stayed. I slouched into one of the green chairs that I'd grown used to and curled up into a ball. I just wanted to sleep this off. I opened my eyes when the only other woman in the room started screaming. I immediately closed my eyes as I listened to her yelling that she wasn't crazy.

The nurse woke me up to go into the room to do the skin assessment. I hated these because I never wore underwear, so it was an expose-all session. Same stuff, different day, except this skin assessment was different. I took off my jacket, shirt, and bra and just looked down at my wrists. Then I took off my pants and saw my leg. I held back tears, pulled up my pants, and put my arms back into my jacket. She told me that I would be in the crisis unit because I was high-risk. I hated that floor. It was filled with the stereotypical people that you would expect to see in a psychiatric hospital. What sealed that deal was the massive "suicide cut" on my left arm. It went all up my arm from my wrist to my forearm. When I made that cut, I had every intention of bleeding to death.

Dreading the next step, I went back into my chair. I fell asleep and woke up to a dark complected girl in a black flowered dress with her boobs hanging out of her dress. She asked me if I was okay in a panicked voice. I turned to look at her, and her eyes were about to bulge out of her head. I said, "Yes, I am just tired." Then I went back to sleep. I woke up to her screaming and throwing her drink across the wall and yelling that she wanted to be put in a straitjacket, so they did just that. After that, all I heard was the lady continuously screaming that she wasn't crazy. I was informed then that I would be going to unit 33, which is what I was used to. I lost my place as a crisis unit patient.

Thank God.

They took me through those familiar locked metal doors of unit 33. The first person I saw was my favorite tech. I smiled, and he smiled back and said that he was so happy to see me and my smile. I had always been called "Sunshine," so it reminded me of my prior self. I suddenly felt comfortable seeing someone I knew who would take part in my treatment.

I immediately fell asleep. Over the years, I learned to be comfortable in places like this. It became my safe haven from myself. I crashed hard and didn't wake up until the dreaded dinner time. I sat at a table far away from everyone. I didn't want to talk to anyone. But lucky for me, Chatty Kathy came and sat with me. Now, I talk a lot, but she definitely takes the cake as a talker. It was exhausting.

  After dinner, I grabbed my 305 Menthol 100's. This time, I came prepared. We get two cigarettes for fifteen minutes. The bigger the cigarette, the more you get. So, I bought three packs and was set for my stay. I sat on the stoop where Chelsea, Jesse, and I sat to be alone. But of course, someone had to join me. I was irritated. His name was Josh, and he ended up talking just enough to be tolerable. I started to feel better, and he became the one who got me out of my shell this time.

  When we came back in, I saw the girl from the waiting room. She immediately turned to me and said, "Hey, I know you from downstairs."

Damnit.

She immediately latched onto me. She admitted that she was on so many drugs when she came in and also came because she had an anger problem. But anyone was better than Kathy talking my ear off, so I was content talking to her.

I spent the next couple of days swinging from high to low. They increased my Vraylar to 6mg and Lamictal to 500mg. They kept me on Wellbutrin and Buspar. I was happy that I had Dr. Powell as my doctor. He had been mine for the past couple of stays, so he knew my mood swings pretty well. When I saw him the first time, I literally could not stop talking. It was like I was waiting to get my word in before he finished. He called it pressured speech. I was manic as hell. Now, it was just the waiting game for the medications to work. I hated this game.

I didn't have a roommate my first two nights, which was nice, but I still didn't sleep. Lucy came in around 8:30 on the third night. I said, "My name is Lauren," but there was no response.

Great.

It's going to be a long stay. I had the bed by the window and had spent days staring out of it at the busy wasp nest in the corner and the airplanes flying by. It wasn't much, but enough to keep my mind occupied. She started complaining about it being cold, so I told her my secret. Get two blankets and make a "tent" over your head so your breath keeps you warm. She still complained about being cold, so I offered one of my sweaters and went to sleep. I got around four hours of sleep, which was good for how manic I was.

I don't know what it was about me, but the oddballs came to me like magnets. Kathy followed me everywhere. She talked about everything and complained about everything. She had 5 days sober, which beat me, but all she did was lecture people about their sobriety and how to stay sober. She was homeless, like the majority of the people there. This time, it felt like a rehab where no one wanted to stay sober. So, just like I learned from my support groups, I stuck with the winners.

I had a major depressive mood swing after a full day of intense mania. It was like an overbearing dark cloud. I couldn't move or cry. I just stared out my window. I said a prayer to feel better and make it through this. I fell asleep for a couple of hours and woke up to half of a rainbow. I felt like I was on the right track.

By the fourth day, I noticed that I was still manic. I could not sit still to watch TV or read or even stay in one place except to look out of that little box that was my window. It's hard being bipolar because, with every good mood or excited feeling, you have to consider that it might be mania or hypomania.

I was taking my meds one day and saw a familiar face. It was Nathan from my first stay at the hospital. He always made me laugh and have a good time. He became my new mealtime buddy, and we played cards all the time.

Every time the phone rang, everyone assumed it was for me, which I loved. I had always struggled with losing Jade and Alyssa. I never understood why and how they could just leave me in the dark like I meant nothing to them. It was like losing them paved the way for even better and more loving friends to enter my life. I was even told how awesome my support system was. I hadn't felt so much love and support in such a long time.

I woke up the next morning feeling fantastic. I got a full ten hours of sleep, and the first thing the nurse, who had been part of my treatment three times by this point, even said, "Wow, you look so good, like Lauren again." What I liked about going to the same hospital was not just the familiar faces but that they see you at your worst and watch you transform into your best.

Another thing I loved about being in places like this was that you learn to appreciate what you have in comparison to others, and you meet others that you can relate to. Morgan was coming off of crack, and God knows what else. I had seen her each time I came in. She was homeless and could not stop wiggling, twitching, and having her tongue constantly on her lips. We went to the recreation room where some of us were playing the game Sorry. She wanted to play, and we had to walk her through it, which was fine. There was music playing, and she was dancing and told us that she was a stripper. I could relate because there was a night in college when I did an amateur night at a strip club called The Dollhouse. I vaguely remember that night, but I know I was dared to do it, so I did. I woke up with dollar bills sticking out of my underwear and all around me in my bed, so that refreshed my memory. So, I couldn't and did not judge her at all.

I went into Dr. Powell's office and finally felt stable, so he let me go a day early. I was ecstatic to start over and begin my new life, until I got home. It was like a switch went off the minute I got home. I immediately started drinking. I ended up being completely insane on the high dose of the medicine I was on. I was staying in the other room of the house so I could vape because Brooke hated it. After a few days of heavy drinking came the pills. I stashed some in my car and took them inside. There were about ten of them. At this point, I was extremely suicidal. I got caught drinking yet again. So, off I went. The bookshelf was knocked over, I pulled out a chunk of hair, hit the wall, and broke another door. I was out of control. Brooke came in to stop me, so I grabbed all the pills and put them in my mouth, but she was able to get them out. Three of them fell into my shirt, but I didn't tell her, and she didn't see them. She left, exhausted from me and my shenanigans. I sat on the bed crying. I just wanted to fucking die. I drank the rest of the White Claw that I had in my cup and took all three 3mg Xanax. That was enough to immediately knock me out. I woke up to Brooke shaking me because she thought I overdosed again. This time, I woke up with a vengeance. I was more insane and out of my mind than I had ever been.

I don't remember much, but I tried to leave, and Brooke held me back and grabbed my keys, and I punched her in the face. I ran outside and just started running, then realized that I couldn't go anywhere, so I went back and there were cops there. They saw how fucked up I was and that the house was trashed and split us up to talk to each of us. Brooke accidentally said that I hit her. She would never rat on me, but it slipped out. He told her that he was going to have to take me to jail for assault. She was crying and pleaded with him not to. He asked her if she was trying to keep me from leaving, and she said, "Yes, I was genuinely concerned about her leaving home." They decided to put me in involuntary confinement in a local state psychiatric hospital, but this time, I didn't fight it.

This was the second time I was in a cop car, and this time, I was put in the back. I begged them to please not take me to a state mental hospital, but they did. I let Lea and my other friends know that I was being Baker Acted, which is called something different in every state. It is involuntary confinement. I got to the state psychiatric hospital and passed out. I woke up a couple of hours later to call Brooke, and she was crying hysterically and apologizing for sending me there. I had sobered up by that point and told her that I would have done something stupid, so she did the right thing.

I waited for twelve hours to meet with the tech for the first round of getting admitted. He asked how I was feeling, and I said, "Doesn't even matter, I'm stuck here for 72 hours." He told me that I wasn't stuck there if I didn't feel like I needed to stay. I just needed to tell the doctor that. So, that's what I planned to do. I waited another four hours to talk to the doctor and told her I was messed up when I came in, but 100% okay now and ready to leave. She told me that I was okay to leave and was a total bitch about it, but I didn't care. I was just ready to leave and go home.

It took another two hours to discharge me and for Brooke to pick me up. The ride home was rough. She filled me in on all that I did and told me that she honestly couldn't take it anymore. This was it. My mom told me I was no longer welcome in her home if I was still drinking. I had finally hit my bottom. I had thought I was at rock bottom multiple times before, but I didn't realize that rock bottom had a trap door leading to a further bottom. I was finally done. I threw in the towel.

When we got home, Brooke asked me if I wanted to go to rehab. I told her that I really thought I would be okay. I honestly wanted to be done. I could not lose my entire family and life to alcohol.

We were very broken, but I knew that because she didn't leave me at my worst, she did love me, and despite all that I put her through, I did love her, too. We laid in bed for hours, which led to days. I started talking to my mom again and repairing that damage. You don't realize the trail of destruction you're literally throwing out behind you until you sober up and look back. There were broken pieces from my entire life scattered behind me, and I was finally willing to start picking them up, sober.

I made it about three days until I started getting cravings again, and then I knew that I wasn't going to win this battle alone. I needed help. I started searching for rehabs that my insurance covered and found another one in Fort Lauderdale. Brooke wasn't able to take me, but my dad was. I packed up all my stuff and started the four-hour drive to clean up my life.

The drive was quiet. I was replaying all of what I had done over the last four months, and it was incredible how much damage I had caused in that short amount of time. The rooms of my support groups always say that alcoholism is a progressive disease. I didn't know what that meant until this point. I had eight years without a drink. Granted, I took pills, but alcohol is my drug of choice. It was waiting for me to come back, and I picked up right where I left off eight years ago and then went down in flames.

Chapter 33

It started to rain, which felt ironic. My dad and I pulled up to the front, and there were three very nice yellow buildings. It already seemed more promising than the last. I unloaded the truck with a massive lump in my throat, then said goodbye to my dad and walked inside. I was immediately greeted by the friendly staff. Sean was who I talked to first. He did my drug test and went through all of my bags. I peed in the cup and told him I was going to bomb the test. I had been sober for five days, waiting until the beds were available, but I had Xanax and Adderall in my system. I took them for weeks. I knew that they would be in there. He said that I was ready to go upstairs to the detox floor. I was pissed. I didn't want to go to detox. I didn't need to detox from anything. But I went along with it.

We took the elevator up. New patients weren't allowed to use the stairs because they could be a fall risk. We walked through the glass doors, and it was exactly how I imagined a rehab would be the first time I went to one. Granite countertops, large windows, baskets of snacks everywhere, couches, and a big screen TV. Each room had two full-sized beds, a massive dresser, and a massive TV. My doubts and uneasy feelings immediately dissipated. My roommate was a bubbly girl named Avery. We hit it off immediately. She was from South Carolina and was another fellow alcoholic. The beds were far apart, and we were allowed to keep our phones all day. I was super comfortable and so grateful that my insurance covered this place.

After talking to Avery for hours, they let us out for a smoke break. By this point, I was smoking a Jul, and I came prepared. I sat out and kind of kept to myself, but everyone was so nice and chatty, including the staff. I stuck with Avery, but she was very talkative and friendly. I met a guy named Connor, who was skin and bones and so shaky. He was a low-bottom drinker. He drank so much that he put himself in the hospital because he was having seizures while trying to quit drinking on his own. We got about twenty minutes outside, then went to our first group, which was a couple of doors down from the front desk. It was all in the same building, which was nice. We never had to leave campus, and they provided meals and every snack, pop, and juice you could imagine. I had lost so much weight from the medication change and all the drinking and Adderall, so I could use some weight gain, but the last time I was in rehab, I gained so much weight, so I tried my best to stay on top of how much I was eating this time.

The first couple groups were a blur. Actually, the first couple of days were just a blur. I met with a doctor, and we discussed my medication change that they did in the hospital. He was pleased with it, and so was I.

I had zero side effects and no food cravings, which was something I had never experienced since I was put on bipolar medication in 2015. Every night and morning, we would line up at the glass-plated windows and take our medications. It was very time-consuming, but in a way, it was nice because they took their time with everyone, monitoring their mood, physical and mental status, and level of cravings. I honestly didn't have any. I felt good and so very hopeful.

I started getting to know more people as they walked through the doors of detox. There was Trevor, who I immediately knew was from the South when he called me "Ma'am" and held the door open for me. He was a contractor from Texas and such a gentleman. He was in for cocaine. Then there was Jack. He was a short, pudgy guy from Louisiana and had a thick accent. He was not very friendly, but I soon came to find out that he just wasn't a talker. Lucas was Cuban and from Miami. I didn't know much about him, but he was very friendly even though you could tell he was very broken from his drinking. Ashley was a bigger girl from Tennessee. She came in on heroin and hid it from her boyfriend for five years. She was incredibly successful in her career, even at the peak of her addiction. Then there was Taylor. She was a black woman and so incredibly angry. I tried my best to stay as far away from her as I possibly could.

We all mingled quite well. Groups in detox were optional, but I wanted to get the most out of this program as I could, so I went to all of them but one. Since it was still COVID era with the new Omicron strain coming through, we had to eat with just one person at each table. For the first time, I was actually wanting to share a table with someone, but we couldn't. The food was very good, but I didn't eat much. I wasn't trying to starve myself by any means. I just wasn't hungry.

Avery and I were like old best friends. We were constantly laughing and having a great time. We shared a bathroom with Nora, who was a rough, trashy girl who always had something to say, blared her music, and would leave our side of the bathroom open when she used it so we could hear everything. She started fights with staff every day and eventually left AMA, which means Against Medical Advice. In that same room was Paige. She was beautiful, skinny, and had long, well-polished hair.

She had two years of sobriety and then went on a two-week binge on crack. Her home group was actually the group across the parking lot, and she worked her ass off to make money, and from what she said, she had a lot. In that two-week binge, she spent $20k on drugs and hotels. She was very nice but very short-fused.

We had our first "meeting," and it was a woman from my alcohol support groups. She went through this program, had years of sobriety, and worked a hell of a program. Only Avery, Connor, Trevor, Paige, and I went out for her group. Paige did most of the talking because they had the same home group. She talked to me, and I said a little bit about myself and my codependency on Brooke and how much I lost to drinking. She cut me off before I could even finish saying what I lost and told me, "No honey, you didn't lose it. You chose to give it away." She was blunt, and I liked it because I needed to get in my head that I didn't know anything, because no matter what I had learned up until this point, I still ended up here.

Avery and I would watch her YouTube channel. This girl was hilarious. I confided in her a lot, and we would gossip about what we thought of others and had a great time. She and I went to a group one day, and on our way, this girl came in and melted in the armchair in the center of the detox unit. She had blonde, curly hair up in a messy bun, a blue tank top that said "Good Vibes" on it, and short pink shorts. She was so fucked up and wore sunglasses inside that whole day. I soon found out that her name was Sydney. She was a hot mess. She spent the first couple of days detoxing from crack and so much wine. But once she sobered up, she became one of my favorite people.

Paige was leaving and chose not to go into inpatient treatment because she was self-pay, and it cost $10k just for a week of detox. She left me with a green puff vape in menthol mint flavor. I was ecstatic to finally have one of my own! She left me a bag to put all my toiletries in and all her hair supplies, face wash, makeup remover pads, and lotion that smelled so good. I had brought stuff, but mine was generic and just what I used at home. She had some nice stuff. She wished me well and left.

I found myself making my bed every day, showering every day, wearing my hair down, and sometimes braiding it at night to make it wavy the next day. I was taking care of myself again. I was having a good time and learning a lot from the little groups, but I was definitely ready to go to residential treatment. I didn't know how many days I had, and I wanted to get to the heart of the true program. I was getting frustrated but trusted the process.

The next day, Taylor, Trevor, and I went to inpatient. As excited as I was to go, that meant that I was rooming with Taylor. We were the first of our tight-knit group to go. She was so excited to room with me, but I couldn't say the same. I was so afraid of her. With my lack of a voice and her overbearing voice, I didn't think we would be a good match.

We took the familiar black van from the detox unit to the inpatient compound. We drove right by the Hard Rock, which was in the shape of a massive guitar, then pulled up to a gate. I walked in and saw a patch of fake grass, lines of picnic tables, and a navy-blue retractable awning over them. The building was an L shape like the last one I went to, but this one was two stories. I found out that we went to groups on-site, which I liked. It honestly gave me a college-town vibe. They told us we were just in time for wrap-up. We walked in, and there were maybe twenty people in chairs in a circle, and we grabbed some chairs in the back. We came in the middle of the group, so we just watched. Each person would say their name, how many days sober they had, how their day was, two things they were grateful for, and how they were feeling. Brandon was the first to go. He had twenty-two days sober, and I tuned out the rest until I heard him say he was grateful for "ALL Y'ALL." And the entire room said "ALL Y'ALL" back. Trevor and I looked at each other. He mouthed, "What the fuck?" Then Brandon said that he was feeling great. The entire group chanted back, "You look like you are feeling great, what do you think bout that?"

What kind of place was this?

  We felt so uncomfortable. They did this until they got to the last person in the circle. Then, it came to our turn. I murmured, "ALL Y'ALL," when it was my turn and got it yelled right back to me. I liked it. Trevor and Taylor went next, and then everyone stood up and circled in the center, where Brandon started the prayer. They said the serenity prayer, but the "we" version:

> *God, Grant US the serenity to accept the things WE cannot change, the courage to change the things WE can, and the wisdom to know the difference.*

  I figured it would be done at that point, but it wasn't. Brandon continued, "Put one foot in for all the troops and first responders, to all the babies born into addiction at no fault of their own, to the people suffering inside and outside of these walls." After each line, the group repeated it.

"Raise your head up," (everyone put their head up and repeated what he was saying) *"because it's been down for way too long."* And then it was over. How awkward but powerful.

We ventured outside while we were waiting to be taken to our apartment. Taylor sat with a couple of people outside of our group that she knew, and I sat with some of the people who were already there. I felt so uncomfortable, but I refused to be a wallflower like I was in my last rehab. I introduced myself and met Riley, who was a fellow lesbian, Allison, who had pink hair, and Donna, who was a very large woman with incredibly fake lashes. They weren't warm and fuzzy to me, but they weren't rude, either. We smoked some cigarettes and talked, and then the tech told us that we could go upstairs.

We walked up the stairs to unit 5. It was nice and big. There was a brown leather couch, a chipped brown granite coffee table, a flat-screen TV, and a kitchen with a dishwasher, disposal, stove, and fridge. Then, the bathroom had a half-octagon-shaped glass shower and a full-length mirror. The bedroom had a dresser, which we split half and half, and each of us had a nightstand. The beds were twin-sized but on complete opposite sides of the large bedroom. There was a huge closet that we split, also. She had tons of makeup and clothes. I had maybe six outfits, my new running shoes that Brooke bought me before I started drinking, and three pairs of Walmart flip-flops. I had to bring extra; in case they broke. We planned our meals with seventy-five dollars a week to spend on food and toiletries. We combined our money to go get groceries, and then, along with this arrogant guy named Dylan, went to Walmart. Dylan had 18 years of sobriety, so he felt better than all of us, but just like us, he ended up here. I was waiting for the day for him to fall off his high horse.

We got our groceries. She packed up on the meats, potatoes, and vegetables. I got my little BumbleBee tuna salad kits, some Belvita cranberry and orange cookies, and lots of Diet Coke and water. We made sure to get coffee, too. Groups started every morning at 8:00 sharp.

We got our groceries and walked into the apartment, and she started cooking. She made homemade spaghetti and meat sauce, and it was incredible. She said she'd cook for us every night, and I told her that I would make sure to keep the place clean. She was like Brooke. She liked everything spotless, whereas I, on the other hand, was a complete slob. So, I admitted that I was, and she agreed to help me. I saw a different side of her. She was really cool.

We did meds every night at 8:00 and every morning any time before 8:00. We would go to the door at the bottom of the L building that was filled with two public bathrooms, two group rooms, and the nurse's office. I went to get my meds and was pleased that the transition of my medication from detox to inpatient was successful. The first night there wasn't bad, but she made a lot of noise in her sleep, which I hated. Ever since I got off of Risperatol, I had to work to fall asleep. I didn't sleep well that night, but I got about four hours. I woke up, put on my best yoga pants, and put my hair in a ponytail. I brought minimal makeup, so I put on my mascara and foundation, pinched my cheeks, and called it a day. I had my cup of coffee and my Belvita cookies on my bed, and then made it, grabbed my notebook, and left my phone upstairs. They warned us about having our phones on us during group hours. We were not allowed to go into our rooms from 8:00am-3:30pm, and if we got caught on our phones, they could take it for the day, or if Andy, who oversaw everything, caught you, he would take it for the entire stay at the program. So I didn't want to risk it, and some time detached from my home life would be good for me.

The day started off with a choice between yoga or a walk. It was Fort Lauderdale, Florida, in the middle of the summer. It was hot as hell, and you couldn't pay me to go on a walk, so I chose yoga. I had only done it a couple of times prior to this, so I had no idea what I was doing, but Melissa, the yoga instructor, and one of the counselors led the yoga class very well. I loved it and promised myself I would go every morning. There was a list of people split into two groups on the door to the big room where yoga was. I was in the first group with Taylor and Riley. Henry was the leader of our group, but I didn't like him. I thought he was very arrogant, so I was instantly very close-minded to the first group. I am not sure what changed throughout the first days, but I ended up loving his group, and he grew on me really quickly.

In the middle of the day, Ashley, Emily, Lucas, and Connor came over to residential. We were so excited to see them before we went to our assigned therapy group. I had Dominica as the leader/therapist, and she seemed cool. In this group, there was Ashely, Riley, Lucas, Taylor, and me. There was also a guy from the Dominican Republic who was very flamboyant and cute, but I never really got to know him. The group was mainly led by the people who had already been there for a little while, but Taylor always had something to say, too.

Taylor was sober for four months but came back into treatment to work on her anger; and boy did she need to. She was married to a woman as well, and I was envious of their relationship. They talked on the phone, video-chatted, and texted all day. Brooke was still so resentful about all that had happened that she wasn't talking to me much, and when we did talk, we just fought. But one thing I learned from the last time at rehab was not to let outside relationships, even my marriage, get in the way of my recovery.

All we did was smoke. In the morning, between groups, and after groups until we had to go to our rooms at 11:00. We got to know everyone really well, and our group continued to grow closer. Jack, Evelyn, and Emma came over. I didn't really get to know them when I was in detox. Heather was a skinny, pretty little hippie. She did a different variety of drugs and was couch-surfing before she checked herself in. Evelyn was a sweetheart from Colorado. She was a one-liter vodka bottle at a time drinker. She had shakes for the first week of detox and, just like Sydney, showed up plastered.

I knew how important taking notes and journaling was to my recovery, so I immediately started writing when I got to inpatient. Even though I went through hell over the past four months and was in treatment for ten days already, my mind was still playing with the idea that I could drink. I knew better, so I chose to do what I did the first time. I prayed.

After a couple of nights, I got comfortable going to sleep with Taylor in the room. I brought headphones and would listen to music while I slept. I showered every day and continued to take care of myself. One morning, I woke up at 6:00 and couldn't sleep, so I walked downstairs. It was still dark out, but there were a couple of people out there. I had my cigarettes and vape and sat at a table with a guy named Carson.

He was in the Marines, had been there for forty days, and was planning to stay for seventy-five. Then there was Dan. Dan was a mess. He was around 70, and everything out of his mouth was a joke. He had been in treatment for ninety-two days. I sat and talked with them about myself and listened to them talk. Slowly but surely, people started coming downstairs, and then I took my medicine and went upstairs to change and get ready for yoga.

At this point in my recovery, I was so lost within myself. I was happy but had no idea who Lauren was anymore. I didn't like myself for what I had done and who I had turned into. I was a shell of my previous self. I told one of the counselors that I wanted to be the old Lauren again, and she looked at me and said, "Well, the old Lauren brought you here. How about you become a brand-new Lauren." That seed was planted so deep into my brain that it became my goal for this treatment.

Groups were great. They were very constructive, and I learned a lot from them. Several different people led the groups, but oddly enough, my favorite was definitely Henry.

I always got put in groups with Taylor, which I hated because she was so angry and so confrontational. I despised confrontation, even if I was just watching it. Most of the time she talked, I would cringe.

We met once a week with our assigned therapist, and mine was Dominica. We had an hour together, and I spent the entire hour talking about my relationship. I knew Brooke and I needed to work on our communication, or else both of us would go back out and destroy ourselves and/or each other. She agreed to have a session with both of us the next week to work on our communication. She called Brooke to get to know her. I was so surprised that Brooke said so many kind things about me after all that I had done. She told her how we were best friends for years, then fell in love. She said we started strong, but then taking care of her mom and the drugs and alcohol ended up causing us to lose what brought us together in the first place. Our friendship. Dominica asked her if she was willing to work together in therapy, and she said, "Absolutely." I was tearing up at this point. I saw so much hope for us, even after all the damage I had caused.

Finally, Sydney came to the residential compound. She was one of my favorites. She was hilarious and was a frequent rehabber. She started doing hard drugs at 30, and she was now 34. She had the kindest, oldest soul but was so lost in her addiction.

I was fully engaged with every group. I talked about my bottom and hitting Brooke, and the responses I got from my peers and staff were incredible. The counselor told me that I was not a mistake, I just made some mistakes. As bad as that bottom was, it needed to happen. It was my moment of clarity that opened my eyes to how far I had fallen. We also discovered that my first cross-addiction once I cut out my drug of choice is people. Mostly my partner. It was that way with Joey, and then grew to be the same with Brooke. I desperately needed to stop this pattern if I was ever going to find myself and who Lauren is.

I started feeling really insecure. I didn't like who I was, so I automatically assumed everyone else felt the same way. On the outside, I stayed happy and was sure to always ask everyone how they were doing. I wasn't even doing it just to be nice. By this point, I genuinely cared about everyone who was there. I found joy in the little things, like Emily waiting for me before group and telling me that she was excited to be in my group, or Trevor and Ashley remembering how much I liked Welch's fruit snacks and always giving me some when I felt down, or the time when I was waiting on my vape so someone gave me one of theirs. They will probably never know how much those little things did for me.

At this point, Riley, Allison, and Donna were gone. At the "coin outs," we would all say good things about the person who was leaving, wish them whatever we chose to, tap the coin on the metal chair leg, and then pass it to the next person. At every wrap-up, I would say my time and be so proud of myself. I would make sure to say that I am grateful for "ALL Y'ALL." I loved it, and I loved everyone there. It honestly felt like we were growing together. We were all so broken when we walked in, and together, we were putting the pieces of our lives back together.

In Henry's group, he always mentioned finding our "deepest secret," which was the core reason why we were drinking. I had no idea what mine was. I always assumed it was just because of my relationship and the situations I put myself into. He mentioned that we cannot sit on our deepest secrets because they will take us back out and possibly kill us.

I loved Henry and his groups, but it drove me nuts that he never remembered my name. I shared my heart with everyone in his groups, and he didn't know my name. It made me realize how much I really wanted this. My best friend from back in Oklahoma, Sawyer, told me that she was mentally preparing for the phone call from someone letting her know that I was dead. She said it probably wouldn't have been intentional, but she was preparing for it. She told me that in the midst of my drinking and drugging, but at that time, I couldn't have cared less. Now, it shook me to my core. It hit me that if I didn't stop, at the rate I was going, I would have died. I never understood how people relied so much on God and the program to survive. But I finally understood it. This was life or death for me. If I didn't get it this time, I wouldn't come back.

  Everyone but Avery came over at this point. We still weren't sure why she wasn't transferred over, but they sent her home. I was super bummed because she was so fun and, we bonded so well. I grew very close to Trevor. We would smoke and talk for hours. Even when I drank, I didn't smoke as many cigarettes as I did in rehab the first time. It was literally our only way to hang out because we weren't allowed in each other's rooms.

I saw the doctor, and this time, it was over Zoom. He had 34 years of sobriety and commended me on my knowledge of my bipolar and my previous years of sobriety.

Which felt nice because, at this point, I had forgotten about my accomplishments and just focused on what I did wrong. Just like the previous doctor, he wanted to keep me on the medication regimen I was on.

I became known for my loving, peppy, and caring personality. I was told how much I made people's day when I would tell them good morning first thing in the morning and with how much I questioned them about how they were feeling. It felt good. I started to realize that this wasn't a front, it was who I was. I really was this nice and positive. Little by little, I was finding myself.

Every week, we had someone from a narcotics support group come in and speak. Not a lot of people went, but I made sure to make everyone that I could. The people who came in made me remember how close to Miami we were. Gold teeth, gold chains, and gelled hair.

The first guy came in and mentioned that we all have our last drink or drug before checking into rehab and told us he did his last hit of heroin in the parking lot of rehab and actually died in the parking lot. It immediately took me back to myself. He mentioned living life on life's terms. He lost his brother early in recovery, but before that, he had been going religiously to meetings and had a home group. Well, when his brother died, he decided that he wanted to use and left his house to go to his drug dealer's house. He said that he didn't remember driving. He was just on autopilot, and next thing he knew, he was parked in front of his home group. He stressed making that routine because our body does go on autopilot, and when the time comes that we are desperate, we already know where to go.

Henry had a group about trust and forgiveness. I was so excited that he finally remembered my name.

About damn time!

I realized that no one trusted me to stay sober anymore, and neither did I yet. I said I would quit so many times and lied so much that I lost everyone's trust. Henry said that trust takes time and to be patient with the process. If you go 15 miles into the forest, you have to go 15 miles back out. Dammit, that really put it into perspective that I had a long way to go. I was fortunate that I was able to talk to my friends from back home. I made my amends and told them where I was and how well I was doing, and slowly but surely, I was gaining my life back.

Chapter 34

We had a group on a Saturday with a counselor that I had never seen before. Her name was Betty, and she was talking about what our childhoods were like. I wasn't in the mood to share, so I didn't, but everyone else did. There were some pretty terrible stories, but I wanted to keep mine to myself. She looked at me and asked how I was doing, and I said I was okay. She looked at me deeper and asked again, "How are you doing? How was your childhood?" I decided then and there that if I was going to heal, I needed to talk from my heart and be completely transparent.

I told her and everyone that I had been bullied my entire childhood. Trevor interrupted and asked how someone could be mean to me. I held back tears and told them how I never fit in. I wasn't a cute kid, and everyone let me know that. I got laughed at a lot and never felt like I fit in or mattered to anyone. I told them the story of when I was seven and my Aunt Jean died. I was very close to her and didn't understand what death was, so I wrote her a letter telling her how much I loved her and missed her, then signed it with my full name, spun around, and threw it into the air. In after-school care that day, kids in my class found it and made fun of me and told everyone how much of a loser I was, then shredded the letter and threw it on the ground. I had never told anyone that story, but I felt some relief. Then, I dug deeper. I told them about the time when I tried to stick up for myself in the 7th grade to this guy who was making fun of me. He just looked at me and spit in my face, and everyone laughed. Nobody stuck up for me. They all laughed and walked away, and I was left wiping his spit off my face. I was crying at this point. I mentioned how I struggled with feeling like I fit in my whole life.

 Luckily, I got pretty, grew thicker skin, and learned to make fun of myself as a defense mechanism, or else I probably would have killed myself years ago. Everyone was shocked. They were silent and then got angry.

They told me how amazing of a person I was, what they all liked about me, and how much I never deserved that. I had never talked about that to anyone, ever. Dan handed over one of the notebooks we were given that had the word love engraved into it and wrote "self" above it in pen and told me to make sure I wrote down how great of a person I was until I believed it for myself. I wiped my tears and was eager for the group to be over.

I was in a stupor after that group. We all sat outside and smoked, and I just thought that group had my brain turning. I was present physically at the table, but mentally, I was on another planet. It hit me like a ton of bricks. Trent and Hunter were my sacred secret.

My childhood and the first two sexual encounters I had were what lingered in that deep hole I had in my soul. I felt a sense of relief, but at the same time, I felt broken because it brought up all those feelings, and I didn't want to share them with anyone. So, I just moved my focus to everyone else and their recovery. Luckily, I had therapy on Monday.

Monday came around, and I was eager to tell Henry that I found my deepest secret. He congratulated me and told me that my recovery would change drastically if I worked on that. After that, I was eager to get to my therapy appointment. She started off the session picking up where we left off from our last session, but I stopped her and told her I learned my deepest secret and wanted to work on that. I started to tell her about my childhood, and I couldn't even hold back the tears. By the time I got to Hunter, I was crying. I told her everything that happened with him and then with Trent. I was fidgeting in my seat, and she told me, "I honestly think you were sexually assaulted twice." We talked about it for a while, and she gave me an assignment. She told me to write down each emotion that those occurrences made me feel and how I acted because of those embedded emotions. I told her I would work on that and left the session feeling like I had an open wound.

I woke up the next day and just felt so sad and angry. I was mad that no one but Trevor ever asked if I was okay or how I was doing. I felt so unimportant and like nobody cared about me. I skipped yoga and went to Henry's optional group first. I just sat there. I didn't say a word. I didn't even make eye contact with Henry. The group couldn't be over fast enough. I wanted to isolate myself, but I couldn't because we were locked out of the room because of the group. I sat with Dan, Carson, and Jack because I knew that they wouldn't talk to me. I was just sitting there thinking when Henry came up to me and pulled me aside to ask me if I was okay. I didn't want to say no, I wanted to be okay and not be vulnerable. But I knew I needed to grow, so I told him no. I told him how I felt like no one cared about me or asked me how I was doing. I told him how I felt unimportant my whole life and struggled with that. I confided in him that I felt alone and that I cared so much about everyone else, but no one felt the same way about me. He just smiled and said, "You're going to share at the next group because you're in my group." I chain-smoked my cigarettes after that and was so uncomfortable thinking about opening up again to everyone.

I sat in the same seat I sat in before and watched as Henry adjusted his hat and smiled at me. He opened the group by introducing the subject of the group that day. High expectations. I felt like it was an attack.

What the hell?

He told me to share with everyone what I had told him outside, and I did just that. I struggled to get the words out because I was so uncomfortable. Trevor and Taylor almost seemed offended because they said they were constantly asking me how I was doing, and they did care. I felt so stupid. They were right, they did say that all the time.

Why did I feel this way?

Then, everyone shared about how they felt. Nothing was intentionally directed at me, but of course, I took all of their comments as attacks. Emily told the group that she does things for people without the intention of getting anything back but just to be nice, which I took as a dig. I spiraled deeper into depression. I wanted the group to be over. I mentally checked out and immediately left the room after it was over and resumed my spot at the table with Jack and Carson. I was so upset. Trevor and Taylor came over to me, and they pried it out of me. I told them about the rape and what happened with Hunter, and I really did feel better after telling them. Then it hit me head-on. Everyone does care. When they do ask, I say I am good, brush it off, and move the focus to them. All I needed to do was say that I wasn't okay. I was so used to people not caring how I truly felt after talking about my childhood that I resorted to shutting down like I used to. All I had to do was say that I needed help. I rushed to Henry and told him what I discovered, and he just smiled and said he thought I'd be one of the ones to make it. That felt good to hear, and it had me on a high for a while until I remembered that I was told that at my first rehab, and then, months later, I went down in flames. That happiness was short-lived, but I did feel like I took a massive step forward in my recovery.

I started to get really close to Lucas. He was so funny but very sad. His drinking caused him to lose his kids, and he was homeless. His last drink, he blacked out and drove 60 miles across Florida. It scared him so much that he wanted to get help. Our conversations started off slow, but we got to know each other a lot better over time. At wrap-up every day, he would look at me to remind him how much sober time he had. We became good buddies.

I started having nightmares, and one night, I dreamed I was being attacked by fire ants. I kept waking up feeling like I had ants all over me. I eventually said, "fuck it," and just grabbed my pack of cigarettes and vape and went downstairs. Sydney and Dan were the only other ones awake. Sydney was blaring music at 4 am. She constantly played the song "Spirits" by the Strumbellas. She would play it over and over and over to where we all would have it stuck in our heads all day. Dan offered me some coffee and said he had a surprise for me. I followed him upstairs to get some coffee, and he pulled out a massive strawberry and said he saved it for me. It was such a small gesture but meant so much. I took the coffee downstairs and only drank about half before I was drenched in sweat. My God, what was in this coffee? I felt like I took a bunch of Adderall. I didn't finish the coffee, but I sat and talked with Dan. He started telling me his horror stories of his drunken temper fits. He told me about all the physical damage he caused other people and the idea that he was this gentle, silly drunk was completely smashed. He was a monster when he drank. Sydney and I talked and listened to music for a couple hours, and then people started to trickle down the stairs.

 I eventually went upstairs and got ready for the day. Linda held the group that day, and she was my least favorite. She always had really controversial groups that just ended up with us all disagreeing with her. This one wasn't that bad, though. We were supposed to share a sticky situation that we had or could have gotten ourselves into. I wrote down, "When I went to a friend's Bachelorette party in Austin in my first year of sobriety." I struggled every day to stay sober. Dan was in that group. He was sitting right next to me, and Linda asked him to read. He started talking and said, "You just got out of rehab, you're driving home at one o'clock in the morning, you get a flat tire, and your phone dies. You are in the middle of nowhere, you go to your trunk to get your spare, and you find a ¼ of a bottle of whiskey. What do you do?" People came up with all different scenarios to stay sober. He just started laughing and said he just made the whole thing up. Linda was so pissed, but we all laughed. I loved being able to laugh after all I went through.

Dan was leaving the next day, so he got my Facebook name and number and immediately started taking screenshots of all my pictures and commenting on them. It was harmless, and I just planned on blocking him after I got out. He did a French exit, no coin-out. Sydney and I were the only ones up early after that until a couple of other people started waking up early, including my buddy, Lucas.

We had a group about faith and spirituality. I mentioned how I found my higher power and what He has done for me. Then I mentioned that I stopped talking to Him when I was drinking. The counselor said that He was there the whole time, waiting for me to reach out to him. Since I had been at rehab, I had become so spiritually centered, and everything seemed to fall into place. Brooke and I were back to where we were when we got married. It reminded me of how Joey was before I got into the program. Everything rolled off of my back. I was so happy to be back in the center.

Later that day, I was sitting outside with Sydney, and I got a video call from Dan. He was hammered. He spent 113 days in rehab, and in two days, he relapsed. It just goes to show you that you can prepare yourself for the outside world all you want, but once you're out there, you must want it badly enough, or you'll slip right back into it. I got in a couple debates about that with counselors and, of all people, Jack. The group was over triggers, which I didn't believe in, either. If you want to drink, you're going to.

The entire group was talking about relapse prevention, putting up post-its of numbers to call, going to new places, and changing little things about your day to break the cycle of your using pattern. I didn't agree with any of it. I played along so I wouldn't seem like an arrogant person, but I did all that. I had numbers to call. I left my chips in my center dish. I knew exactly what to do in that situation. I had utilized my toolbox numerous times, and it can save your life and sobriety, but it all comes down to whether or not you want it badly enough. Each time I relapsed, I avoided looking down at the chips, I didn't pick up the phone, and I didn't go to meetings. A mind made up is a mind made up, and every time, nothing could stop me. I suggested in the group that I could change my Febreze in my car to another scent, so I didn't seem like a jerk. But I knew now that I didn't just want to be sober, I wanted to live sober, and I had to, or else I wasn't going to make it.

Chapter 35

We had a group in the gym one day with Henry, and he wanted us to write a letter to our drug of choice in five sentences. I loved doing stuff like this. He asked me to share mine, and I read off of my paper:

> *"You are an asshole. You caught me at my weakest and brought me down further than I thought possible. You taught me that there was a trap door at rock bottom. I will never be able to forget what you have turned me into and what you have done to my life. I will do anything in my power to make sure you will never control my life, ever again".*

And I meant every word of it.

He then put a cup on a chair and told us that alcohol is an object, and we are the ones who give it the power. Without us picking it up, it stays an object. It seemed so simple when he put it that way. We have control over what happens next. I hope to God I don't go back. It seems so easy to do when I am in rehab, but I know things are difficult when I get out. I just HAVE to stay in the center. Nothing has ever seemed so certain to me.

I had been working on my assignment, and my emotions were anger, guilt, shame, failure, and a new one that I realized, fear of abandonment. All of those emotions led to me being a people pleaser, thinking less of myself, not having a voice, and all the things that I wanted to change about myself. We discussed it in my last therapy session. She told me to make sure I find a trauma therapist and continue this process. She then cut my therapy session short, which I didn't appreciate, but I had a better understanding of why I am the way I am now because of what happened to me years ago. Later that day, I looked Trent up on Facebook. He was married with two kids. It just pissed me off that he had this little family while I was stuck picking up all the broken pieces from what he did to me. I talked to a counselor about it, and they told me that forgiving someone who doesn't apologize is something you do for yourself in order to heal. So, I decided to let that anger go. Hunter, too.

I had let their terrible actions affect my life for far too long. I got to the point where I liked myself. I even loved myself. I loved my life and had goals and felt that my life had purpose. After closing those heavy metal doors in my heart, I became that brand-new Lauren I wanted to be. This Lauren was kind, strong, determined, and spiritually fit.

I knew that if I didn't love myself, then there was no way I could love anyone else. I was prepared for the day when I would have no one to rely on but myself and God.

After that accomplishment, rehab just became fun for me. Groups were fun, and I still engaged and listened, but I was more eager to have our smoke breaks. By this time, I had my own money and ordered vapes. I had gone through six packs of cigarettes and three vapes before I got the new vapes. I was already getting a smoker's cough. I was upstairs eating dinner and then came down and heard whispers about a new grumpy lady who had just come over from detox, and she was already complaining about Sydney's music. We were all so tight that we didn't like the idea of someone negative coming in. We had made so much progress in our recovery.

Later that night, we were outside smoking, and I saw Lucas lying in the fake grass by himself. I sat next to him and asked him how he was doing, and he told me that he was sad. It was his son's birthday, and his son had blocked him. We talked for a while, and then he showed me pictures of his kids. We laid in the grass for hours, smoking and talking about his life before alcohol. Next thing I knew, it was 11pm, and we were told to go upstairs.

I woke up at 3:00 the next morning and could not go back to sleep, so I went outside. Sydney was not even up yet, so I sat at the table with a new tech named Cindy. Sometimes I get an overwhelming feeling that someone is against gay marriage, and I got that vibe from her, so we talked, and I told her a little bit about my life but made my "her" into a "him." We talked for about an hour until Sydney woke up. Then, Sydney and I listened to music and exchanged songs. Sydney always felt like she was failing by being 34 and not married or having kids. I told her that I was 33 and couldn't work because of my bipolar and was having to get put on disability. I sent her an article that I read a while back about very famous people in history who didn't achieve their careers or goals until they were our age or older, and the article even went on to say how many times they failed before then. It made both of us feel better.

Lucas had been begging me to go running with him at the gym at night, so I finally caved and ran a mile and a half. I almost died, but it was fun. We played "Eye of the Tiger" and ran our hearts out, and then I laid on the cool floor for the remaining 30 minutes while Lucas and Brandon finished their workout.

I got a runner's high for sure and felt even better about myself. We went back to the compound, and I showered and took my meds, then went to lay down.

Gwen, the new older lady, wasn't as bad as we all thought she would be. She just would cough all over the place and wouldn't wear a mask or go on bed rest. We spent all day with her in groups and did a homeless food drive with her, and it turned out she had COVID, so we went on lockdown. We all had to take COVID tests that day. We all passed, but we had to do all our groups on Zoom and couldn't linger outside smoking. Luckily I could get away with vaping inside our room. By this point, I would fall asleep with it in my hands.

Zoom groups were terrible. The connection was so sketchy, and I couldn't pay attention or write notes like I had been. By this point, I had almost the entire notebook filled with my entries, notes from groups, quotes, and advice I got from the videos that they made us watch. I just put the phone camera off, laid in bed, and smoked. I felt bad because I knew it wasn't the staff's fault, but we found out that COVID was rampant at detox, and they didn't test her before she came over. We were all pissed.

We would come outside to smoke and had to sit six feet apart, but that didn't last long. We had all been sharing drinks and vapes for so long that we figured if one of us had it, then we all did. After dinner that night, Lucas was lying in the grass again. I laid next to him, and we looked up at the stars. He was playing the most depressing stuff, so I told him I was taking control of the music and started playing oldies. He was Brooke's age, so I started with the main song from the movie Grease. He smiled, and then we started playing songs all night and talking. We had a great time. I started talking about my life, and we stayed up until 11:00 when the tech made us go upstairs.

I was woken up the next morning by Cindy knocking on the door. They do checks every hour, so I didn't think anything of it, but she told me to come to the door. She had a gold bracelet in her hands that had love written on it. She told me, "I know we aren't supposed to pick favorites, but I wanted you to have this and remember how loved you are by so many." She told me that I had a brighter presence about me and that I needed to keep that when I left rehab. I thanked her and put it on. What a kind gesture.

We finally got off quarantine because we all passed the COVID testing, but it was a sad day. We had six coin-outs, and Taylor and Trevor were two of them. The whole group spent every minute together. Trevor was staying the weekend because he was having a lady friend come to visit. I was complaining that I had to stay until 10 the day that I was leaving. I was being discharged the day he was leaving. He told me we should hang out, go to the beach and a meeting, then he could take me to the airport. I was excited about that idea. It helped me feel better about him leaving and made it not as hard to abruptly say goodbye.

Coin-out was rough. We all said what we needed to say about each person and tapped each coin on our chair. The "ALL Y'ALL"s and chants were so loud and powerful. Brandon was sick (turned out to be COVID), so Trevor did the final prayer and chants. When we put our foot in, I teared up. This was it, the last time we would all be together. I swallowed in between words and felt the huge lump in my throat. We got done and prepared ourselves for our last night together. We had a cookout, and I was so bummed that everyone was leaving. I was going to skip the gym, but then Lucas came out with his headphones and his sweatbands on. His smile faded when he saw that I wasn't ready. So, I went, and I ran two miles. One more and I was going to be ready to start races again.

I woke up at 3:00am to see our first friend leave. Then another left at 4:00am, and then Taylor left at 9:00am. We joked about what I was going to eat after she left, but she surprised me and left me dinner in the fridge. Then came Trevor. Even though I was seeing him tomorrow, it was still sad. There were 8 of us left after all of them were discharged. My coin-out was that afternoon. One of the other guys who came the day before tested positive for COVID, so we had a group about how to distance ourselves and that they were going to continue the group.

It was my turn to coin out. Everyone had the nicest things to say about me, my growth, my genuine heart, my sense of humor, and how grateful they all were that they met me. Even old Al, who never said anything about anyone, had nothing but nice things to say about me. The prayer was quiet, the chanting was weak, but It was dawning on me. I was leaving tomorrow. I told Lucas that I didn't want to run that night. I just wanted to listen to music with him and Sydney. We laid in the grass like we did so many nights before. This time, Sydney, Emma, and Evelyn joined us. We all stayed up until 1:00am, talking and listening to music. It was the best night of my whole stay. No one talked about me leaving, we just pretended like it was any other night.

Sydney told me that she and Lucas were going to wake up early to spend more time with me because Trevor was picking me up at 11:00. That next morning was the first time in weeks that I slept in. I woke up at 7:50am to the tech yelling at me to get my ass out of bed. I walked downstairs, and I was so sad that I had overslept. Groups breezed by, and then the time came. I had to say my goodbyes. I hugged everyone. I gave Sydney and Lucas an extra squeeze when I hugged them bye.

Trevor had given me $50 to take an Uber to and from his rental and to the airport, so my Uber picked me up and took me to Trevor. We got there, and it was a small efficiency apartment. We sat and watched a movie and then decided to go to the beach. He rented a Slingshot car, which is a small car that has three wheels, no roof, and half of a windshield. We were about twenty minutes from his place when it started pouring. There was traffic and no roof. Our cigarettes got wet, and he was so embarrassed because people were honking and laughing, but I told him that if it was me, I would be laughing my ass off, too. After another grueling ten minutes, we got out of the rain and to the beach. We forgot towels, but luckily, I had a black shirt that a construction worker gave me through his window when we were stuck in the rain. Trevor jumped into the seaweed-filled water while I just sat in the sand and reflected on the last years of my life. I honestly felt like a whole new version of myself. I was so positive and hopeful of my future, as well as my future with Brooke. Trevor came up and sat in the sand with me for about thirty minutes, then we noticed more rain clouds, so we bolted and headed to a meeting.

We walked into the meeting he chose in Pompano Beach. We walked to the front, and my jaw dropped. This was where I got my thirty-day chip after my first rehab. I didn't recognize it at first because we walked in through the back when I went with the guys from the last rehab. I enjoyed every minute of that meeting. There was so much power in every share, and I stood up to get my thirty-day coin because that day was my thirtieth day sober. Trevor and I went out to the car and sent a picture of us and me holding my coin to Henry. It was highly suggested that we get to a meeting within 24 hours of leaving rehab. I sent the picture with a text telling Henry how much I enjoyed the program and how much he personally helped me grow and find myself again. He texted me back and told me that he would surely miss me, that I was special to him, and that he was here for me if I ever needed him. We drove back to the house and smoked a couple more cigarettes before I got my bags ready and called the Uber. It was time. I had to say goodbye to Trevor. This one was tough, but I knew we would stay in touch. He helped me put my bags in the car and shut my door.

I had gained a new self, knowledge, and the drive to succeed and take control of my sobriety. I got that same lump in my throat that I had before as we drove out of the parking lot.

When I got to the airport, I felt so confident in myself for the first time in a long time. I waited for what felt like forever for my flight to leave. I always wanted an aisle seat. I still somewhat had a fear of not being able to get easy access to a bathroom. I hated the thought of having to wake up someone to go to the bathroom.

My flight went by quickly, and I was so very excited to make it home.

Chapter 36

I had put my all into this rehab and myself, and I was eager to show my family how I was doing. I planned on going to meetings. I called my sponsor, Amy, whom I kept up with throughout rehab. I went to my meeting across town, and it was nice seeing the familiar pictures on the wall. Amy was not there, but I shared my experience. I was ready to start over.

Despite my progress, Brooke and I were not doing well when I got home. I had created so much resentment from her with all that I had done, so we were arguing a lot. One day, I decided to go to my mom's to give her some time. I texted Amy about what happened, and her response was that she could not work with me anymore "because I put myself in a dangerous situation within 72 hours of being home." And "to let her know when I really want this program."

What the fuck?!

In hindsight, I realized what she meant and that it came from love, but at the time, I was pissed, so I blocked her. Now I was starting over, and I didn't have a sponsor. I called my friend Faith, from where we used to live. She told me that she would temporarily sponsor me until I found someone else who could. Since I was still staying with my mom, I decided to meet her at a meeting. I liked being there. It was where my base program was located.

I walked into the room and saw Katie; someone I worked with in the past. She had been a constant in my recovery. She had amazing sobriety and always pushed me to come to meetings and reached out when I would go MIA. She always called me "Sunshine," even when I was at my worst. She became a really good friend over the years, which I was very happy about. I also kept up with my friend Peyton. She was from New

York, and I met her after my first relapse. She was bold, with bright red hair that matched her fiery personality. I felt at home again.

After some time, I moved back to Tampa, but I was still going to meetings three times a week where my mom lived. Working with Faith was fun and great. She worked a really good program, and I just adored who she was.

She was blunt and direct but had a heart of gold. She always told me how she felt and how much she loved me. She was quick to say when I was doing well and when I was straying away. She never judged me and helped me move beyond my past to become a better person and a better wife.

One addiction that I could not conquer was cutting myself. I no longer cut my arms because I did not want anybody to know about it, so I cut my upper thighs instead. By this point, I was ashamed of it. The only people who knew that I did it were my close friends and Brooke. They were not supportive by any means, but never got upset with me or made me feel less than. In a way, I replaced the urge to drink with my cutting. I had about twenty cuts on my leg at a time. Brooke had accidentally broken in a scale, and I took the pieces of glass and hid them in a vase in the spare bedroom, which I was still residing in. Brooke would always try to hide things that I could cut with, but she never knew I hid them.

I went to the meetings by my mom's house every Tuesday and Friday. Fridays became a day with Faith and her family. She took care of her mother, and she was an amazing woman who reminded me of my grandma. She was always happy and a very caring person. We would sit in her room and talk for hours. She always made me feel loved, even when I didn't love myself or my life at the current moment.

Brooke and I were still not doing well. She was not happy with who I became. I had been codependent our entire relationship up until I went to rehab. She took me being more independent as me not loving her as much, but by this point, I loved her more than ever. I knew I needed to do some work to save my marriage and myself. I was determined and ready to put the hard work into my sobriety.

About three months into my new sobriety, I started the struggle with not sleeping. For three days, I stayed up all night writing instead of sleeping. Well, I knew better. I remembered what the doctor said years ago. One all-nighter alone could cause a manic episode. But I was so eager to write that I didn't sleep. So, during the day, I fed my long-lasting addiction, caffeine. I would have numerous energy drinks to last throughout the day. This can also trigger a manic episode. Along with not sleeping for days, I should've known that I was doomed for disaster.

I had gotten pretty close to Katie and Peyton as they helped me grow in sobriety. Both had more than ten years sober. Sometimes I felt undeserving of their friendship. I was three months in, and they loved me more than I loved myself. Hazel was also special to me. No matter how many times I called her drunk, she was always there, no matter what. There was a time when she would get hard on me but loved me despite my addiction. She had been a friend since high school. Sawyer and I struggled together to get sober, but we also helped each other out. She eventually got sober around the time that I did. She was someone that I could truly be my weird self with. Audrey was a friend who moved to Gainesville years ago. I drunk-called her a couple of times during my relapse, which led to a wonderful reunion of friendship once I got sober. She always knew how to make any situation light and funny. Between all of my friends, I had the best support system that I could ever ask for. Little did I know how much I would need it.

I was still struggling with sleep and soon became manic, as expected. I could not sit still. I was always in my car, which was where I got my alone time and privacy. Just like with my mania while I was dating Joey, I became impulsive and nasty. I would cut myself any time I had any stress or when Brooke and I would argue. I felt guilty for all I put her through. She was happy I was sober but still resentful for all that I said when I was drunk and all of my lying. I understood that. I promised her and myself that I would put in all the work and that I would become a better version of myself. As much as I didn't sleep and had all the signs of mania, I still wasn't aware that I was manic.

I started suffering from blackouts. There was one time that I called Jessie and talked to her for hours. I could remember glimpses of our conversation but didn't remember the majority of it. The same thing happened with some other people in my support group. I didn't catch onto this until after the fact. I was staying with my mom that night. I woke up after getting a few hours of sleep, and I knew that I needed help. I called Brooke the next morning, and she was very supportive of my choice to go back to the psychiatric hospital. I was so discouraged that I had to go back, but it was what I needed.

Chapter 37

Brooke offered to take me to the hospital, but I was already at my mom's, and I couldn't wait. I got to the hospital around 10:00 in the morning. My mom and I stopped for cigarettes on the way, and I wore the long pants I had been wearing for days. Luckily, I was wearing a jacket without strings. Brooke promised to bring me more clothes. At this point in our relationship, she knew what to bring me. For the first time in what felt like weeks, I fell asleep in the waiting room. I woke up to someone coughing up phlegm. I looked at the clock, and it had only been two hours. I looked to my left and saw a guy with a black hat, and the girl next to me started talking to him about using Fentanyl. It got really old really quickly. I was sober and could not relate to using that. They just kept talking about it, and at this point, I was wide awake. No matter how much I tried to sleep, I couldn't. I waited six more hours just to talk to the new admission nurse.

It was a guy, which I was not used to, but he was funny and made the process light. I told him about the blackouts and nights without sleep. I had become slightly suicidal at this point, but I knew that I was heading the way to complete suicidal ideations. I was honestly worried I would eventually act on it. Deep down, I didn't want to die. I shared this with him, and he commended me for doing the right thing. It was time for the dreaded skin test. Since it was a male, he brought in a female to assist in the test. You would think I would know to wear underwear by this point, but I didn't. So he had me cover myself as I showed him all the cuts on my thighs. At this point, I had them on both sides of my legs. After the skin test, he told me I would be admitted and put on suicidal precautions. I waited another two hours in the waiting room, and then he told me that I'd be admitted to unit 33. I was so happy to hear that.

We walked up to unit 33, where I immediately saw Jennifer, one of my favorite technicians.

She was so excited to see me, which made me feel even better. She called me "skinny mini" because I had lost forty-five pounds since the last time I saw her. All of the nurses said hello. What I loved about unit 33 was how much I felt at home in such an uncomfortable time. They put me in room 602. It was right next to the nurse's station. I was very pleased to see that I didn't have a roommate yet, but the bed was by the door, and I was not happy about that because I always liked looking out the window. I accepted their choice and went to lie down, though, because I was just happy to be in a safe place.

It was around 9pm by the time I got upstairs to the unit. I turned off the lights, and not even ten minutes later, two nurses came in panicking and made me get up. I didn't even realize that I didn't get the metal detector test before I was admitted. They did a pat down and checked under the mattress. There were tears under the bed, so they made me move to the bed by the window. They took the mattress out of the room and told me that I would not have a roommate until they got a new bed. My lucky day! This had never happened here. I crawled into the bed by the window, and I did my best to sleep.

Just as expected, I only got three hours of sleep. I got up to look at the clock on the wall several times that night. Each time I would check, I had to walk into the main room to see the clock, only to see that just a couple of hours had passed. I did this until 7am when I got up to do my vitals. I had gotten so used to this process. I had done it consistently for seven years. My blood pressure was very low, which concerned them. I didn't really know what that meant, so I just got up and got in line to go to breakfast. I hated the first meal of a hospital stay. When we got downstairs, I sat at a table completely across the room. Luckily, no one sat next to me.

We went out for a smoke break, and this time, I brought Kool Menthol 100s, the cigarettes that I smoked when I was 17. It was bold and oddly familiar. I walked to my usual spot on the stoop, but someone was already sitting there.

Damnit.

I asked him if I could sit next to him, and he said, "Of course." I sat down, and he started talking. His name was Blake, and the conversation was actually very interesting. He had traveled all over the world. He came in for depression and a place to stay. He was homeless. Time passed quickly, and we went upstairs.

Again, what goes up must come down. I became severely depressed. I would lay in bed and stare at the busy wasp nest outside my window. My view was of the other building, so I didn't really have much else to look at. I felt empty. Like I had a dark cloud over me.

Now, I was actually suicidal. I was so tired of being bipolar. I feared this would be my entire life. Now that I wasn't manic, I fell asleep. The staff knew that I hadn't had a good night's sleep in over a week, so they let me sleep all day.

I woke up to them telling me that the doctor wanted to see me. I walked in and saw Dr. Powell. I was thrilled. He had been my doctor every time I had been there. He told me that he saw my name downstairs on the patient list, and he asked them to be my doctor. Then he started researching the symptoms that I'd been having. He gave me the option of Depakote or Lithium. I honestly didn't want either of them. I told him that the Depakote didn't work on me, so we chose Lithium. He told me that Lithium would help control my mania and also help with the suicidal thoughts. I had so many side effects from Lithium before, so I wasn't too happy, but honestly, I didn't have a choice. He mentioned that he would only put me on a small dose so I would not have a lot of side effects. Only time would tell, I guess.

I came out of the office and sat next to Blake, and just as before, the conversation was great. I looked over at the long, wooden table on the other side of the main room and saw Nathan. He had been a constant in my hospital stays. He had severe depression and beat my record number of hospital stays. He had been to the hospital thirty times in ten years, which made me feel "normal." I moved over to talk to him, and he was drawing Micheal Jordan, which was what he always drew. You'd think he would draw something else, but he didn't. I told him how nice it was to see him. He mentioned that he was leaving the next day, and that really bummed me out, but I was happy that he felt better.

It was lunchtime, and I sat next to Nathan. He knew I was married to a woman and told me that I was too pretty to be a lesbian.

Ugh.

He had made it through three other hospital stays without saying anything about it. Guys were always saying stupid shit about me being married to a woman. Overall, it ended up being a nice lunch. We went out to smoke, and I sat with Blake again. After our thirty-minute break, we had to go back inside.

I crawled back into bed and resumed staring out the window. I reflected back on the past seven years. I felt like a broken person. I didn't see any hope to get better, but to my surprise, I was able to fall asleep again. Even better, I stayed asleep until the next morning.

I woke up to Nathan being gone. He didn't say bye to anyone, just left. We stood in line, and I had a new guy all over me. His name was Justin. He even looked like a creep. He had a bald head and wore a green shirt. He was

Cuban and told me that I was too pretty to be here. He was a very close talker, which weirded me out. He kept talking about how pretty I was, then told me that he wanted to get my number. I didn't know how to respond, so I said sure. I knew that I wasn't going to give it, but I said yes anyway. I quickly started talking to Blake to get the hell away from him.

We had four people in wheelchairs. There was Maryanne, who was this itty-bitty older woman, and Herbert, who had one tooth and was quite the talker. I didn't talk to the other two during my entire hospital stay, though. I had gotten so tired of coming here that I didn't take the time to get to know everyone.

Before breakfast, I made sure to get in line after Justin so he wouldn't sit next to me. I sat alone this time. I was happy, but I didn't have much of an appetite despite being on Lithium. We were called to get our cigarettes one by one. I got my two cigarettes and went outside.

Justin was far behind me, but when we walked outside, I noticed that Blake was not on the stoop. I walked over to him and quietly asked him to please sit with me. He immediately caught on to why I was asking that of him, and I am so glad that he did because, just as I expected, Justin came up and started talking. Blake gave him the cold shoulder, and so did I, but even with every hint that we didn't want him to sit next to us, he still did. All he talked about was how much money he had and how nice of a life he had. It felt like we were outside for an hour, just listening to him talk. We were called up to the front to come inside, so we rushed away from Justin and went inside.

The first thing that happened when I got inside was Justin asking me for my number again. He also asked if I was married. I told him yes and that I was married to a woman. Again, just like most men in the hospital, he got disgustingly excited. He mentioned that he would come and play cards with my mom and wife after this hospital stay.

Why in the hell would he think that I would want him to come spend time with my family?

It quickly reminded me of where I was. I eventually told one of the nurses about it, and she pulled him aside and talked to him. After that conversation, he left me alone.

Thank God!

A couple of days passed, and the medicine started to balance me out. I was sleeping and wasn't so manic. I had brought a book and was actually able to read. I had been starting to read again at home and was thrilled that I was stable enough to read again. I spent hours in my room reading. It was so nice because I still didn't have a roommate. Taking showers was what I did to relax and "reset" when I was in the hospital. I didn't have to worry about putting away my stuff, and I had the whole room to organize all the clothes that Brooke brought up to me. I had plenty of clothes to change into. I was able to find shampoo and conditioner without alcohol in it. I no longer had to use the 3-in-1 stuff that made my long hair tangled. I was surprisingly very comfortable during this stay.

Dr. Powell was great. He knew me so well, and he was able to notice that I was doing better, so he told me that I would only be staying for a couple more days. My entire support system that I had built called me and supported me throughout my stay. Over the years, hospital stays were always a little difficult for me. I would think of Jade and Alyssa. They were always there to pick apart my messy brain, calm my nerves, and make me feel somewhat normal. I didn't even realize until this stay that I already had that. Katie called every day. Never missed a day, sometimes even called a couple times a day. It dawned on me then that I lost Jade and Alyssa only to have someone more loving and selfless in their place. Closing that door in my mind and heart made me feel like I could finally let go of the past. Brooke was checking on me every day, also. We were slowly rebuilding our bond again. I was seeing the light at the end of the tunnel and this part of my life, finally.

That night, after spending several hours reading, I fell asleep. Not long after, I woke up hearing someone throw up.

What the fuck?

I didn't know if it was a male or female doing it, but regardless, it was gut-wrenching and absolutely terrible. It lasted for hours. I wished to God that I could go back to sleep, but I was up, and I knew that wasn't going to happen. I turned on my light, which I could still do because I had the room to myself. It ended up being a long and terrible night. I was nauseated and just focused on reading. I was almost done with the book.

I woke up the next morning, eager to find out who the hell kept me up all night. It was a transgender man, and he was mid-transition. He had pink hair and a peach-fuzz mustache. He chose the name Carl, which I found odd. Out of all the male names to choose, he chose Carl? But that's none of my business. I had an unnecessary resentment towards him for throwing up all night and keeping me up.

We went to breakfast, and I sat with Blake. At this point, I really enjoyed his company. We always sat together for meals and sat on the stoop together. I was always hesitant to share my sexual preference with whom I shared my time with on the stoop because I was afraid that they would be against it. It would crush me to have someone be vocal about not agreeing with my marriage. I told him that day that I was married to Brooke. He was super supportive and told me that his brother was gay. He was the first guy out of all my hospital stays to not say something ridiculous when I told him. I made a comment about still having a room by myself, and he told me that I was such a frequent flier here that I earned the Presidential Suite. We both laughed, then it was time to go inside.

When we got inside, I was so happy to see Chase, the tech. He told me that he was thrilled to see me. He said he didn't want to come to work because he had just gotten back from vacation, but he saw my name on the list and suddenly wanted to come to work. I loved Chase. We always talked about running, and he was always so kind to me.

It was my last day there, and I had finished my book. That was the ticket. Since I was able to finish a whole book, we knew then that I was stable. When my moods are swinging, I cannot read to save my life. Now, I finished an entire book. I came out to the main room, bragging about finally finishing my book, and everyone gave me shit about never leaving my room. I pushed Herbert to the nurse's station, and I guess he overheard that I was married to a woman. He felt the need to tell me that he would get me to switch back to men.

..with one tooth, no thanks.

As I laid on my bed, I looked at my reflection in the window as the sun shined into my room. I thought about what Dr. Powell had told me about my first visit with him during this stay. He told me that I had a severely fragile mental illness. That wasn't the first time I had heard that, but this time felt different. I looked back on the years of medication changes and hospital stays. Wow, I really did have a major mental illness. It became a hard pill to swallow. It dawned on me that I will never be normal. I decided then and there that I just had to find my own normal.

My last day went by quickly. I was told that I was leaving, and hours before I left, Chase came in to say goodbye and wished me well. Somehow, I knew that I wouldn't be coming back for a while, and so did he. Jennifer did the same thing.

I left and walked out to Brooke with her arms held open. It was so good to see her, and I was ready to be the wife that I knew she deserved.

Chapter 38

I went back to my life before the psychiatric hospital. I went to my support group meetings and was growing in my sobriety. It was so nice being supported by my friends and having them love me so much. I finally felt deserving of their friendship.

Brooke and I grew so much closer through all that we had been through together. I was in a really good place. I talked to all my friends every day. I was finally able to be that good wife, daughter, and friend that I always knew I could be. I was making friends in meetings and even some friends in Tampa. Life was good, I was happy. Very happy, even. I should have known this pattern. I just cannot trust a really good day. I went up, then crashed down. This happened a couple of times just a week after I left the hospital. I was so tired and hopeless. Just like it had been since 2015, the mood swings can come untriggered. I went to one of my meetings back where my mom lived and noticed that I didn't want to talk to anyone but didn't think too much of it at the time. I was sitting alone, and friends sat down next to me. I took the meeting in, but when it was over, I could not get out of there fast enough.

As I was driving home, the thoughts started coming. I knew that I could reach out to Brooke, and when I did, she said that she was depressed herself. Then, I thought I could call Katie. She was always my go-to, but she was having such a good day. What kind of friend would I be if I dumped my depression onto her? So, I drove home listening to music. As I started driving on the highway, I noticed that things were moving so slowly yet quickly at the same time. The colors were dull and flat, and the song "The Sound of Silence" by Simon and Garfunkel came on. Just like they had years ago when I had my first mixed episode, the lyrics spoke to me. I felt every single word. I knew then; that I was in a depressive swing. I knew that because I identified that I was feeling like a burden to all my friends. I was just so tired of living this way. It just comes up whenever it wants to and affects every aspect of my life. I knew better than to just lay in bed because that would only make things worse, so I just kept busy. Everywhere I went, I put a mask on, figuratively. I hid my feelings and didn't want anyone to know that I was literally dying inside. I was exhausted by keeping up this façade that everything was okay. I had heard so many times that I bring light into the room, but I hated my life.

I hated being bipolar and was hanging on by a thread. I came home that night, laid next to Brooke, and stared out the window. The movement of the bay water was relaxing most of the time, but this time, it made things worse. As the water moved, it swayed my mind back and forth. I was playing with the idea of suicide. My life ending seemed calming. Not having to worry about ruining people's lives anymore. Not being a disappointment to my family and friends and Brooke. Lastly, I was just fucking tired. Tired of fighting to balance my moods. Tired of not knowing how I would feel in the next hour. Tired of not sleeping and going crazy high and manic to the bottom of the barrel depressed. All these thoughts raced in my head, back and forth, until eventually, I fell asleep.

When I woke up the next morning, the lights were still dull. I felt like I had a ten-ton weight on my chest. I couldn't move. I laid there and thought that if I got up and got dressed, I would feel better. Faith always taught me to "suit up and show up" every day. Well, I did that, and I didn't feel better. I had finally had it. I had enough of all this bullshit that comes with having bipolar. I didn't ask for this. I didn't want this, and I was tired of burdening all of my loved ones with all of it. I poured my large pill bag onto the bed. There were Lamictals, Busbar, Vraylar, and Wellbutrin all over the bed. I thought about taking the Vraylar, but it was such a hassle to get it filled.

Even though I wanted to die, I was still considering what would happen if suicide didn't work. I decided to take the Wellbutrin. I picked up five pills and cupped them in my clammy palm. My hand was shaking, and I used my other hand to grab my cup of water, then hesitated for quite some time.

I debated all that I had felt for the past couple of days. I honestly felt like I was doing everyone else a favor. My eyes welled up with tears, and the small black writing on the pill bottles blurred together. I breathed in deeply, put the pills in my mouth, and swallowed them. I sat back for a second, then thought that only taking five would just make me sick. I needed more. So, I grabbed five more and repeated the process. Then, I did it again. Now I had taken 15 Wellbutrin, and I started to panic.

What did I just do?

I told Brooke what I did, and she immediately called the cops, which pissed me off, so I just left the house. She sent me a text saying she would make sure they found me.

They were going to Baker Act me and send me to a state psychiatric hospital again. The hospital I usually go to was in another county, so they legally wouldn't be able to take me there. I decided to go back home, and when I drove up, I saw two police cars. That was a sight I was used to by then.

I walked upstairs, and they were in the house waiting for me. I told them that I lied about taking the pills and that I only said that for attention. I did not know the harm of lying about it at that time. I felt sick, I was clammy, and my cheeks were flushed. They had an EMT come and check my vitals, and they came back clear. The cops stayed while Brooke talked their ears off about baseball cards. I was so ready for them to leave, and after twenty grueling minutes, they did.

Brooke wasn't happy, but I told her that I had some errands to run. I really enjoyed driving around and being in my car, so I stayed out for about five hours. I made some appointments, got some new makeup, and called all my friends. Sunset was approaching, so I headed home. I was just a couple of blocks away when I started to feel funny. Things were bright but had an orange hue around them. It was similar to when I did mushrooms. The sunset was beautiful, and bright orange was smeared across the sky. I had no idea that this tranquility would soon lead to chaos. I sensed that something was really wrong, but I didn't know what. I parked my car and walked up the steps. I struggled to make every step. I came in, and Brooke was in our bedroom. I did not want to get sent to the psychiatric hospital, so I told her that I drank. This lie alone almost took my life. I did not think that through. Brooke got upset and said she was taking me to the mental hospital. At this point, I was scared, so I agreed to go.

I didn't even grab any clothes. We immediately walked down the stairs, and that was when my legs gave out.

I couldn't walk. Brooke had to help me walk to my car. Then, I blacked out.

Chapter 39

I slowly opened my eyes to a dim blue room. I felt Brooke holding my hand, which was attached to an IV. I looked down at my hand and saw a wristband that said "Jane Doe3100592752."

What the hell happened?

I asked Brooke, and she told me that I had multiple grand mal seizures and had been on a ventilator in the ICU for the past two days. I was in shock. I couldn't even cry. I just wanted to know what happened. Honestly, I wanted to know what I had done to myself.

Brooke told me that she thought I was just drunk while we were walking down to my car. She put me in the front passenger seat of my car but then decided to take her car instead. When I tried to get out, I wasn't able to figure out how to open the door. I just couldn't figure out how to unlock it. That was when she knew something was really wrong and decided we should hurry and get on the road. As we were driving, I laid my seat back and told her that I needed to go to the emergency room. As she turned the car around, trying to find the nearest hospital, I started to hallucinate. I was starting to mumble about seeing other people and bright lights.

I sat up suddenly, and my face hit the dash. At that moment, I started having a grand mal seizure. My hands were posturing up next to my chest because I was seizing so intensely. Brooke pulled up next to a BP gas station on the road by our house and told them that she needed an ambulance. They were quick to respond and had two ambulances show up in a matter of minutes. She verbally gave them my information when they asked who I was. While Brooke was telling them my information, I went silent and still. I was completely dead weight. Brooke heard the lady watching me yell my name and try to wake me up, but nothing was working. I was out cold. Six EMT's gently took me out of the car and put me in the back of the ambulance. Brooke was not allowed in the back. They told her that I was going to St. Stephens, one of the nearby hospitals, and then they drove off.

Brooke didn't know what to do, so she called Katie. Brooke was crying and telling her what happened, and because Brooke was so upset, Katie called St. Stephens. They told her there was no one there by that name. They did tell her, however, that there were two other St. Stephens hospitals in the area, so she called around. One was a rehabilitation center, and the other was a behavioral health center.

It did not make any sense. I was not where they said I would be. Katie called the police and asked them where I was taken. She gave my description, but they would not give her any information because they did not know her relation to me. Brooke went up to St. Stephens, demanding that I was there. She told them that she was my wife and wanted to see me, but they would not let her. Katie, always thinking on her feet, found a picture on my Facebook of our marriage license and used it to show them that Brooke was truly my wife. After arguing with them for hours, they let her back, only to find out that the reason they could not find me was because I was registered under the name "Jane Doe."

Brooke went to the back to see me, and when she walked into the room, she saw that I was on a ventilator. I was having major seizures and then would go unresponsive over and over again. She was wondering why I was put on a ventilator, so they informed her that I not only needed assistance breathing due to falling in and out of consciousness, but they were also worried that I would vomit and choke. They said that it would make things so much worse if that happened, so they took precautions. She was not allowed to talk much or touch me because any extra brain movement or excitement could have thrown me into another seizure. I did not need any more brain activity than I was already having. She was crying and held my pinky and prayed that I would be okay. She called my mom, and it only rang once before going to voicemail. She tried a couple of times, but no answer. My dad was on a trip in Arkansas, so she called my Aunt Catherine. She answered the phone, and because it was the middle of the night, she asked, "Who is it?" Referring to who was dead or in the hospital. Brooke responded with, "It's Lauren." Both of them tried to get a hold of my mom. No answer. My aunt remembered that my mom always put her phone on *Do Not Disturb,* and you need to call twice in a row for the call to go through, so they were finally able to get a hold of her, and she made her way to the hospital.

When my mom arrived, I was out of the emergency room, and they had moved me to the Intensive Care Unit. I was still on the ventilator and continuously having seizures. I would fall into a massive seizure and then go back to being unresponsive. There were two large fluid bags attached to my IV line. I was loaded up with Fentanyl and Benzodiazepines. They were meant to stop the seizures from happening but were not working very well. Eventually, they had to put me in restraints to hold my hands back from curling up to my chest when I would seize, only to have me break through them moments later.

The first day and night passed with no major changes. They wanted me to be somewhat awake to take the ventilator out. They did not think that I would vomit at this point, and I seemed to be breathing on my own, so they decided to go ahead and remove it. Once they took it out, I was just mumbling. I wasn't having any more seizures at this point, but I could not form any words. The nursing staff told Brooke to start making arrangements for me, which was a nice way of saying I was not going to make it. Devastated, Brooke called Katie first and told her what was happening and what they said. Then, she called Audrey. I usually call her my iguana. Just like she does, she made any situation as light as she could, and it cheered Brooke up for a minute. Then, reality was quick to come back. Both told Brooke that they would not only pray for me themselves, but they would have everyone in their support group meetings pray for me as well. It was the only option they had at this point.

Brooke was holding my hand when I woke up. I vaguely remember feeling her hand in mine and seeing bright colors. I heard mumbling voices start to grow louder, and then I was able to make out the voices of Brooke and my mom talking. I snapped out of it and muttered, "Now I know that I am talking a bunch of bullshit." I couldn't even get the words out of my mouth that I was going to throw up before I did, all over myself. That was when everyone sighed a breath of relief that I might actually pull through this.

Then, I fell back into a blackout. Brooke told me that she helped clean me up, and they decided to put me into involuntary confinement in the hospital, so they moved me upstairs to the lockdown unit.

Chapter 40

After being informed of what happened and what I had done, I asked her how long I had been there. She told me that I spent one night in the emergency room, two days in the ICU, and one day in the lockdown unit. I quickly realized that I was still on the lockdown floor when I heard a man yelling that he wasn't crazy from a couple rooms down. Now *that* I was used to it. This was my level of expertise. I looked over and saw a curtain.

Great, another roommate.

Brooke filled me in on all that happened in those few days and all that Katie did for me. I was left speechless. Then she told me to look at my wristband. I glanced down and saw that she was right. It was "Jane Doe3100592752" in bold black letters. Now it all made sense.

Holy shit.

After all of the suicidal ideations and attempts, I actually almost did it. And the funny thing was, I didn't want to die anymore, at all. I was so happy that I didn't die. My old therapist, Mary, used to say, "suicide is a permanent fix for a temporary situation." All of those stories I used to hear about people with bipolar committing suicide almost became *my* story. I started to cry. I was so incredibly grateful that I made it.

Brooke handed me some of the books that I had been reading before all of this occurred. Ironically, all of them were addiction and mental health recovery stories. After a couple hours of talking and laying together, Brooke left to go home to sleep and shower. I was so bummed. I wanted to be with her now more than ever, but I knew that she had been at the hospital with me for days and needed to go, so I kissed her goodbye and fell back asleep.

I woke up shortly after because I had to pee, then looked down at my IV.

Shit, I had to drag this across the room with me.

I went to stand up, but I could barely stand.

Why didn't they have someone here to help me?

I staggered across the floor, stumbling along with the IV cart, and made it to the bathroom. Took me about ten minutes to get there. As I walked past my roommate, I saw an older, rough-looking woman. Her raspy voice matched her appearance. She told me that her name was Carol, and I honestly don't remember anything else that she said because I was so focused on not falling. I crawled back into the elevated hospital bed and quickly fell back asleep.

When the next day came, I was mentally messed up. I really almost died, or should I say, Jane Doe almost died. Other than my mom, the first person I wanted to talk to was Katie. I couldn't even grasp the kind of friendship she gave me. When I called her, all I remember was her crying and telling me not to ever do that again. She also told me that everyone was praying for me. I could not believe how loved I was. I mean, when I took those pills, I had no idea the impact of what leaving this world would do to everyone in my life. I felt so ashamed for even considering doing that to them. I started to slide into guilt, and then I let that take over. Luckily, I was put by the window, so I just gazed outside. My mind was moving slowly but intensely as I pictured myself with a tube down my throat and a brace around my neck. I looked down at my arms. I had the IV and two more holes: one on the top of my hand and the other on my forearm. I couldn't even imagine how Brooke must have felt, not even knowing where I was in the state I was in. And my poor parents.

Attempting suicide was the most selfish thing I had ever done.

I did my best to try to rest and relax, but I kept having to get up to use the bathroom. It was a pain, but it did get easier. I was able to walk better than before. I was getting better mentally as well. I was starting to look at the elephant in the room, weighing heavy on the situation. Not the guilt, shame, or stress, but the fact that I didn't die. I mean, out of all the things I had been through and experienced in my entire life, I knew now that I was meant to be alive. I started talking with my roommate, mostly because she wouldn't stop talking. The doctor finally came in to do a brain scan. I hadn't fully realized the extent of what two full days of seizures could do to my brain. They brought the machine in and put about twenty little sticky pads all over my head. And we waited. She told me that she would let me know the results, and then I would be allowed to leave. Thirty minutes felt like five hours. She came in and told me that I had no permanent damage. They put me on Lexapro instead, which I was content with. At this point, I did not care. I was just ready to get home and live my life.

Once my Baker Act was lifted, I called Brooke to come and pick me up. They insisted that I come down in a wheelchair, which I was embarrassed to do, but then I quickly remembered how I looked when I came in and was quick to feel better. I was assisted into the front passenger seat with my paperwork and prescriptions. She looked at me with those beautiful, piercing green eyes from the driver's side, and said, "I am so happy that you're alive. I honestly don't know what I would have done if you didn't make it."

As we drove off to go and get my prescriptions filled, I stared out the window. The colors were so bright, and the air so crisp. I saw my reflection in the side mirror. I thought about my life up to this point. My life had been shattered into a million pieces over the past 7 years. I had lost myself multiple times, been to the psychiatric hospital eleven times, two drug and alcohol rehabilitation centers, and had more medication changes than I could count. I struggled with being bipolar and an addict for years. I looked death straight in the face and walked away stronger and better than I ever was before. I accepted myself for who I was and what I had. I loved myself and knew now that I could handle anything that was thrown my way. For the first time in my life, I didn't feel so damn broken.

We pulled up to the grocery store, and Brooke helped me out of the car. I was so ready to feel like myself again. As we walked up to the sliding glass door of the store, I heard a familiar sound. Wind chimes. There was so much emotion attached to that sound for me. My parents had wind chimes in the backyard of my childhood home. It brought me back to when times were so simple.

Back then, I didn't have bipolar, I wasn't an addict, and I didn't abuse my mind and body. I always made my parents proud, and I had an amazing childhood at home. I had no idea what real pain and struggles were. I started to smile thinking about that, but then my smile quickly faded when my mind went to the old high school senior photo that was hanging up on their wall. My stomach fell at that thought. Two boys tainted and ruined the spirit and body of that sweet and innocent little girl. My life unraveled at 17 and has never been the same since. I wiped the tears that welled up in my eyes with my sleeve, and I walked through the glass doors.

I looked down at my feet, slowly putting one foot in front of the other. Then, it hit me. Everything I had been through brought me to where I was in that very moment. I not only struggled, but I clawed and scraped my way through my life. I struggled to exist. And deep down, I always hoped that there was more to life than I was living.

By 33 years old, I had experienced and been through more than many people may ever experience for themselves in their entire lifetime. But the advantage that I had was that I was able to dig so damn deep into myself to finally find out who Lauren is and what she is capable of.

I finally had friends who unconditionally loved me through every relapse and hospital stay. I gained a new best friend who overfilled all the shoes that previous ones had painfully left behind. I had my ride or die. Our friendship started when I was just 18, and she stayed with me for the past 18 years through all my bumps and bruises. Over those years, we grew closer and grew up together. And lastly, a wife who never left my side. She loved me and held my hand every step of the way. I was finally able to love that little Lauren inside of me who was always made fun of and abused. I was able to do that by learning something that I had never been able to do before, using my voice. I am not defined by what ailments I have.

Today, I identify as Lauren, a loving, kind, strong, sober woman who is capable of anything that she sets her mind to. The millions of shattered pieces of my life finally started coming together in my mind.

I had always asked myself when my life was really going to start. It dawned on me at that very moment, next to the bananas at the grocery store, that it already had. I took a deep breath in. I have arrived. It is now time to stop existing and finally start living.

You, like me, have the ability to rise. To reclaim. To shine. This is not the end of my story, or yours. It is just the beginning.

www.ingramcontent.com/pod-product-compliance
Lightning Source LLC
Chambersburg PA
CBHW020242010526
44107CB00039B/1470/J